Mussolini's Defeat at Hill 731, March 1941

Mussolini's Defeat at Hill 731, March 1941

How the Greeks Halted Italy's Albanian Offensive

John Carr

Pen & Sword
MILITARY

First published in Great Britain in 2020 by
Pen & Sword Military
An imprint of
Pen & Sword Books Ltd
Yorkshire – Philadelphia

ISBN 978 1 52676 503 1

A CIP catalogue record for this book is
available from the British Library.

Typeset by Mac Style
Printed and bound in the UK by TJ Books Limited,
Padstow, Cornwall.

Pen & Sword Books Limited incorporates the imprints of Atlas,
Archaeology, Aviation, Discovery, Family History, Fiction, History,
Maritime, Military, Military Classics, Politics, Select, Transport,
True Crime, Air World, Frontline Publishing, Leo Cooper, Remember
When, Seaforth Publishing, The Praetorian Press, Wharncliffe
Local History, Wharncliffe Transport, Wharncliffe True Crime
and White Owl.

For a complete list of Pen & Sword titles please contact

PEN & SWORD BOOKS LIMITED
47 Church Street, Barnsley, South Yorkshire, S70 2AS, England
E-mail: enquiries@pen-and-sword.co.uk
Website: www.pen-and-sword.co.uk

Or

PEN AND SWORD BOOKS
1950 Lawrence Rd, Havertown, PA 19083, USA
E-mail: Uspen-and-sword@casematepublishers.com
Website: www.penandswordbooks.com

Contents

S. ALBANIA AND N.W. GREECE

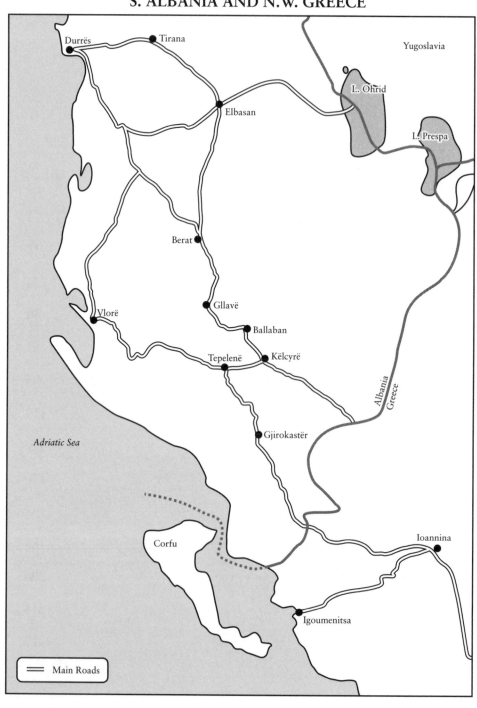

BEGINNING OF THE BATTLE

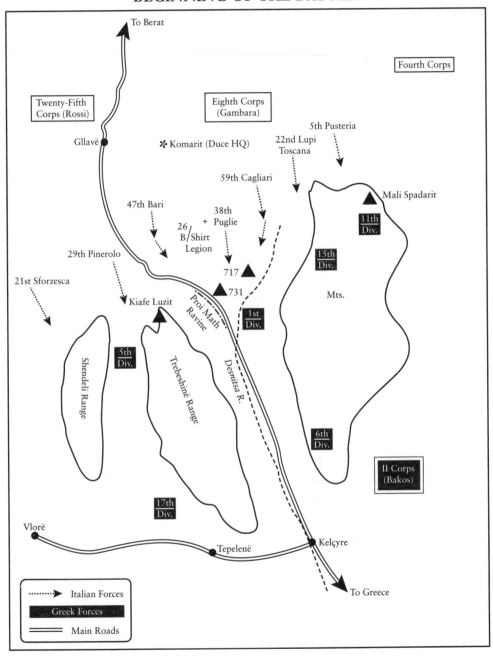

To Berat

Fourth Corps

Twenty-Fifth
Corps (Rossi)

Eighth Corps
(Gambara)

5th Pusteria

Gllavë

✳ Komarit (Duce HQ)

22nd Lupi
Toscana

59th Cagliari

Mali Spadarit

47th Bari

38th
+ Puglie

11th
Div.

26
B/Shirt
Legion

29th Pinerolo

15th
Div.

717

21st Sforzesca

731

Mts.

Kiafe Luzit

Proi Math
Ravine

1st
Div.

5th
Div.

Shendeli Range

Trebeshinë Range

Desnitsa R.

6th
Div.

II Corps
(Bakos)

17th
Div.

Vlorë

Kelçyre

Tepelenë

To Greece

········▶ Italian Forces

Greek Forces

══ Main Roads

GREEK 1ST DIVISION DEFENSIVE POSITIONS 9 MARCH

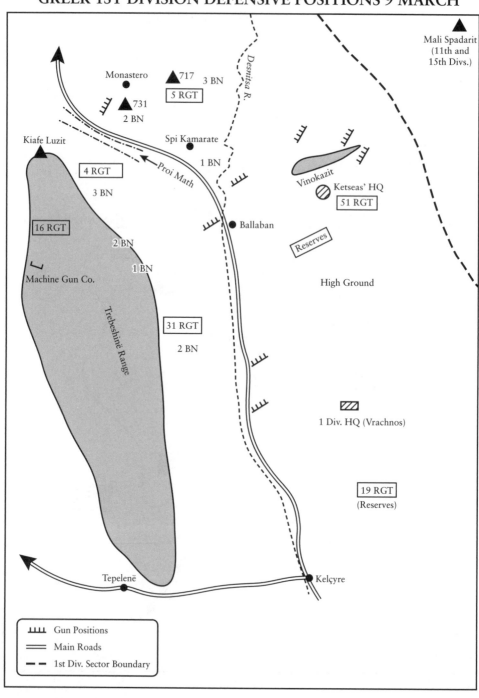

List of Illustrations

Illustrations to be found in the plate section in the centre of the book.

1. Mussolini viewing the Greek positions from Komarit.
2. Major Dimitrios Kaslas.
3. An Italian attack on Hill 731. The second man from the right appears to have just been hit.
4. Bersaglieri go into the attack on or near Hill 731.
5. Mussolini and General Gambara (right).
6. Members of the Greek Army 1940 Re-enacting Team simulate the defence of Hill 731.
7. Framework of an ammunition-carrying mule saddle against a background photo of a Greek Army supply train.
8. The Greek Army 1940 Re-enacting Team demonstrating a machine gun defence.
9. Unknown artist's impression of the final moments of Captain Giorgio di Borbone, 19 March 1941, on a memorial postcard.
10. Italian-made Gnutti 51cm bayonet (restored).
11. The view north from Kelçyre along the Desnitsa Valley, with the Trebeshinë range on the left.
12. The Proi Math ravine, as seen from what remains of the Kelçyre-Berat road.
13. The summit of Hill 731 as it is today.
14. Mortar grenades and helmets recovered recently from Hill 731.
15. Somewhat neglected memorial to the 38th (Puglie) Division near the summit.
16. Italian shell discovered by the author on the east slope of Hill 731.

17. Hills 731 and 711 (left and right respectively), as seen from the south.
18. Hill 717 and Mali Spadarit beyond, seen from Hill 731.
19. The Greek war cemetery at Kelçyre.
20. Evangelia Fatsea with a photograph of her grandfather, Sgt Maj Halamabos Kyriakakis of the 14 Regiment, 5th (Crete) Division, still unaccounted for, at the Kelçyre war cemetery, October 2019.

Prologue

Someday some historian will seek the truth about what happened then, and delve into dusty archives to find it. Then he will give the world a picture of the superb action of the battalions and batteries, but in brief, and thus completely cold. What will be missing is the mental uplift of the warrior as well as the enthusiasm of deciding on the ultimate sacrifice. And, searching through some book or orders of the day he may find some entry such as: '… March 1941. Soldier X is hereby deleted from the regimental roll as killed, fighting heroically on Hill 731.' And after some years a researcher will with difficulty try to read the soldier's name, but in the meantime the ink will have faded. And later still, more historians will be completely unable to read the soldier's name as the writing will have been entirely obliterated.

Those words were, in a way, about me.

The 'someday' was in early 2019, and I was the 'some historian' who was 'delving into the dusty archives' of the Hellenic War Museum in Athens. As I read this I sat bolt upright at the desk and looked up from the yellowing pages, listening to this faint yet distinct voice from the past. That voice had been muted for many decades, waiting with infinite patience for someone to tap into it. The experience was a healthily humbling one; it fired me up to try to do justice to those brave men on both sides – inexplicably neglected by the great bulk of World War Two historiography – involved in the epic battle for Hill 731. Would I actually be able to call up even a small part of that 'mental uplift and enthusiasm for the ultimate sacrifice' that is so politically incorrect (not to say incomprehensible) in our digitally-dulled and much less noble age?

Whether or not I have succeeded in this, only the reader can decide. Which historian, writing at a remove of, say, two or three generations from his subject, has indeed any hope of reproducing the unique and indescribable experience of a battlefield in the mind of a reader? But it is our job nevertheless to try. This book will attempt to recapture the sheer intensity and, yes, horror of the month-long battle of Hill 731 between the Greek and Italian armies that has never before been adequately told in English.

The words beginning this prologue were written in 1949 by George Kitsos, a Greek military officer, in the preface to his work, *The Italian Spring Offensive.* In that year, memories were still fresh of the desperate battles in the Albanian mountains in 1940 and 1941 when Mussolini's troops invaded Greece, hoping to neutralize that country as a potential British ally, but instead found themselves driven back by an unexpectedly hardy foe. Among the 'dusty' tomes of the Hellenic War Museum I sensed someone figuratively looking over my shoulder in silent encouragement and perhaps gratitude that someone in the second decade of the twenty-first century was taking the trouble to find out what happened on Hill 731, one of the most blood-stained heights in modern military history. Kitsos' words are also a sobering reminder of the relentless march of time, the enemy of all remembrance – an enemy against which the conscientious historian can wield only flimsy weapons.

Hill 731 was one of those notorious heights that pop up regularly in military history: one thinks of Cemetery Hill at Gettysburg, Monte Cassino in Italy, Crucifix Hill at Aachen, Iwo Jima. Known to the Italians as Quota 731 Monastero, from a monastery that stood on a nearby eminence, Hill 731 is not one of the better-known encounters of World War Two. But it was extraordinarily ferocious. Perhaps the closest analogy in that same global conflict can be found in the battle for Iwo Jima exactly four years later. In both cases, the attackers made a desperate and bloody attempt against considerable odds to secure a strategic height – Hill 731 in Albania and Mount Suribachi on Iwo Jima. And with brutal similarity, the fight dragged on for weeks, with appallingly high casualties and supreme displays of heroism on both sides.

Over seventeen days in March 1941, the attacking Italian Eleventh Army, despite its great resolve, was seriously bloodied. Unlike the Americans at Iwo Jima and the Confederates at Gettysburg, the Italians in Albania at no time were adequately equipped and armed for the task; in fact, much of their equipment proved inferior to the Greeks', especially in artillery and machine guns. Above all, the Greeks prevailed in morale. Though many Italian soldiers, to be sure, believed and internalized the national Fascist line that the Duce was leading Italy back to her long-lost days of Roman greatness and that lesser Mediterranean nations (such as Greece) should submit, many others – possibly even a majority – had unwillingly shouldered their rifles and hoisted their backpacks to fight a nation they had never previously imagined to be their enemy at all. By March 1941, the *Regio Esercito* (Royal Army) had suffered four months of reverses in the freezing crags of Albania; in that terrible winter, many a man and beast on both sides had literally frozen to death where they stood. Now the Italian *Soldati* were assured that one more massive push would crack the stubborn Greeks and finally send them reeling back. The wonder is that, despite the eroding morale in the ranks and the severe ordeals of an Albanian winter, the majority of Italian soldiers rushed into the meat-grinder of Hill 731 so heroically. After the war, a Greek historian wrote: 'One could think that the battle was staged by some diabolical film director to give the impression of horror, awe, bloodshed and heroism.'

The winners, as always, get to shape the historical memory. We are all familiar with photographer Joe Rosenthal's iconic snapshot of the raising of the Stars and Stripes on Mount Suribachi, one of the most reproduced images in history, the subject of books and films. But would that picture have been taken if the Fifth US Marines had been driven off Iwo Jima? Similarly, in Greece the military successes of 1940-41 against the Italians are justly held up as a significant military achievement and are officially commemorated annually to this day. The battle of Hill 731 ended in a Greek tactical victory, albeit a costly one. Yet it was the attacking Italians who suffered the most and who rest unseen, as it were, in the shade of history. Who remembers the thousands on both sides who perished on the shell-blasted slopes of Hill 731, apart from those who built the few crumbling stone memorials that are seldom visited, and which is certainly not on any of the world's battlefield must-see lists? Understandably did both sides equate the hill with Golgotha, the site of Christ's crucifixion.

I am aware of only two instances where the Greek-Italian War provides an incidental background for works of English-language fiction: Olivia Manning's *Friends and Heroes* (1965) and Louis de Bernières' *Captain Corelli's Mandolin* (1994), both of which were made into films. That conflict, in fact, suffers from a relative lack of historical 'visibility', and partly for that reason the battle for Hill 731 has not been easy to research. The sources are fragmented and often contradictory, with frustrating gaps in the recorded sequence of events. The library of the Hellenic War Museum in Athens contains a fairly adequate number of sources from the Greek side, and many thanks are due to the librarian, Dimitris Roulias, and his deputy, Commander Haralambos Sklavounos of the Hellenic Navy. These sources contain official Greek military assessments of Italian strategy and tactics and theories of how in the end Mussolini failed, as per the title of this book.

The book, however, could not have been written without the unstinting help of the Hellenic War Museum's public relations and media director, Yannis Korodimos, who has often helped me with other projects in the past and was instrumental in enabling me to visit Hill 731, which even today is not easy to get to. I owe a great debt of gratitude to the Hon. Giorgos Sourlas, a Greek former cabinet minister who now heads the Association of Relatives and Friends of the Fallen of 1940-41 and who accompanied me to Albania at the end of October 2019. Also with me were Lieutenant General (ret.) Aristodemos Bouloukos and his wife Dimitra, who handled the logistics of the trip. In Albania Orpheus Betsi of Gjirokaster and Alexander Selfo of Kelçyre provided vital transport services. I must praise the stamina and good cheer of Ioanna Gourgioti of Art of Travel who shepherded us to Albania and back, on her feet for many hours at a stretch and never without a smile even in the most trying moments. Special thanks also go to Andreas Marcou, the head of the Greek Army 1940 Re-enacting Team (who also produced some rare combat photos), as well as to ex-journalist and parliamentarian Nasos Athanasiou, who first set me on course to delve into the subject. I would also like to thank copy editor Christopher Trim whose eagle eye snagged several textual bugs that I thought I had eliminated.

If there is one potential criticism of the book which I hope to forestall, it might be that some readers will consider it a bit top-heavy on the Greek side. This was because my research turned up more material on the Greek side than on the Italian; in a way this was unavoidable, as the Greek military history tradition since World War Two has heavily promoted the successes in Albania while postwar Italy, trying to erase the stain of its Axis membership, remains reluctant to bring its war record too much into public view. But no nation, whatever the 'rights' or 'wrongs' history has labelled it with, should hide the brave deeds of its soldiers.

It has become a truism among World War Two writers that Mussolini's six-month-long failure in the Albania campaign was colossal folly on his part. American historian Barbara Tuchman defines folly as 'the pursuit of policy contrary to self-interest'. Yet that definition begs the question of what 'self-interest' actually is at any given time. Mussolini doubtless thought he was right when he invaded Greece, based on his conception of Italy's self-interest at the time. The unpredictable processes of war, rather than any 'higher' moral considerations, simply thwarted his plans. And nowhere was this more evident than at Hill 731.

Some Greek historians claim that Mussolini's failure at Hill 731 forced Hitler to intervene in Greece and put back his planned invasion of Russia, but the evidence for that is thin; Hitler had to juggle more complex factors. Of far greater significance is that Hill 731, more than anything else, marked the beginning of the end for Mussolini's own political career as dictator; from now on it could only be downhill. The severe Italian losses brought home to a growing section of the Italian officer corps what a mistake the war against Greece had been. At the time, Alexander Kirk, the American ambassador in Rome, wrote to Washington of the distinct possibility of an Army revolt against the discredited Duce – a revolt that was to materialize two years later.

To avoid reader confusion, I have spelled out the numbers of the Italian army corps (e.g. Fourth Corps, Eighth Corps) and written the Greek corps in Roman numerals (e.g. I Corps, II Corps). I have standardized the enumeration of divisions, regiments, battalions and companies for both sides, hoping that the context will make clear which is being referred to at any one time.

JC
Athens, November 2019

Chapter 1

The Duce Takes a Look

T he staff and troops of the Italian Army's Eighth Corps were up well before dawn in the morning of 9 March 1941. This was going to be no ordinary day of battling the mud and cold winds of the southern Albanian mountains – not to mention the Greeks who had been fighting them constantly and bloodily for the past four and a half months in inhospitable and rugged terrain that would tax the endurance of even the most hardened military man.

General Gastone Gambara, the corps commander, made sure that his staff were smartly made out, as a distinguished visitor was at hand to witness the opening of what had been meticulously planned for weeks: a sledgehammer blow that would smash the advancing Greek Army against the crags of Albania and rescue Italy's military reputation that had been severely mauled by a bitter winter of almost constant Italian reverses. The high-level visitor was Benito Mussolini himself, determined to personally witness – and of course take credit for – the operation that hopefully would restore glory to Italian arms and reflect sorely-needed credit upon himself.

Small wonder that his famous jut-jaw was set more aggressively than usual as, dapper in his field-grey uniform, gleaming polished boots and fore-and-aft hat, he emerged at 4 a.m. from his field quarters in the hamlet of Agip and settled himself into a staff car for the two-hour drive over dusty roads to the point from where he intended to observe the start of the great counterattack. At 6 a.m., it was light enough for the dawn mists to dissolve and a brilliant icy blue sky bathed the mountain peaks in a pink glow. At a spur of Mount Komarit, Mussolini got out of the car and strode quickly up the steep slope to his observation post in a small concrete embrasure buttressed by sandbags. Close behind was Achille Starace, secretary of the Fascist Party and one of the Duce's closest confidants. 'What do you think of the troops' morale?' Mussolini asked his aide. Starace, of course, had little choice but to reply, 'Very good, Duce. Everyone seems to be eagerly awaiting the signal to attack.'

Starace was not a soldier, despite his black Fascist Party uniform. A former dealer in prostitutes and drugs, with a police record, he owed absolute and slavish allegiance to the leader who gave him prominence and kept him out of jail. This is not to say he was devoid of abilities, but they were of the efficient Mafia-don sort: he knew how to organize a monolithic party and its public relations stunts and was as obedient as jack-in-the-box. Speaking on the telephone to his boss, he would stand to attention and order everyone else in the room to do the same. In sum, according to Mussolini's biographer Denis Mack Smith, 'he was someone the Duce could despise yet depend on.' And he was certainly not the only one with that facility.

So why did Mussolini bring Achille Starace all the way to inhospitable Albania? The party secretary had recently fallen out of favour – one scapegoat among several for the Italian failures in Albania – but he had somehow wheedled his way back to his Duce's side. Mussolini, despite his outward show of iron resolve, was actually an insecure man who was heavily influenced by whatever influential people told him. At a juncture such as this, where the reputation of himself and all Italy was in the balance, he needed someone who would serve as a faithful flatterer and be an echo chamber for his own thoughts, and Starace – not one to dampen enthusiasm with military realism – was the man.

Starace was one of several high Fascist Party figures (known as *squadristi*, or party group leaders) who had been drafted into the Army, given middle-grade officers' rank, and sent to the front to assuage well-founded public suspicion that they were a privileged caste of armchair strategists. He may have had a hand in penning a ditty designed to raise morale for the task ahead:

Soon it will fall to us,/ the squadristi of Milan,/to burst through the front,/ knives and grenades in hand./ The Duce has guaranteed/ that now the war is come,/ the Greeks will be thrown/ back to kingdom come.

Mussolini might have been excused if he regarded the cold cloudless sky as an auspice. The Air Force, the *Regia Aeronautica*, would have a perfect view for bombing and strafing the enemy positions. At a height of 800 metres on Mount Komarit, he scanned the formidable peaks and valleys to the south where the Greeks were entrenched. The embrasure was quite crowded. Flanking Mussolini was General Ugo Cavallero, the Army commander on the Albanian front; the obese commander of the Air Force in Albania, General Ferruccio Ranza, sporting an aviator's tunic; and the commander of the Eleventh Army, General Carlo Geloso, whose troops would be primarily involved in the great push. Also there was General Gastone Gambara, whose Eighth Corps would bear the brunt of the offensive. Gambara wore a non-regulation *bersagliere* tunic which he claimed had always given him luck in the field.

This was the somewhat theatrical opening of the Duce's great military showpiece, the Spring Offensive (*Offensiva di Primavera*), a grand plan that would stop four months of humiliating Italian reverses on the Albanian front and finally turn the tables on the aggressive Greeks. The offensive had been planned in some organizational detail, though its strategy was based on the simple doctrine of relentless frontal attack, apparently without much concentration on contingency plans if the offensive did not go according to the initial plan. As such, it had come in for criticism by some senior officers but, as it was Mussolini's pet scheme, there wasn't much they could do about it. On paper, at least, the Spring Offensive's basic aim was a reasonable one: to eliminate the Greek positions around the towns of Kelçyre and Tepelenë and use the freed-up mountain valleys to drive down to Greece.

The instruments for the offensive would be three corps, the Fourth, Eighth and Twenty-fifth, comprising fifteen divisions. The Eighth Corps would spearhead the attack with the 24th (Pinerolo), 38th (Puglie), 47th (Bari), 51st (Siena), and 59th (Cagliari) Divisions, plus the 26 Blackshirt Legion. The Twenty-fifth Corps had formed up on the right, with seven divisions, and the Fourth Corps on the left abutting the Ninth Army that could be called upon if needed. But this was clearly intended to be the Eighth Corps show – at least in the opening stages – and General Gambara honoured the event by sporting his lucky tunic.

The constellation of brass flanking Mussolini at the observation post lapsed into silence as, at precisely 6:20 a.m., fifty gun batteries opened up with a shattering cannonade aimed at the Greek 1st Division that was blocking the planned Italian route south through the Desnitsa River valley. The guns vomited a wall of flame along the entire Italian line, from the Twenty-fifth Corps on the right and the Eighth Corps in the centre to the Fourth Corps on the left. The front was made as wide as possible so the Greeks would not be able to divine, from the local intensity of the fire, where the expected infantry assault would concentrate. The ground under the Duce and his generals shuddered as more than 100,000 shells shrieked over the few kilometres and slammed into the Greek positions over the next two hours. At 8:30, the gunners lengthened their range to fire over the heads of the advance infantry units that were ordered forward at the same time.

'The Greek positions are completely covered in a literal rain of fire and steel,' Cavallero wrote in his diary.

> The advance of our units was quick at first. But after a while, the first attacking sections came up against the stubborn defence of the enemy who, taking advantage of every feature of the terrain, stuck to the bare rocks of his positions and fought with unheard-of efficiency.

Apart from the unexpected Greek resistance, the Duce was concerned about air cover. 'Why is the air force late?' he asked. The *Regia Aeronautica* was supposed to be droning overhead, adding its own bombs to the saturation shelling. But the sky was empty. Cavallero and Gambara tried to make excuses for this lack of coordination, saying something about poor visibility in the sector. But presently the aircraft appeared, diving out of the clear sky to bomb and strafe the Greek positions. The whole Greek line, in fact, appeared to be one vast inferno of flame and smoke in which nothing could possibly be left alive.

The Greek 1st Division, however, had dug in well. And somehow the Italian assault troops massing for the opening charge knew it, despite the comforting claims of the senior commanders. The first objective was the most formidable one. Hill 731 rose like a rampart guarding the mouth of the Desnitsa valley. Compared with the higher and rougher peaks in the vicinity such as the Trebeshinë and Tomorrit ranges soaring up to 2,400 metres, Hill 731 was a mere molehill, but a vital one, for it stood right at the entrance to the Desnitsa valley and the main road running through it, which in turn was the way to recapturing the strategic town of Kelçyre (also known as Klisura); sixty more kilometres would then bring the *Regio Esercito* to the Greek border, which it had last seen in November 1940, hounded northwards by the counterattacking Greeks. By then, the brass hoped, Hitler would speed to Mussolini's aid to crush the Greeks and the long-suffering Italian *soldato* could at last go home.

To one Italian soldier, looking out one evening, the view of the enemy-held Trebeshinë range, which had to be taken, sent shivers down his spine: 'It looks harsh and menacing, and somebody says, "See? There's the line." And it's like he's saying, "There's death up there."' The soldier, whose name and rank are unknown, was one of the new December arrivals and had experienced an abrupt baptism of fire.

You see the flash of our batteries deployed in the valley and on the slopes, and hear the whoosh of grenades over our heads, exploding in the enemy lines, while you count the minutes and then the seconds until you have to sprint ahead, searching the faces of the men as you fire your machine gun... Mount Trebeshin... a mysterious and terrible thing, an ugly shape, caked in mud and rocky like a hundred others. No-one cares except those who have made war among the rocks and in the mud and have left behind fallen comrades and a piece of their heart.

Now they had to go up against it all. Again. And this time, they were told, they had to win.

As the first guns fired their salvoes, the front echelons of the 38th (Puglie) Division and 24th (Pinerolo) Division crept towards the bulk of Hill 731, flanked by the 21st (Sforzesca) Division of the Twenty-fifth Corps on the right. The area immediately in front was known to be riddled with Greek artillery and machine-gun posts, especially on the spurs of the feared Trebeshinë range. Watching the advancing lines of field-grey men through his binoculars, the Duce had his attention drawn to that rocky range which, he was told, not only had to be wrested from the enemy but retained as protection for the base town of Berat, a few kilometres to the north.

No-one expected the offensive to be easy; the past four months had demonstrated the stamina of the Greeks all too well. By mid-morning, the sounds of battle began to filter back from the first clash of opposing forces. Yet the first communiques from the front, arriving at about 9:30, were encouraging: key eminences on the flanks of the drive such as Bregu Julichi, Chafa Mezgorani and Chafa Lusit were reported to be already in Italian hands and Hill 731, one message claimed, was as good as taken. The Spring Offensive, it seemed, was getting off to a good start.

If there was one operation on which Mussolini was staking his entire reputation and standing as a world leader, the *Offensiva di*

Primavera was it. For too long, cartoonists in Allied countries had been picturing him as a theatrical buffoon; the Greeks, especially, held him in supreme contempt. To be fair, however, he was concerned about the image of the Italian fighting man. For too long the Italian had been stereotyped in Europe as a romance-addled bon viveur, spoiled by *mamma*, averse to hardship and prone to petty crime. He yearned to change that stereotype by toughening up the Italian military to make it as efficient and ruthless as the Germans or as practical and unemotional as the British. He had hoped to accomplish that in the wild crags of Albania. Partly he had succeeded; the Italians fought very well in the circumstances, but the Greeks knew the terrain better and had better commanders and had relentlessly pushed the Duce's men back. It was high time the tables were turned.

But as the morning of 9 March wore on, the Duce realized that not all was going to plan. His generals might flatter him with overly optimistic despatches from the front lines, but he was smarter than to uncritically believe them. As the distant clamour of battle crescendoed, he turned to his Air Force chief, General Francesco Pricolo. 'If this offensive doesn't succeed in the next two or three hours,' he grumbled, 'it's not going to work out at all.'

Later in the day, he was driven back to his headquarters in a sour mood. All he knew at that point was that the first wave of 3,000 men of the Cagliari Division, tasked with gaining the peak of Bregu Rapit (also known as Hill 717) on the left, had not made as much headway as expected. The division commander, General Giuseppe Gianni, had been off sick and absent from the battle. 'Those generals who become ill on the very day of the offensive make me think,' Mussolini growled to Pricolo on the way. 'They have a poor spirit, not enough bite, and no initiative at all!' He gazed out of the car window into the impenetrable Albanian night. 'Look at Rommel. With just one division he has re-balanced the situation in Libya.' And three divisions of his own had been unable to seize a handful of miserable Balkan heights from the Greeks. Despite the initial upbeat messages from the front, General Alberto d'Aponte and his 38th (Puglie) Division had fallen short of their objective of Monastir Ridge, the last step before tackling Hill 731.

It was always this way in the end, the Duce reflected grimly. He, the saviour of Italy, the restorer of her military reputation, the true heir of the Caesars, was constantly being let down by his wimpish pen-pushing generals. To quote a German officer of World War One referring to the British, his *soldati* were lions led by donkeys. One week before, he had taken the trouble of personally flying a Siai-Marchetti SM79 bomber from Bari, protected by a cocoon of a dozen Macchi 200 fighters, to Tirana, the Albanian capital, to see for himself what was going on. On the way, he hadn't said much to his main passenger, General Pricolo, instead choosing to concentrate on his flying. At Tirana, he was met by the commander of the Italian forces in the Albanian theatre, General Ugo Cavallero, a short and stout man with high intelligence and an incisive military brain. At once, Mussolini, Cavallero and Pricolo got into a staff car for a tour of the front. Pricolo, the Air Force chief, noticed that his boss looked 'hesitant and anxious'.

The Duce's mood had brightened at Berat as the car passed the marching men of the 47th (Bari) Division, few of whom had any inkling that they would soon be thrown into a meat-grinder. Many of the men cheered – they, too, were tired of having to retreat before the Greeks. The same happened with the 51st (Siena) Division farther down the road. The men's enthusiasm restored some of the Duce's confidence. 'Get well soon,' he told one wounded soldier, who replied eagerly: 'The important thing is to win!' As the staff car rolled past a constant stream of foot soldiers, lorries and baggage trains winding over the precarious tracks, he may well have reflected: lions led by donkeys indeed! Too many of his senior officers may have been untrustworthy, but the average soldier, judging from the wounded man he had just passed, had what it took to win. (It is not often realized that Benito Mussolini was the only national leader of a combatant power in World War Two who actually stood on the front line with his soldiers.) The imminent Spring Offensive just had to prove that, otherwise his standing in the eyes of his senior partner, Adolf Hitler, would receive a fatal blow. Much was riding on the impending battle, nothing less than the apotheosis of his career. He could not afford to fail.

Fifty-eight years old and in apparent good health, Benito Mussolini had been at the helm of Italy for nineteen years. Canny politician that he was, during that time he had evolved through various phases to keep himself in power. The 1920s and 1930s were decades in which the twin sirens of fascism and communism were attracting devotees in all the countries of Europe; those doctrines promised to do away with the messy complexities and corruptions of parliamentary democracy and the inequalities of capitalism in the interests of the working people. Mussolini's theory of the fascist corporate state, where capital, labour and the state were fused together into large blocks and forced to work for the common good, appealed to many Italians, even when the Duce resorted to thuggish tactics to enforce it.

He was no coward. Despite having been a radical pacifist in his youth, when he was called up in 1915 and sent to fight on the Austrian front, he acquitted himself reasonably well, reaching the rank of sergeant. (His political views were still too radical for him to get a commission.) While he was training with a grenade-thrower in February 1917, the device blew up, killing several soldiers. Mussolini was riddled with grenade fragments, though none proved especially serious, and after a spell in hospital he was invalided out of the Army. It was, however, an army that, as in 1941, was badly led. Morale plummeted, leading to the disastrous defeat at Caporetto on 24 October 1917. The stubborn and heartless Italian commander, General Luigi Cadorna, made morale infinitely worse by enforcing the dreaded ancient Roman punishment of decimation, where every tenth soldier was tied to a post and shot.

'Nothing in [Mussolini's] life caused him greater humiliation,' writes biographer Denis Mack Smith. The mass executions shocked him, and most likely left him with a deep distrust of top military brass. Italy, too, was deeply humiliated. Incompetent politicians and generals, it was argued in the cafes and the newspapers, were ultimately responsible for the disaster; the corollary was that the country needed a dictatorship to rebuild itself and get rid of the lightweights and scoundrels who were running it. And Mussolini believed he was the man to do it.

On 28 October 1922 (ironically, the date on which he would attack Greece eighteen years later), Benito Mussolini led his blackshirts on Rome, where the weak government quickly crumbled and King Vittorio Emanuele III saw little alternative but to install Mussolini and his Fascist Party in power; the king himself, though no extremist, hoped that the new government would put an end to chronic anarchy and corruption. A great many, perhaps a majority, of his countrymen agreed with him. Several influential Italians around the world, including Guglielmo Marconi of radio fame, applauded the development. Prices on the Italian Stock Exchange soared. In Mussolini's view, the Italians as a southern European people simply had not had the time that the northern Europeans had to develop more or less stable parliamentary democracies and thus were prone to abusing political liberty. The only way to force the volatile Italians into a working polity was through strong-arm methods. The alternative was anarchy.

The model he chose to employ was a military one, larded with a dose of state socialism. From the outset, he organized eager young men into action groups called *squadre* whom he used to cow opposition and carry out the occasional gangland-style killing. He was always quite open about his contempt for democracy. 'Revolutions are not made by saints,' he said, almost echoing Lenin, a onetime role model. On his first day as prime minister, he took personal control of the nation's police. Then, in his second year in power, Greece suddenly intruded into his affairs.

Like the then-unknown Hitler, Mussolini despised the 1919 Versailles Treaty ending World War One. He claimed it deprived Italy of 'ethnic Italian' territory in central Europe and the western Balkans. Though one of U.S. President Woodrow Wilson's fabled Fourteen Points had been the 'readjustment of the frontiers of Italy... along clearly recognizable lines of nationality,' what Italy actually gained was a portion of South Tyrol and a strip of territory in what is now Slovenia on the Adriatic Sea. It was not enough for many nationally-minded Italians, especially their new leader. The nation's population was pushing forty million, and much agricultural produce and industrial coal had to be imported. Small wonder that many were quite ready to be mesmerized by Mussolini's bombast that the successor state of ancient Rome deserved more – much more. Some in Italy were already suspecting that he would turn out to be another typical politician, long on talk and short on action. That was an image he could not countenance. So the first fight he decided to pick was with nearby Greece, a much smaller power.

The Greek island of Corfu, the largest of the Ionian Islands, retained a strong Italian cultural tradition from the days when they were all Venetian colonies. They lay temptingly off the west coast of mainland Greece; their possession, especially of Corfu, would secure Italian control of the Strait of Otranto, the southern gateway to the Adriatic Sea and hence an important sea trade route. Mussolini was prepared to bet that Corfu could be wrested from weak Greece as 'the first stage in a triumphant march of fascist legions on the road to national greatness' with little trouble. With luck, the rest of the islands would eventually follow. Of course, outright naked aggression, so soon after the horrors of World War One, would not work, so a *casus belli* had to be manufactured.

In July 1923, Mussolini ordered the military to draw up plans for a landing and occupation of Corfu and sent naval units to make a show of strength offshore. Corfu had no defensive guns, and its Greek garrison could not have coped with a full-scale attack. The required *casus belli* came with the murder of an Italian general, Enrico Tellini, on the Greek side of the Greek–Albanian frontier. Tellini had been heading an Italian–French–British mission sent to Albania to delineate the disputed frontier as part of the post–World War One Balkan arrangements. Without the slightest evidence to back up the claim, Mussolini at once blamed the Greeks. Before a denial from Athens could be sent, he personally fired off an ultimatum to Athens to take the blame for Tellini's murder or lose Corfu. Days later, an Italian force landed on Corfu and occupied the whole island; the commander of the naval force offshore, acting without orders, ordered the shelling of the old town and citadel of Corfu, killing a number of children, among other casualties.

Public opinion in Europe, especially Britain, was outraged. Mussolini responded by threatening war against Britain, a move that alarmed his senior naval staff. Why, he stormed, he might even smash the newly-hatched League of Nations if it stood in the way of his ambitions. Such extreme rhetoric, of course, was quite the wrong kind in a Europe still trying to recover from the most devastating conflict in history up to that time; Britain displayed strong support for Greece, and a month later the pressure of international condemnation forced Mussolini to pull his troops out of Corfu, his first attempt at annexation thwarted. He was outwardly humiliated, but something in him was boosted by the rash act. The attempt at Mediterranean bullying had centred world attention on him; he was finally somebody on the global stage. He had got the corrupt bourgeois leaders and decaying aristocracies and newspapers of the West to take notice of him. Italy was no longer just a sunny land of spaghetti-eating, wine-bibbing opera singers where sex-starved northern women went to find romance; Italy, at long last, was a steel-tipped military power. In his own words, 'it is a crime not to be strong.'

There is nothing inherently 'fascist' or even callous about that statement. Winston Churchill, for example, would have heartily agreed, as would almost every leader of a democratic country that wishes to preserve its security. The fact that these days it is quite politically incorrect to utter such a phrase does not detract from its stark validity. The problem is: when does being legitimately 'strong' progress to dangerous aggressiveness? To Mussolini, the line was very thin, if it was there at all, and it is true that through the 1920s he made a point of making rather a nuisance of himself on the European stage. General Jan Smuts, the South African leader, saw him as 'running around biting everybody'. Mussolini was one of the first leaders to recognize the new Soviet Russian regime in 1924, seeing in Vladimir Lenin a mirror image of himself on the far left. For a time he eyed Turkey as a potential location for an Italian colony. But it was the Balkan peninsula with its string of relatively weak countries – Yugoslavia, Albania and Greece – that whetted his appetite the most. Especially Greece, with its long and convoluted coastline, that offered far too many advantages to the British Mediterranean Fleet to hole up in and threaten Italy's domination of its *Mare Nostrum*.

The Italian military establishment was, in general, heartened by its new, loud leader. The disgrace of Caporetto had left a lingering bad taste in the national mouth. Mussolini's declaration that Italians had to cultivate in their minds a 'permanent state of war' no doubt boosted the status of all three services. The Italian Air Force he intended to build up was, he declared, destined to rule the Mediterranean skies. Much of this, of course, was mere posturing, and he knew it. But if it kept patriotic Italians happy (and himself in power) and caused foreigners to think twice about crossing him, then it worked.

One major institution of Italian life, however, retained its strong scepticism about Mussolini and his Fascist movement, and that was the Roman Catholic Church. The Vatican, however much it may have approved the suppression of socialist and communist threats and freemasonry, was nevertheless extremely uncomfortable with Mussolini's doctrine of near-unlimited state power which went dead against age-old Christian ideals. It also could not forget Mussolini's earlier extreme anti-clericalism: one of his early published writings had been titled *God Does Not Exist* (it was quickly withdrawn from circulation when he came to power). But, belatedly perceiving the centrality of Catholicism to all aspects of Italian life, he initiated a series of contacts with Pope Pius XI that in 1929 ended nearly half a century of frosty relations between the Papacy and the Rome government with a concordat that delimited the Pope's domain to the present dimensions of the independent Vatican City and regularized relations. His cordiality to the priests, however, was only skin-deep; their use to him was solely to keep believers docile and occasionally be used as tools for his foreign policy against Protestant and Eastern Orthodox powers.

The 1930s saw Mussolini, now enshrined as the Duce, at the apex of his aggressive abilities. By now he had accurately judged the Western and northern European democracies for what they were: timid governments ruled by money and media whose overriding fear of another war made them pushovers for stronger characters. He perceived what many people north of the Alps still don't – that southern Europe is fundamentally different from the north in mentality and historical culture. Great Britain, for example, might correctly regard itself as the paragon, albeit imperfect, of parliamentary rule. But in Mussolini's eyes, Britain was a declining power paralysed by the militant working-class left and enervated by the languidness and moral decay of a conservative nobility living off the fat of empire. Empires should be the rewards for ruthless leadership and a vigorous and hard-working people, not supercilious aristocrats. And, in 1934, the Duce began to show the world how he thought it should be done.

The majority of Italians gave him their eager backing. So far, in the twentieth century, they had been acutely aware of their 'have-not' status in the shadow of the wealthier powers. The British Empire embraced about one-quarter of the land area of the globe and half a billion people. Next came the Soviet Union, with 170 million under its red banner, and France third, not to mention the growing

United States across the Atlantic. Italy was pretty small beer in comparison. The average Italian worker was paid about half of his British or French counterpart; Italian businessmen lacked the capital to compete with their richer British or American or French rivals. Small wonder that both the (controlled) trade unions and the Italian business establishment helped lead the cheer for the creation of Italy's own empire. And in case anyone failed to get the message, the Great Depression of the early 1930s seemed to confirm that authoritarian fascism was the best way to keep a decent plate of pasta on every table.

Mussolini never had much use for the League of Nations, and he was certainly not the only one in Europe to view it as anything more than an elite debating society; even the United States had refused to join it, even though one of their presidents, Woodrow Wilson, had conceived it. Like Hitler in a newly-rearming Germany, Mussolini correctly divined the lack of backbone in the League. Still, he took a distinct gamble when in late 1935 he attacked the only remaining free and uncolonized African country, Ethiopia. With the liberal use of indiscriminate aerial bombing and poison gas, the antiquated Ethiopian forces quickly succumbed. But Ethiopia was to be no mere colony on, say, the British model; the country was fully and formally annexed to Italy on 9 May 1936. True, the League reacted to this naked aggression against one of its members, but the sanctions imposed were too little and too late. The Duce had correctly out-bluffed Britain and France, whose timid diplomats feared pushing Germany and Italy together if any stronger penalties were applied and thus sold Ethiopia down the river.

The year 1936 was a crucial one. With Ethiopia now in the fold, Mussolini looked for a way to secure combat experience for his military and found it in the Spanish Civil War. As soon as the fighting broke out, he sent shiploads of weapons, tanks and aircraft, plus 100,000 soldiers and technicians, to help Nationalist General Francisco Franco's forces. This aid helped Franco win the bitter three-year conflict, while the democratic nations of the West dithered ineffectually. The Italian contribution in Spain was not as trouble-free as Mussolini claimed. Many of the men were ill-trained Blackshirt 'volunteers', as the regular Italian Army was quite reluctant to get involved. But no, the Duce insisted, the Spanish Republicans would be beaten within a few weeks. It was not to be, and the Italians suffered considerable casualties, with perhaps up to 6,000 men dead and missing, not to mention the huge financial cost. He would make the same mistake a few years later against Greece.

By 1939, the message that both the Führer and the Duce read into international politics was that, yet again, might made right (an idea, in fact, going back to classical Athens in the fifth century BC). For the latter, the Balkans now seemed to be ripe for the picking. 'My will knows no obstacles,' he enthused as he pulled his men out of Spain and prepared to send them to Albania. That dirt-poor country had, in fact, been under Italian economic control for some time, but Mussolini needed to make it official, which he did on 8 April 1939, formally annexing the country. He got away with this gamble as well; aware that it could trigger a European war and perhaps knowing that the Germans didn't care for him acting recklessly in the Mediterranean, he exulted in this new flexing of military muscle. Albania, above all, would be a base from which Greece could be threatened and pressured, and if necessary invaded, to prevent the British Royal Navy from using Greece's convoluted coastline and multitude of islands.

Chapter 2

The 'Walkover'

In the early hours of 28 October 1940 the Italian ambassador in Athens, Emanuele Grazzi, was driven to the home of Greece's prime minister, Ioannis Metaxas, to wake him up and deliver an ultimatum, which in peremptory tones accused Greece of 'violating neutrality' by helping the British and 'threatening' neighbouring Albania. In response to all this, Grazzi's note said, Italy would need to 'occupy some strategic points in Greek territory,' and if any resistance were put up, it would be 'met by force'. No national leader worth his salt could ever agree to such a crudely-put demand, and Metaxas replied simply, in the diplomatic French, usual at the time: *'Alors, c'est la guerre.'* 'Well, then, it's war.' Less than three hours later, Italian forces poured over the Albanian border for what the Duce and some of his top military brass fondly imagined would be a 'walkover' to Athens.

It wasn't. One of the incurable optimists was the commander of the Italian expeditionary force, General Sebastiano Visconti Prasca, whose 23rd (Ferrara) and 3rd (Julia) Divisions, followed up by the 131st (Centauro) Armoured Division, ran into a brick wall of Greek resistance at Kalpaki Hill north of Ioannina. Within days, the Julia had been outmanoeuvred and encircled while the tracks of the Centauro's small Fiat tanks (those not pounded into blazing hulks by the Greek artillery) slipped and skidded helplessly in the mud. After less than a week, Visconti Prasca's army had been pushed back over the Albanian border, and for the next four months, under relentless Greek pressure, it gave up the key town of Korçe (Koritsa). Then the bitterest of winters set in, with the extreme cold a worse foe than the enemy, until the end of February 1941, when the Duce figured that the Greeks must be worn out, in worse shape than the Italians, and hence easy meat for a grand Spring Offensive.

In the meantime, Visconti Prasca, the optimist, had been dismissed and replaced by General Ubaldo Soddu, who likewise proved unable to stem the relentless Greek advance. On 4 December 1940, a major change was made at the top when General Ugo Cavallero was appointed Chief of the Military Staff. A man of rare intelligence and considerable managerial talent, Cavallero was undoubtedly one of the most capable senior officers Italy had ever had. He had become a general at thirty-eight and had the rare attainment of fluency in German and English. He, too, was a military optimist, but a rather more realistic one than Visconti Prasca. He had kept himself well-informed of the progress of the Albanian campaign so thoroughly that he claimed Mussolini, at one point, had exclaimed: 'He knows Albania like his own hometown!' According to Cavallero, much of the reverse in Albania could be put down to the pessimism and near-defeatism of his predecessor as Chief of Staff, Marshal Pietro Badoglio, who simply had not planned things properly. Here was Fascist Italy, the new rising power of Europe under its iron-willed Duce, unable to subdue a handful of Greeks! All it required was the proper application of power in the right places.

On the very day of his appointment, Cavallero flew to Elbasan in northern Albania to confront Soddu at the Ninth Army headquarters. From now on, Cavallero would assume an active role in directing the campaign, relegating the ineffectual Soddu to the sidelines. His first conclusions were dispiriting. The Italian line, stretching in a rough southwest-northeast direction from just north of Vlorë on the coast to Lake Ohrid in the east, so far had managed to defend Tirana, the Albanian capital, and other major towns such as Elbasan. But there was always the danger of a Greek breakthrough. The report of the Quartermaster-General, General Antonio Scuero, was grim: the soldiers were only just getting enough to eat, there was an almost total lack of woollen clothing, medical supplies were dangerously low, stocks of infantry ammunition had run out and the artillery was scraping the bottom of the barrel for shells.

The Ninth Army commander, General Mario Vercellino, was in an even blacker state of mind. On the left of the front, at the source of the Shkumbin River, he claimed his Third and Twenty-sixth Corps were outnumbered five to one by the enemy; he was also woefully lacking in artillery. However, the Third Corps had recently recaptured a strategic height on its front, thanks to the spirit of a reserve battalion of the 19th (Venezia) Division. Vercellino held a poor opinion of the Air Force, which he claimed was habitually late arriving at its objectives: 'It must support the troops more and not occupy itself overmuch with distant targets.' Vercellino, in fact, had decided to give his troops a week's rest until hoped-for reinforcements could arrive. General Geloso's Eleventh Army, on the right, was probing ways of recapturing the approaches to Kelçyre and hopefully retaking the town itself but, so far, the 51st (Siena) Division was being held up by the Greeks.

Other parts of the army bore the scars of the recent reverses. Colonel Giovanni Manai, the commander of the 41 Regiment of the 37th (Modena) Division, had been court-martialled for caving in under a Greek attack and opening a ruinous breach in the line. Losses had been grievous. For example, casualties in the 8 Alpine Regiment of the 3rd (Julia) Division reached eighty per cent. The 139 Infantry Regiment of the 47th (Bari) Division had to fall back in the midst of battle when it suddenly found itself out of hand grenades and bullets. The Julia commander, General Mario Girotti, urgently pleaded for the division to be retired for a rest and refit after the rough handling it had received in the first week of the invasion of Greece.

Fairly typical was the fate of the 7th (Lupi di Toscana, or Wolves of Tuscany) Division of the Twenty-fifth Corps that had been conducting a rear-guard action through the slow retreat northwards. On 17 January, the Greek 15th Division staged a push around the town of Ballaban under cover of artillery fire. The division's 7 Regiment picked up Italian grenades found abandoned in the snow by the Lupi and lobbed them in their general direction. They caught up with the rearmost elements of the Lupi near Vinokazit, on the main road between Hill 731 and Kelçyre and took them prisoner – all of four soldiers and a lieutenant shivering around a fitful fire. A far more useful discovery was a store of tinned food, cheese, jam and brandy, all of which was loaded onto the Italians' backs for the long night walk back to the Greek lines. The supplies decently fed a battalion of the 7 Regiment for several days.

Cavallero's report for that day says that the Wolves of Tuscany would have prevailed against 'fanatical' Greek attacks if the division's 77 Regiment had not broken under 'torrential' Greek artillery fire, leaving the 78 Regiment's left flank unprotected and forcing it back. This in turn opened a breach between the 21 Regiment and the Julia Division, which the latter struggled to close. The truth was worse than Cavallero's careful prose suggested; the great bulk of the 77 Regiment – including its commander and the sorry handful of men caught around the fire – were marched into captivity, while the 78 Regiment was effectively rendered helpless. (Shortly afterwards, Prince Peter of Greece, a liaison officer with the British, visited Italian prisoners of war in Ioannina. He asked to see the renowned Wolves of Tuscany. There was a jeering call: *'Lupi! Lupi!'* to which only a few demoralized men responded.)

The general feeling, however, was that the Italians had a sporting chance of recovering the ground lost since November, especially as the Greeks had so far failed to take the key towns of Berat, Tepelenë and Vlorë, this last-named all the more important as it was a vital supply port. After listening to his commanders' pessimistic reports, Cavallero moved on to Tirana to telephone the Duce and suggest forming a triangular solid Italian section whose base would be the roughly 100 kilometres of coastline between Vlorë and Durreş (Durazzo) and its apex inland at Tirana. From this position, he said, with Soddu listening in, the army could be amply replenished with new units and materiel for the push south. Notice of this was taken in Germany, whose foreign minister, Joachim von Ribbentrop, launched the official line that 'Italy [is] at this moment engaged in a stabilization of the front [and that] the Italian retreat is a transient phenomenon, a military accident that often happens in war.'

One commander could well have shaken his head at such vagueness and may well have done so: he was General Pricolo, the Air Force chief accompanying the Duce. Though he was an airman, he seems to have displayed a keener and more realistic sense of the military realities on the ground than many an army officer, Cavallero included. In fact, it could be argued that as an airman, and hence a more-or-less detached observer, he could see more clearly. On 17 January, Pricolo had sent a thousand-word report to Mussolini implicitly warning him against being too optimistic in dismissing the Greeks' fighting capacity. He noted that the Greeks almost always attacked from higher ground and combined their mortar and light artillery units to good effect. He also acknowledged their superior morale, though he believed that if the Greeks were stymied in their plan to seize Berat, their morale would suffer a severe blow: 736401

> So far in the operations [Pricolo wrote] the Greeks have displayed tactical ability and good staffing, especially in senior officers, iron discipline, ever-high morale and a spirit of initiative. At the same time, however, they are less able to take advantage of easy successes. They show an exaggerated concern for their flanks which they try to protect with effective flanking connections. They seem to have administrative problems, especially in providing supplies to high mountain locations.

For his own side, Pricolo placed the total number of troops in the Italian Ninth and Eleventh Armies at some 300,000, against an estimated 350,000 for the Greeks. The two armies comprised six army corps, or twenty-one divisions, three Bersaglieri regiments and three cavalry regiments. That would look good on paper, but since the start of the war at least ten divisions had been roughly handled – the 19th (Venezia), 53rd (Arezzo), 49th (Parma) and 29th (Piemonte) of the Ninth Army (Third and Twenty-sixth Corps); and the 51st (Siena), 5th Alpini (Pusteria), 3rd Alpini (Julia), 47th (Bari), 37th (Modena) and 131st Armoured (Centauro) of the Eleventh Army (Fourth, Eighth and Twenty-Fifth Corps).

Mussolini was anxious to make a good impression as, on 19 January, he was due to meet Hitler at Salzburg and wanted to impress him with Italy's military clout. The day before, Mussolini had probed Cavallero's deputy staff chief, Colonel Salvatore Bartiromo, for details of what was happening in Albania. According to a report of this tense exchange, the Duce was indignant. 'The Greeks already have a salient of fifteen kilometres,' he said. 'You've got to wage a war of manoeuvre. I've been hearing the same thing over and over – "The Greeks have formed a salient!" "We retreated in order to level out the front." Enough of this passivity! You have to attack, not level out with retreats.'

'But, Duce, we were never ready,' replied the deputy staff chief. 'There was always something lacking.'

Bartiromo excused the 'passivity' be explaining that there were not enough men to seize the strategic initiative. 'But you have the divisions,' Mussolini said. Yes, the colonel replied, but the divisions are under strength. The enemy had taken a lot of prisoners (at least 300 of them from the 77 Regiment of the crack Tuscan Wolves, or Lupi di Toscana, he might have added). The Duce cut him short: 'Bartiromo! There's no way other than to attack, attack! I've been saying this for a fortnight.'

'His Excellency Cavallero has that intention, but there's always something missing, munitions in particular.'

One can imagine the Duce shaking his massive head in impatience at this string of excuses from a staff officer. 'Bartiromo, you have to counterattack and break this spell that has been costing us territory for ninety days, from position to position. At this rate we'll find ourselves in the sea.'

A few moments later Mussolini got to the real point: 'I'm going to Germany. The first thing they're going to ask me is whether I'm going to stop at the present line. What do I reply to them?'

'That His Excellency Cavallero is confident of holding the line.'

'Then go and talk to "Excellency" Cavallero,' the Duce retorted, ending the talk on a note of contempt.

The Germans, of course, were under no illusions about the Albanian campaign; they could see perfectly well that the Italians so far had been humiliated. It is quite likely that they leaked a plan to themselves invade Greece on 15 March 1941, which Mussolini took seriously. And Hitler had never wanted his Axis ally to waste his men in a futile Balkan adventure in the first place. On the way to Salzburg, Mussolini was in a sour mood. What was he going to tell the Führer? 'If on 15 October [three months before] anyone had predicted what had actually happened, I'd have had him shot,' he growled to his foreign minister, Count Galeazzo Ciano. At Salzburg, Hitler treated the Duce cordially and tactfully, avoiding mention of the Italian debacle in Albania. But he made perfectly clear his own intention to move against Greece, the unavoidable implication being that Mussolini was going to fail. But failure was not yet in the Duce's vocabulary; he returned to Rome in a slow burn, grimly determined to restore Italy's military prestige against Greece before Hitler could steal his thunder.

The Germans in fact flatly dismissed Mussolini's forecast of a victory on the Albanian front, as evidenced in their minutes of the Salzburg summit:

It is totally impossible for the Italians to possess the forces required for an attack on the Albanian front in the time foreseen [two and a half months]. It is therefore ruled out that there can be any positive Italian help in case of a German attack on Greece via Bulgarian territory.

In the margin someone, possibly the Führer himself, had written: 'The German attack will provide some serious relief to the Italian front.'

Just in case any in the Fascist Party at home were inclined to point to Albania as a disappointment, the Duce assembled a conference of party cadres in Rome's Teatro Adriano on 23 February to reassure them that Italy's struggle against 'the masonic-democratic-capitalist world' would not let up. Though most of the 3,500–word speech was designed to shore up party morale in wartime, he could not avoid referring to Greece. His justification for the attack was that Greece, as Britain's last ally in the Mediterranean, needed squashing. But in his subsequent defence of the campaign per se, he sounded curiously apologetic:

On this point the agreement of all responsible military factors was absolute. I add that the operational plan, drawn up by the Armed Forces Supreme Command in Albania, was approved unanimously, without reservations of any sort.

Had there been any criticism of the military in high places? The Duce's language offers strong hints that there was. The casualty lists from Albania would have been reaching into many a grieving Italian home. Perhaps with those families in mind, he noted that 'the Italian soldiers in Albania have fought superbly' and that 'the Alpine troops, in particular, have written pages of blood and glory that would have been an honour for any army.' This was doubtless true in some cases. But he was far too clever to delude himself and must have stepped down from the stage of the Teatro Adriano wondering whether his words would have any effect.

Mussolini's directive to Cavallero was unequivocal:

On the eve of our attack you will convene the army corps and division commanders and announce the following: the attack which we will unleash can and must bring about a radical change in the situation, especially from the viewpoint of the troops' morale.

The directive went on to insist on complete surprise and to make the paramount point that nothing less than Italian military prestige was on the line. The tone could hardly mask the Duce's deep inner distrust of the officers leading the 'superbly fighting' men that had led him to take the field personally, in the hope that his mere overwhelming presence might turn the tide. Cavallero, for his part, decided that too many wounded, sick and frostbitten soldiers were being sent home, so he allowed only the most serious cases to board the hospital ships; the rest were to recuperate in the rear, to be available as reserves should the need arise. The losses in junior and middle-grade officers had been acute; green replacements were sent out fresh from civil life with little knowledge of the military life and no idea of the hellish conditions of combat. But a leader has to fight with the army he has, and in the early morning of 9 March Mussolini could fold his arms across his barrel chest and stare southwards into the Albanian mountains where the enemy waited.

The Duce might be expecting great things from his commanding general, but Cavallero's own strategic objective was sensibly focused: the hub of Kelçyre had to be gained at any cost. That town and Tepelenë to the west were key points on the road from the port of Vlorë, the army's main supply route. Geloso's Eleventh Army, spearheaded by the 58th (Legnano) Division of the Twenty-fifth Corps, was tasked with pushing down the Desnitsa valley and seizing Kelçyre. Once that was accomplished, Cavallero planned to wheel northwest and encircle the Greek 1st, 11th and 15th Divisions in the central sector, after which it would be a simple matter to drive the Greeks back over their border and proceed as far as the northwest

Greek town of Ioannina, some fifty kilometres south of the frontier. Unlike his reckless predecessors, Visconti Prasca and Soddu, Cavallero intended to stop at Ioannina. His hoped-for occupation of that north-western wedge of Greece would be a counterweight to the Germans' expected drive from the direction of Bulgaria – at the very least, a justification for the blood that Italian soldiers had already shed.

Even this limited objective was asking a great deal of the *Regio Esercito*, which was far from being the best-equipped army of its time. Uniforms and boots were generally of poor quality, with a tendency to disintegrate under the rigours of a winter campaign. Letters home and later reminiscences are full of references to 'strips and rags' hanging off tunics and trousers, as well as boots falling apart as soon as they got wet. Rations were often meagre and too often were lost when supply mules fell into raging rivers or were blown up by enemy cannon fire. Giovanni de Pizzol, a country boy from Treviso, noted in his diary that when rations finally reached his unit at 2 a.m. one morning, they consisted of 'a bit of cold broth with bad-smelling meat and a sopping wet piece of bread'. The wounded, including de Pizzol, received rather better fare such as *caffè latte*, chocolate, brandy and maybe a cigarette or two.

Accommodation was elementary in the extreme. Tents were flimsy and fragile, offering little protection from freezing wind and rain. The troops slept on thin straw palliasses. De Pizzol wrote of one rainy night when rainwater seeped through holes in the tent roof and dripped onto the soldiers. His corporal at last had to get up, light the tent candle and plug the holes with pages from a newspaper. Every soldier hoped for a spell of duty in a town or village where he could have a real roof over his head and sleep in a proper bed. As regards ammunition, that was also subject to the vagaries of the supply situation. A platoon with a heavy machine gun considered itself fortunate. De Pizzol's task was to carry his platoon's ammunition case; his lieutenant one day posed proudly with his men with their

Breda gun for a group photograph. 'This is our salvation,' he said, 'this gun with eight cases of ammunition.' De Pizzol recounted how a long burst of seven hundred rounds would stop the Greeks in their tracks and 'tear big holes in their lines'. The Bredas, however, often jammed and carrying them and the heavy cases through intractable mud was a distinct ordeal for all concerned.

In such conditions, the morale of the average Italian *fante*, or infantryman, could not have been very high. Thrown into an unfamiliar and implacably hostile environment, he would have been hard put to adjust. Private Matteo Pecoraro of the 8 Regiment, a native of Salerno near Naples, tried to keep his spirits up. Eager to do his duty to 'the Country and Mussolini,' he had embarked with his regiment at Brindisi on 23 December, ending up at Berat on Boxing Day. 'The trip was long and miserable,' he wrote in a letter home the day after his arrival. 'Don't worry if you don't get news from me. Don't cry because I've been sent down here. Just pray to the Good Lord to protect me from any danger. We're now waiting for our assigned zone.'

That zone was the north end of the Trebeshinë range where the Greek 1st Division had carved out a strong position. Hill 731 was the tip of this position. To its west is the Proi Math ravine, through which the main Tirana–Kelçyre road runs, overlooked by the Trebeshinë range. To the east is Hill 717, also known as Bregu Rapit, again separated by a ravine. This depression joins up with the Proi Math to form the Desnitsa river that flows alongside the Kelçyre road. Beyond that, to the east, rises the height of Mali Spadarit. In 1941, oak trees grew on the lower slopes of Hill 731, petering out as they neared the summit which was quite bare. The only reliable water source was a fitful stream at the bottom of Proi Math, though melted snow doubtless met the Greeks' water requirements. The north slope of the hill falls away sharply, studded with small clumps of trees and bushes, but offers a splendid view of anything approaching from the north. Cavallero wanted to level the Greek salient, of which Hill 731 was the most serious, before inaugurating his grand southward push.

Pecoraro's upbeat personality made an impression on his fellow-soldiers, one of whom described him as having 'a thin face, lit up by two large shining eyes...a face that gives off an inner light'. Shivering in their tents in the relentless snow-bound landscape, the men learned what war really was. Pecoraro's friend wrote:

> War is a hard and arduous thing, totally different from what you'd imagine: all the time you find yourself hitting against its harsh reality, such as itching, fleas, sudden awakenings, muscle tiredness, mud and misery. The mess is such that you see men die stupidly, you go on the attack without really understanding the use of it, because all you see is the tiny bit of front that you are in, and you feel you're going forward with blinkers on, like horses.... So men die and you don't know why and start wondering whether it's all just to send reports to the Corps... Then you discover a man like Matteo, and it's like rediscovering your lost self.

All that the war meant so far, for the majority of lower-ranking Italians, was 'snow and wind, wind and snow, without let-up' - the worry that you might escape a Greek bullet or shell only to die of cold in your sleep. It meant burying your dead comrades, with whom you had been laughing and joking only yesterday, in deep holes in snowdrifts. The words accurately convey the almost total absence of that vital concomitant of military morale, the belief that your country's cause justifies the inevitable hardship and danger. There was a pervasive melancholic sense of a lack of purpose, a gnawing 'what's it all for?' 'It's sad to think of dying so far from home, where no-one of your family can ever come to find you or say a requiem, and that nothing in the end will remain of you.' For Matteo Pecoraro, that would come very close to being true.

Little of this sentiment, of course, reached up to the higher command. The Eleventh Army was to have a monopoly of the Spring Offensive down the Desnitsa Valley on a six-kilometre front. Gambara's Eighth Corps would spearhead the movement with the initial assault assigned to the Cagliari, Puglie, Pinerolo and Bari Divisions beefed up by the crack 26 Blackshirt Legion of two battalions (the 152nd and 155th) targeted right at Hill 731. Flanking the attackers on the right of the line would be 24th (Pinerolo) Division that would outflank Hill 731 and the main Greek 1st Division defences and seize Kelçyre, while a secondary objective was to dislodge the already-fatigued Greek 5th and 17th Divisions from the Trebeshinë range. Supplementing the pressure on the Greek left would be the 21st (Sforzesca) Division of the Twenty-Fifth Corps. On the Italian left the 22nd Cacciatori Alpini (Alpine Hunters) and 5th (Pusteria) Division of the Fourth Corps would keep the Greek 11th and 15th Divisions busy and unable to help the centre, and hopefully the left and right would entrap the whole Greek II Corps in a pincers *coup de grâce*.

Cavallero could pride himself on drawing up a truly Clausewitzian – if not Napoleonic – plan, but the rest of the Italian command was by no means so sanguine. They had seen too much of the Greeks' mountain fighting abilities to be very confident of any sort of spectacular victory that Cavallero preached. The discredited Soddu had perceived this early on. In what seems an incredible lapse in staff work, no-one had bothered to inform Vercellino of the Ninth Army to the northeast that the offensive was scheduled to kick off on 9 March! (Cavallero later would protest his innocence here.) True, the Ninth Army's task was to hold off the Greek III Corps on the Yugoslav border as well as the Yugoslav Army; but that cannot excuse the fact that Vercellino, one of the two second-ranking senior officers under Cavallero along with Geloso, was kept in the dark about Mussolini's Spring Offensive. At the very least, the Ninth Army would have been held in reserve, to move in case the Eleventh Army encountered obstacles. In fact, Vercellino learned about the 9 March attack on that very day, when there was little, if anything, he could do. Perhaps his distrustful attitude to the whole campaign had put him outside normal communication channels.

Gambara's corps was to strike at the Greek 1st Division of the II Corps in a three-pronged attack, the centre prong of which would move down the Desnitsa Valley while the other two prongs carried out diversionary moves. Once Kelçyre was retaken (the thinking went), the Greek 1st Division would be outflanked as well as its neighbouring 5th and 17th Divisions then the Greek 11th and 15th Divisions – hopefully weakened by the hard winter campaigning – could be brushed aside in an unstoppable drive to Ioannina.

However, the Italians – as admitted even by their enemies – were experts in consolidating and fortifying positions once they had secured them. 'Overnight,' wrote a senior Greek staff officer after the war, 'they would set up fortifications and within a few days turn them into heavily-defended ramparts.' This would force the Greeks to launch costly frontal assaults with little chance of flanking moves. In fact, the Greeks would learn the lesson fast and apply it in reverse at Hill 731.

Cavallero had at his disposal twenty-five divisions comprising fifty-four regiments and twenty independent Blackshirt battalions, against forty-two Greek regiments. But these Greek regiments were better prepared than their enemies imagined. Their radio intercepts, aerial surveillance and prisoners' reports all converged on the imminence of a major offensive. On 7 March, the Greek command ordered a dry run of firepower to test readiness; while the 2nd and 17th Divisions were pressing towards the Tepelenë-Kelçyre road, the 1st Division commander, Major General Vasilios Vrachnos, ordered his artillery and mortar fire units to launch barrages northwards to test the enemy's reflexes and reactions. The Italians, believing a major Greek assault to be in the offing, replied with an equally fierce barrage that merely helped the Greeks pinpoint more Italian artillery positions.

Italian losses so far had been heavy: in just four months of combat 497 officers and 5,239 NCOs and soldiers had been killed. Command turnover at all levels had been high. On 28 February Geloso had issued an order of the day to his Eleventh Army; its contemptuous tone is worth recording:

The Greek slaves, powerfully armed by the British Empire, today will confront you, the Italian soldier whose unconquerable pride no-one can beat. Our country is pleased with you. Soon it will call you to the attack... And we will see the backs of the enemy for whom the English gold and weapons will not be enough to save them from the advance of the soldiers of the Eleventh Army.

The ingredients of propaganda are all there, condensed: the demonization of the enemy ('Greek slaves'), the glorification of one's own soldiers, the bogeyman ('British Empire', 'English gold'), in a standard formula (not much different from the mass media agendas of the present day, in fact). No doubt some Italian soldiers took Geloso's absurd bombast at face value, but most would have treated it with deserved cynicism.

On 1 March, the Duce, visiting his sons at the Grottaglie air base near Taranto on the heel of Italy, turned to Pricolo, his air chief, and told him to get an aeroplane ready as he intended to fly to Albania at 8:30 the next morning. Pricolo, thunderstruck, was momentarily speechless. 'Is there a problem?' the Duce pressed. After some hesitation, Pricolo worried aloud that as the news from the Albanian front was not very encouraging, the Duce 'might not want to associate [his] name' with a failure.

'But I'm not going operationally,' Mussolini replied. 'I want to inspect the front.' Pricolo at once saw through the deception – it was obvious that the Duce craved a chance for at least the pretence of leading his soldiers in war, but as Pricolo had no choice but to obey his chief's orders, a Siai–Marchetti SM79 bomber was duly readied at Bari. Mussolini took the controls for the one-hour flight to Tirana, accompanied by Pricolo and a dozen Macchi 200 fighters plus a couple of CantZ 506 seaplanes. He was grim and wordless all the way. Welcoming him at Tirana were Cavallero and Ranza, among others. There, the Duce got into a staff car and was driven down to the front. On the way, he passed detachments of the Bari Division who cheered him as he passed. As his mission was supposed to be an official secret, many men would have taken heart at his surprise appearance.

At Gambara's headquarters, the Eighth Corps commander bent over maps to explain the grand plan. Much was expected of the Cagliari in the first phase, as that division would have to break the Greek front east of Hill 731. Then the Puglie would join in, followed by the Pinerolo to roll up the Greek line down the Desnitsa Valley. Given that the *Regia Aeronautica* all but ruled the Albanian skies, about 28,000 men would do it, Gambara said airily. Moreover, some 200,000 shells were already stockpiled and ready for use. 'With these alone we can shake the Greek formation from end to end, without the enemy suspecting the main points of our action,' Gambara concluded, jabbing his finger on the map between Hills 731 and 717.

Mussolini kept his poker face on. He asked Gambara if he thought the Greeks had cottoned on to what was coming. 'From what we know, they haven't suspected a thing,' the general assured him. The Duce still wasn't so sure. Stemming the recent Greek advances around Trebeshinë and probes towards Monastero, just north of Hill 731, had been costly. The meeting broke up at 3:30 p.m. The next day Mussolini arrived at the Twenty-fifth Corps headquarters where the corps commander, General Carlo Rossi, confidently predicted that he would encircle the Greek centre in short order. But as Rossi was speaking, the thunder of Greek artillery pounding Italian positions around Tepelenë was rolling over the hills.

Besides the strictly strategic aspects of the Spring Offensive, Mussolini was haunted by a bigger problem. He knew that the distrustful and cynical Germans were looking over his shoulder; almost certainly he also was aware that Hitler and his generals knew perfectly well that the Spring Offensive was being carried out solely to maintain the Duce's prestige and was not expected to have any real effect on the wider war in Europe. But the day was still young. He had just seen some 100,000 shells fired at the unseen Greeks in two hours. Who could survive such an inferno? This was his fight, and his alone, and he had to win big.

Chapter 3

'This mountain will be our grave'

The initial rain of Italian fire and steel on Hill 731, experienced from the receiving end, was shattering. The first thing that Major Dimitrios Kaslas, commander of the Second Battalion of the 51 Regiment of the 1st Division, saw was a shell falling on a mule train, blowing the animals to pieces along with an accompanying officer and NCO. That first salvo also wounded Kaslas' executive officer, Lieutenant Kyriakou, and peppered his own raincoat with shrapnel holes. In Kaslas' words, as aerial bombing came to complement the shelling:

> Hill 731, where my battalion was, shook constantly. The air was heavy with dust, fire and smoke. It was hard to breathe from the gases of the explosions, a fiery hell, surrounded by flame and smoke, we couldn't see what's happening ten metres away.

Within minutes, the hill had been completely stripped of its crown of trees and bushes and resembled a churned-up, smoking volcano. Soldiers cowered in shell-holes, trying their best to protect artillery and machine gun emplacements. Kaslas ordered the exposed weaponry to be covered with blankets as some small protection against falling rocks and earth; nonetheless, the two machine guns on Hill 731, two 6.5 mountain guns and an anti-tank gun were destroyed. But Kaslas had his grimly-clear orders from the 51 Regiment commander and sector chief, Colonel Themistocles Ketseas: 'Defend your positions till the last.'

Greece had eleven infantry divisions in Albania: the 2nd, 3rd, 4th (reserve) and 8th (I Corps); the 1st, 5th, 6th, 11th, 15th and 17th (II Corps), plus a cavalry division and the 21 Infantry Brigade. The II Corps was rather deeper into Albania (consequently with a far harder job to do), as the I Corps was held back to commence the drive on Vlorë, by which time the weather should have improved, and then join with the II Corps, as most Greeks hoped, to drive the Italians 'into the sea'.

Hill 731 had been the final prize of a long and arduous Greek counter-attack in the mountains of southern Albania at the height of winter. Much of the credit for the Greek successes must go to the Greek commander-in-chief, Lieutenant General Alexandros Papagos. A haughty and austere man with something of a French stuffiness about him, he had proved to be an able strategist, wisely leaving many tactical decisions to his corps and division commanders, and leaning above all on the incomparable morale of the average Greek soldier, incensed at Italy's unprovoked aggression. It would be no exaggeration to say that morale in the Greek Army, not to mention the totally supportive home front, was as high as it could get in any army in any era, precisely because of that righteous fury. (A more familiar example might be the American sense of national outrage after the Japanese attack on Pearl Harbor.) In terms of numbers, each Greek company theoretically had to confront an Italian battalion. Many soldiers had grown up poor and in rural areas, with the result that they knew how to get by on hard bread and goat's cheese and scramble up the mountains on torn boots.

Early in the campaign, in early November 1940, the agile Greeks had taken quick advantage of a prime tactical error on the part of the 3rd (Julia) Division, which raced ahead of the main force to try and outflank the Greeks and seize the town of Metsovo. The Julia promptly found itself surrounded and forced to beat a retreat along the muddy Aoos River valley, the once-proud black feathers of the Carnia and Val Natisone contingents drooping in the rain, through which the red-eyed, unshaven troops trudged in the first serious Italian reverse of the campaign. The heart and soul of that Greek action was Colonel Konstantinos Davakis, the commander of a special mobile force of 2,000 men of the 8th Division. Barely had Davakis got the upper hand against General Mario Girotti's Julia than he took a bullet in the chest. He survived the wound but could take no further part in the fighting.

As indices of morale, war correspondent Spyros Melas recorded how the soldiers he was accompanying threw themselves flat on the ground at the approach of three Italian bombers. 'Hey, macaroni-face!' one boy taunted the pilot above him. 'Too bad I haven't got wings to get up there. Why don't you get down here and I'll show you!' After dropping a few ineffectual bombs, the Italian aircraft flew off. An NCO had been getting a shave in a barbershop set up in a village stable. 'Why did they leave?' he asked.

'Because the village didn't have any more windows to break,' deadpanned the company barber.

In one despatch Melas described a typical day's battle, this one to secure Hill 1602:

> I'm right in the front line of fire with our boys. I've abandoned the car I'm driving and riding in an all-purpose vehicle... I range over the whole vast space from the peaks to the deepest part of the Devol valley, this graveyard of the imperialistic dreams of Italian fascism. I live the Greek triumph in all its greatness. With each burst of enemy machine gun fire, our bugles sound the signal to charge, and right away comes [the officer's] fearful cry: *'Aera! Aera!'*... 'Come on boys, let's go!' A machine gun burst silences him in mid-shout. He's down. But instead of frightening the men, their impetus is redoubled. Everyone lunges forward and soon the height is taken.

Nearby, the captain of an artillery battery smiles at the correspondent while ranging his guns. 'Look,' he said, 'they're running away!'

He gives me his binoculars. I see the first Italian units doing the Marathon run: it's the 84 Regiment of the [19th] Venezia Division that's breaking up as it flees, scattering into the foothills... A young soldier from Chios appears, leading four prisoners. A reserve officer, a lawyer from Athens, captures three more and sends them to the rear, handing them his business card. I address them in Italian, and they reply: 'Of our battalion only a hundred and twenty men are left.'

Given the military censorship of the time, we may grant Melas some poetic licence in the interests of home-front morale and patriotism. But even allowing for that, there is not the slightest doubt that the morale of the Greeks was far higher than that of the Italians. They were fighting an invader, for one thing, while a great many Italian soldiers, as we have seen, had serious doubts about what they were ordered to fight for, and were generally poorly led into the bargain. To his credit, however, Melas was careful not to impugn the collective honour of the Italian foe, as it was all too easy to do: 'It's a pretty fairy tale that the Italians do not put up any resistance. They stick stoutly to their defences, and it's not their fault if the Greek is resolved to die rather than be enslaved.'

Able men and high morale enabled Papagos to steadily, if bloodily, push back the Italians well into Albania between the declaration of war on 28 October to the end of winter 1941. At the end of January, an unexpected shock hit the Greeks: their wartime leader Ioannis Metaxas, technically a fascist dictator but firmly on the side of the Allies, died unexpectedly after a short illness. More than anyone else, Metaxas had been the guiding spirit behind the Greek counterattack. His replacement, a mild-mannered banker, had nothing of his iron drive, and was eventually to succumb to despair and suicide. But for the men at the front, Metaxas' death had little if any appreciable effect on the general morale. King George II in Athens was maintaining the wartime spirit for the public, while Papagos handled the military side. The intractable winter of 1940-1 had essentially stalled the campaign on both sides. But by the end of February Papagos, of course, knew perfectly well from various sources (including captured Italian officers) that a spring offensive was in the works and had already taken steps to reorganize his army accordingly.

On 16 December Papagos, less than two months into the war, had moved his command headquarters to Ioannina to be closer to the action in Albania. Yet he was acutely aware of one major disadvantage to the move: with the threat of an Axis invasion from the direction of Bulgaria ever-present, he needed to be available for that sector as well if needed. Therefore, on 12 February he hived off the north-west command into a separate one: the Epiros Army Detachment based at Ioannina, with the authority to act more or less independently. The Detachment, known by its Greek acronym TSH, comprised the I Corps and II Corps. To its east was the similarly-arranged West Macedonia Army Detachment (TSDM) – essentially the III Corps – to keep an eye on the Bulgarian front.

January 1941 saw intermittent clashes on the snowy peaks and in the valleys between them where, on some days, frostbite and sheer cold claimed more soldiers on both sides than enemy action did. The names of the actions are those of the endless Albanian heights that were fought over: Bregu Psarit, Bregu Rapit, Bregu Math, Mali Spadarit, Guri i Topit, alien-sounding names to Greek and Italian alike. There was very much an edge-of-the-world feeling to this unforgiving place that no-one had really known about before the war. For the Greeks, hunger was almost as severe a menace as the cold as, all too often, mule supply trains couldn't make it up the snow-clad crags to where the men shivered.

Private Georgios Zachariou, a grenadier in the 2 Infantry Regiment (II Corps) near Frashër, east of Kelçyre, got so hungry on the freezing night of 12 December that he feared he might starve unless he broke regulations and went out clandestinely to look for food in local houses. He was a large man and felt the lack of nourishment more than most. To reach the outskirts of Frashër, he and a friend sneaked out of the lines and across a ravine, in pitch blackness and a light fall of snow. The village technically was in Italian-held territory, and if caught by a patrol, the two men could have been shot as spies. Their platoon commander was in on the scheme and promised not to get them into any trouble as long as they could return with some food. Zachariou and his friend arrived at a prosperous-looking house with a light in the windows. Just in case, he flicked the safety catch off a couple of grenades and knocked on the front door. A well-dressed elderly gentleman opened the door and welcomed Zachariou in fluent Greek: he was the village *mukhtar*, or head man.

Still on his guard, Zachariou spun a tale that he was the advance guard of a whole platoon that had surrounded the place, and then got to the point: he and his comrades were in urgent need of food. In short order, the *mukhtar* went to his storeroom and brought out sacks of maize flour, sides of beef and mutton, a supply of Italian canned goods, feta cheese, honey and tobacco and cigarette papers. For good measure he filled their water flasks with fiery *raki* to warm themselves and take the edge off their privations. Loaded down with the goodies, Zachariou and his friend raced back to their position to where their grateful platoon commander waited. The *mukhtar's* gifts may well have saved some lives in Zachariou's unit, as the supply trains didn't reach the position until more than a week later.

The 10 Company of the Third Battalion, to which Zachariou belonged, was placed on attack alert at midnight on 22 December by Colonel Ketseas. The company commander, Captain Manolis Tzannakis, walked among the men, service pistol in hand, quietly issuing instructions: the battalion was to crawl towards an Italian-held height known as Hill 1150, with bayonets already fixed for a surprise assault. It would be Zachariou's baptism of fire. Just before dawn, the men set out, hugging the earth as silently as possible. About two hundred metres from the Italian lines, as the first rays of dawn broke,

Captain Tzannakis yelled the order: *'Aeraaaaa!'* The cry, taken up by dozens of men, multiplied as it echoed off the surrounding cliffs.

The screaming wave, bayonets levelled, slammed into the unsuspecting Italian 68 Regiment line. Tzannakis fell seriously wounded at the head of his men. The Italians at first broke but re-formed halfway up Hill 1150 and stood fast, hitting back with machine gun fire and offensive grenades. Zachariou saw an Italian soldier pierced with multiple bayonet wounds as well as bullets, covered in blood, reflexively putting up his hands to ward off death, staggering away and then falling headlong down a slope, spurting blood. At once a Greek NCO ran over to the dead Italian, turned him over, rummaged in his backpack and remove a blood-soaked loaf of bread which he began to devour 'with great gluttony, as if it was all quite normal'. Zachariou considered it far from normal.

Zachariou had a hand in capturing three of the enemy – a company barber and cook, and a senior NCO. He tried to put them at their ease; *'Non aver paura, io sono amico,'* he said in the little Italian that he knew. ('Have no fear. I'm a friend.') The barber handed over his razors, which eventually found their way to a Greek field hospital. The cook happened to have the 68 Regiment flag with him, which of course was taken as booty. The cook's backpack also contained a change of all-woollen underwear 'of unimaginable luxury' that soon replaced Zachariou's own sorry lice-ridden shorts.

In the following days, the Third Battalion staged similar attacks on several enemy objectives but failed to make headway. The front broke on 27 December, with the Italians in general retreat. Zachariou's unit was tasked with rounding up as many prisoners as possible by outflanking and encircling individual units. He saw a lone enemy soldier, waited until he came within grenade range, and called out: *'Non aver paura. Bella Grecia! Noi siamo amici vostri. La guerra é passata per voi.'* ('Have no fear. Greece is nice! We're your friends. For you the war is over.') The bewildered Italian put up his hands. A dozen more prisoners were rounded up this way.

Then disaster struck. One of Zachariou's fellow-soldiers, without warning, lifted his rifle to his shoulder and aimed at the prisoners. 'For God's sake don't shoot!' Zachariou yelled. But the other loosed off two shots, though without hitting anyone. Immediately a burst of machine gun fire sounded from the Italian lines and Zachariou's friend fell dead at his feet, the side of his head blown off. Pandemonium ensued, with no quarter given. In the shock of the moment, Zachariou hurled his grenades at the Italian prisoners, the survivors of whom fled.

Private Pecoraro and his unit went into action on 13 January at Bregu Psarit in one of the moves designed to blunt the Greek advance and stabilize the Italian line before the Spring Offensive got underway. To get there they had to march, in soaked and mud-encrusted greatcoats and ragged tunics and boots, through a forbidding fog-shrouded valley where 'it seemed the Greeks were shadowing us all the time; at times they would come alive with their mortars... as if to say, "We're here, you can't rest even for a moment."' This was a typical night's experience:

The cold was frightful, you heard the wind howling like a soul of the damned... you're on duty and expect death, and death indeed came for some – we saw four soldiers who in the morning, with the first light, lay stretched out of the ground and went to wake them, thinking they were sleeping. They were stiff as sticks, shrivelled up, dead of the cold, their faces as white as wax. We had to bury them there in the snow... In desperation you think that no-one will return home alive even if no Greeks appear.

Pecoraro's officers in the 8 Regiment wore gloomy expressions. Patrols sent out to get food sometimes failed to return. The men were all too aware that the Greeks were near and could attack any time and that the sparse ammunition they were able to carry wouldn't be of much use in a serious fight. Such was the cold that if anyone was so incautious as to touch the barrel of his weapon without gloves, chances are that some of the flesh would stick to the metal, assuming that the forefinger pulling the trigger had any feeling left in it at all. 'We all think: this mountain will be our grave.'

During an evening rest, a lieutenant appeared out of the snow with the news that the Greeks were attacking the mule trains with mortars; the unit had to get to its feet and, in the snowy darkness, continue climbing up to the peak ahead, otherwise the Greeks would be in a position to dominate the whole area. A break in the fog revealed a line of men coming down from the height. 'Get yourselves in loose order and take positions behind snowdrifts,' the lieutenant ordered. 'Have your weapons ready and let's see what happens.' The line of men disappeared behind an outcrop and reappeared, nearer. They turned out to be their own men, 'a line of wounded, supporting one another, trying to get to us'. As they staggered on, a salvo of Greek mortar fire sent them scattering. The fire was devastatingly accurate, picking off the wounded men one by one until they ended up 'motionless, their arms spread out, their faces in the snow'.

The men of the 8 Regiment could only watch, sickened. They might have been able to deal with the unearthly cold, the extreme privations, the losses, the howls of men hit and the groans of wounded men abandoned on the field, if they had known and believed in what they were fighting for. But that evening there wasn't time to brood on it too long; someone raised a shout: 'the Greeks are coming!' This time, a long line of men was seen winding around the slope below – this time it was the enemy, who had outflanked the Italian units on the height.

This may or may not – the information we have is vague on this point – have been the action reported later by the commander of the 8 Regiment, Colonel Vittorio Ranise, in the regimental diary. Ranise described an enemy encirclement in the driving snow against which his own artillery didn't have much of an effect. He sent his second-in-command, Lieutenant Colonel Scotti, with a column, slogging through half a metre of snow to try and get in the rear of the Greek line. As the snow and enemy fire held up the move, Ranise decided on a frontal assault on the main Greek position on the height of Bali, a part of the Bregu Psarit. The charge was launched with vigour; the regiment got within grenade distance of the Greeks, who responded with a fearsome hail of machine gun and mortar fire. After an hour's bitter combat, Ranise had to call off the attack, beaten by an enemy whom he described as 'furnished with automatic weapons, mortars and machine guns... more precise and deadlier than our very obsolete equipment.'

Ranise was most likely referring to the Greeks' most effective weapon, the French-made Hotchkiss M1929 heavy 13.2mm machine gun. In firepower, it definitely outclassed the Italian 12.7mm Breda M37 heavy and the 8mm Fiat-Revelli Model 1935. The result was that the average Italian soldier and junior officer, having been breezily informed that the Greeks were inferior in weaponry as well as in numbers, experienced a rude awakening – not to mention sudden death – when faced with the deep *chug-chug* of the Hotchkiss spitting out from behind every rock and snowdrift. At Bregu Psarit, Colonel Ranise counted the cost to his regiment: three officers and seven enlisted men dead, five enlisted men wounded and seven missing, one officer and one enlisted man taken to a field hospital. The conclusion of his report is telling:

> Physical condition of the troops: bad. Moral condition of the troops: passable. Functioning of the supply services: severely hampered by weather and a lack of transport. The troops are on dry rations. Atmospheric conditions: strong winds and snow through the whole day.

The colonel's discreet description of his men's morale as 'passable' is almost certainly a diplomatic attempt to mask its true, much worse, state which would not reflect very well on himself. One of the seven enlisted men missing was Private Matteo Pecoraro.

On 7 January, Papagos had ordered the suspension of operations along the front as the snow and extreme cold had made any major movements impossible. But two weeks later, seeing an opportunity to improve his positions, he launched a drive to seize the Desnitsa river valley through which ran the main northbound road from Kelçyre. As this was precisely the main route that Cavallero wanted to take towards the Greek border, the move had to be countered. Cavallero also saw a threat to the approaches to the port of Vlorë that was the main landing point for men and supplies. To keep that approach free, he had to hold the Tepelenë area at all costs; Tepelenë was eighteen kilometres from Kelçyre, and like the latter, guarded the southern passages to Greek territory; both had to be in Italian hands if Cavallero had any hope of taking the war back to the Greek mainland. And that, of course, was precisely why Papagos planned to create a long salient to the north of Kelçyre that would threaten the Italian base at Berat as well as the military supply route from Vlorë.

At 9:00 a.m. on 22 January, the Greek 16 Regiment of the 1st Division, II Corps, under cover of artillery fire, moved on a farming hamlet called Spi Kamarate east of the main Kelçyre–Berat road and overlooking it. Half an hour later, two companies of the 7 Regiment stormed the Italian position, held by the Val Chiese, or 6 Alpini Regiment, 2nd (Tridentina) Division. The men of the Val Chiese, a proud unit going back to 1915, put up a stiff resistance, halting the Greek attack and inflicting losses. Observing the action was Colonel Themistocles Ketseas, the commander of the 51 Regiment on the right, who ordered his mortar company to begin shelling the Italians. Encouraged by spirited bugle calls, one company of the 7 Regiment got to within about four hundred metres of the main Italian stronghold on the conical peak of Spi Kamarate but under severe fire could advance no farther.

At about 10 a.m., the Val Chiese counter-attacked, sending the right-hand company of the 7 Regiment reeling back. The setback was momentary, however, as Greek reserves were rushed in, as well as the Second Battalion of the 5 Regiment on the right. The bulk of the 7 Regiment's force slowly crept closer to the enemy position until both lines converged in a stubborn grenade and bayonet duel. Both the Greek and the Italian artillery were forced to lengthen their trajectories to avoid shelling their own men. At one point, Second Lieutenant Georgios Moutsopoulos, in command of the company that had to fall back, saw a handful of Italians throwing up their hands. As a relatively inexperienced reservist, he was probably unaware that he was walking into a trap. As he went forward to take the 'surrender' a burst of machine gun fire cut him down. Moutsopoulos' men avenged their commander with a hail of fire of their own.

Ketseas ordered his artillery to step up its bombardment of Spi Kamarate, forcing the Val Chiese to eventually break under the pressure and begin abandoning the hamlet, leaving behind two anti-tank guns and many dead. This was the signal for the 7 Regiment's Second Battalion to stage a bayonet charge at the retreating foe. As the lines closed, an inspired Greek bugler began to sound a popular mountain song called 'Sons of Eagles', spurring the cheering men on. Only a few of the Val Chiese's Second Battalion had the courage to stay, holing up in scattered houses of Spi Kamarate, but these few resisted stoutly with rifle, machine gun and grenade, firing from behind doors and through windows. Only constant fire from Second Lieutenant Leonidas Konstantinidis' machine gun platoon overcame the resistance.

It was not yet noon when the remnants of the Val Chiese threw down their weapons and raised their hands. This time the surrender was for real. A total of three hundred and forty-five soldiers, including twenty-two officers, were disarmed and marched to the rear. Among them was the Second Battalion commander, Major Francesco Laboratore. In the aftermath of the battle for Spi Kamarate, the

Greeks were too dazed to pursue the retreating enemy; the houses of the hamlet brimmed with Italian dead and wounded. The Val Chiese had also left behind a 7.5cm cannon and several motor vehicles. At the same time, Kaslas' battalion, after a hard slog to the north, captured one hundred and sixty-five of the enemy including another battalion commander. Laboratore, under questioning at 1st Division headquarters, had to ruefully admit that he didn't expect the Greeks to attack him with such spirit. The battle cost the Greeks thirty-three dead, including three officers. Among them was the first man to have crossed the Desnitsa river in the first move to create the salient.

Cavallero blamed the collapse of the Val Chiese Regiment on a supposed 'lack of contact between the soldiers and the leadership'. As usual with Cavallero (and most Italian senior officers), his buck-passing observations were only half true. Major Laboratore was closer to the mark when he attributed his debacle to the determination of the Greeks. For the lower Italian ranks, it was a nightmare. One Italian reserve lieutenant in his diary described 22 January as 'a day of hell'. As the dead and wounded around him multiplied, he was assailed by the constant order: 'Resist to the last man! Resist! Resist!' But he, for one, was convinced that the order was absurd as the unit was holding an untenable position. He saw 'masses of Greeks' fording the Desnitsa river, shortly followed by masses of Val Chiese prisoners crossing in the other direction. 'The dead are without number...' The lieutenant himself was marched into captivity the next day, the stubborn regimental orders of 'Resist! Resist!' still echoing in his ears.

With the seizure of Spi Kamarate, the way was clear for a Greek advance up the Kelçyre-Berat road to the north end of the Desnitsa valley, where two heights dominated its entrance: Hill 731 and the smaller Hill 717 (Bregu Rapit) to the east, separated by a narrow gully. But Papagos didn't intend to stop there. The plan was to keep going in a northwesterly direction; the II Corps was to pass Ballaban to sever the Berat road at Gllavë and then push westwards across the

Vijosë river (Vojussa to the Italians and Aoös to the Greeks) towards the prize of Vlorë, while the I Corps would advance in the same direction from its line anchored at the port of Himarë and ending at the southern end of the Trebeshinë range, its right joining the II Corps left.

At midmorning on 23 January, a red flare and twelve shots of mountain artillery were the signal for two battalions of the 5 Regiment, the Second and Third, to renew the advance. The former, under Kaslas, overcame sporadic enemy resistance; Ketseas was waiting for the 33 Regiment to cross the Desnitsa river and turn up but, at noon, encouraged by Kaslas' success, he ordered a general attack on heavily-defended Hill 717. Kaslas' battalion was hit by a sudden Italian counter-thrust which temporarily halted him but was dealt with by Greek mountain artillery and mortar fire. By 5 p.m., Hill 717 was in Kaslas' hands.

On the left, however, the going was tough. The 7 Regiment's Second Battalion, despite losses, proceeded in small jumps throughout the day under withering enemy fire from the flanking heights, but by evening managed to join up with Kaslas' battalion. Italian units held Hill 731 and its spurs, firing desultorily. A night attack on them was out of the question, as both Greek battalions had suffered considerable casualties and were fatigued after a day of mountain combat. But unexpectedly, at 10:30 p.m., fatigue had to be forgotten as columns of the Italian Twenty-fifth Corps emerged from the darkness to storm Hill 717 and hit Kaslas' battalion with full force. The Greeks resisted desperately in an hour of hand-to-hand combat, before the defenders' mortar fire forced the Italians back. But only momentarily. Half an hour before midnight, the Italians rushed at Hill 717 again, and this time came very close to clawing it back in ninety minutes of bitter close-order fighting before pulling back again, leaving behind the usual grim quota of bodies. Kaslas didn't know it yet but holding on to Hill 717 was a dress rehearsal for his defence of Hill 731 six weeks later.

The Greeks, despite their greater familiarity with mountain territory, were not having an easy time of it. They suffered from privations and frostbite as much as any Italian; those soldiers from the sun-drenched Aegean islands, for example, could barely withstand the polar conditions. Private Takos of Ketseas' 51 Regiment had nothing to keep him warm when he and his unit scaled the snow-covered Trebeshinë range on 25 January; the shivering troops were given raw sheepskins to keep warm in. Two weeks later, he would be sent on with the rest of Major Kaslas' battalion to secure Hill 731. 'For a month we worked on trenches and shelters by night, as we were fired on by day,' Takos wrote much later. 'Hill 731 was called Golgotha.'

On the night of 23 January, the Second Battalion of the 33 Regiment began to cross the Desnitsa river, its right flank aiming for the village of Bubesi midway between Hill 717 and Mali Spadarit. It immediately came under severe fire, and the crossing had to be abandoned. Throughout 24 January, the 33 Regiment's attempts to move towards Bubesi were foiled; that night Captain Dionysios Arbouzis (later Lieutenant General Arbouzis, Chief of the General Staff), the Second Battalion commander, tried to find a way through to Bubesi in driving rain and the ubiquitous mud, made worse by confusing and conflicting orders from regimental headquarters. Finally, on the morning of 25 January, Arbouzis, at the head of his column, forded the Desnitsa (with the loss of one man) and linked up with Kaslas' battalion, which had just had to abandon Hill 717 after a bitter see-sawing fight the previous evening. Arbouzis' battalion rallied that of Kaslas, and both units counter-attacked successfully, thanks to help from the artillery and mortar platoons, taking sixteen Italians prisoner. Hill 717 was again in Greek hands.

It was the task of the 5th (Crete) Division to secure the Trebeshinë range – or as much of it as could be secured. Second Lieutenant Hesiod Tsingos of the 14 Regiment wondered which was the worse foe, the Italians or the extreme cold. It was 29 January, and the mere sight of the ghostly white, beetling height was daunting. Yet it had to be taken as it dominated that all-important road threading through the Desnitsa valley between Berat and Kelçyre. The sector was held by the Legnano Division's Val Cismon Regiment of specialized mountain troops, flanked by the 67 and 68 Regiments, which had dented the Greek lines a few days before and were poised to pounce to seize the road. The nights were so desperately cold at the summit that the Val Cismon units had temporarily descended to warmer quarters on the west side, intending to go back up in the morning. Tsingos, in provisional command of the Eleventh Company, replacing an officer crippled by frostbite, was awed by his tough, resourceful Cretans who were used to handling firearms since boyhood. 'They didn't sell their lives cheaply,' he recalled years later, in his nineties.

> They [were] undisciplined, insolent and insubordinate, but you had to admire them for their warlike qualities, the only thing that matters in war. You loved them for their humanity, and you had their love wherever and whenever it was needed.

'Christ and the Apostles!' the 14 Regiment commander, Colonel Nikolaos Spendos, exclaimed, throwing up his hands, when he saw the almost sheer cliff his three battalions had to scale – and with an evening blizzard about to break as well. It was fine for the staff in the rear to sit in stove-warmed rooms and pore over maps and order the height taken, but to the men at the scene it seemed impossible. The top of Trebeshinë soared nearly 2,000 metres into the lowering sky. Officers and men alike were muffled up in thick hoods, and the officers had removed the stars from their shoulders so that they wouldn't reflect light and give away their positions. 'Maybe we'll go up tomorrow,' Spendos said.

Tsingos, however, seized by what he called a momentary craze, volunteered to make the attempt at once. 'I'm going up,' he said. 'Anybody who wants can come with me and God help us.'

'Come on, mate,' one of his men, a former convict freed for military service, said in encouragement. 'Let's get it done.' (There was little regard for military etiquette here.) All four dozen men of the Eleventh Company followed him. Tsingos, along with another second lieutenant, a sergeant and four privates, was the first to the snowy summit, after a supreme effort that one of the soldiers later wrote he 'didn't care to remember'. The effort proved to be well rewarded when they stumbled on lavish stores of Italian weapons, ammunition, booze and biscuits.

At dawn the following day, the men, duly nourished and rested, hunkered down to wait for the men of the Val Cismon to climb back up to the post they had left for the night. Tsingos arranged his men in a defensive line, with the Italians' own machine guns locked and loaded. A column of grey-green Alpini uniforms appeared below and voices were heard. Tsingos ordered his company to keep absolutely still, threatening to shoot anyone who made a sound.

'They're going to capture us,' one nervous soldier whispered.

'I'll give the signal to aim the machine guns,' Tsingos said. 'The enemy has to get very close so that their air force and artillery can't help them.'

When the first of the Val Cismon were just a half dozen metres away from their shelter, Tsingos' men opened fire, spattering the snow with blood. A short time later, Colonel Spendos, with an advance platoon turned up, having scaled the eastern slope. From now on, Trebeshinë would remain in Greek hands, and a steady barrage of Greek II Corps artillery fire in its defence would henceforth assure that it would stay there.

The national shock of Prime Minister Metaxas' unexpected death on 29 January did not prevent the 1st Division from surging forward and securing the whole southern half of Trebeshinës. Cavallero saw an immediate enemy threat to his main base at Berat. His diary entry for that day reveals his fear that Tepelenë might also fall.

I am ordering an acceleration in our plans for a new offensive which, I hope, will forestall that of the enemy and not let us lose the tactical advantage we secured in our recent operations.

This 'new offensive' would turn out to be the Spring Offensive, designed to crush the Greek II Corps once and for all.

Meanwhile, a clamour arose for a scapegoat on which to pin the reverses, and one was found in the Eighth Corps commander, General Emilio Bancale, who in turn blamed the supposed incompetence of his Blackshirt units. 'I assure you that the Blackshirts are worthless,' Bancale rather ignobly wrote to Cavallero. 'When the Greeks realize that they have them in front, they attack at once.' This biting criticism of the Fascist Party's elite units earned Bancale his dismissal as corps commander; he was replaced by General Gastone Gambara, he of the lucky non-regulation *bersagliere* tunic.

Cavallero was right to fret about the threat to the supply routes from Vlorë. On 12 February, with the worst of the winter over, the TSH command ordered the I Corps to capture the port of Vlorë, through which Italian supplies were being ferried, and the Vlorë–Tepelenë road over which the supplies and fresh troops were fed to the front lines. At the same time, the II Corps was assigned to hold the heights around Gllavë (including Hill 731) and link up with the I Corps to hold the line from Vlorë inland. The 2nd (Athens) Division of the I Corps hammered at Mount Shendeli to the west of Trebeshinë but couldn't budge the 21st (Sforzesca) Division whose Blackshirt contingent, by the way, belied General Bancale's belittling description and stood its ground.

General Georgios Lavdas, the commander of the 2nd Division, had attempted at first to secure the high ground south of the Kelçyre–Tepelenë road, but intense shellfire from the Sforzesca on Shendeli pinned his Athenians down. A British artillery officer, acting as observer with the division, thought it would be impossible to advance through such an inferno. But Lavdas called in his own artillery, which engaged the Italian guns in a duel that sent the Sforzesca's advance units reeling back. The Greeks intercepted Italian radio communications whose content could be summed up as, 'What on earth is going on over there?'

Meanwhile, in the teeth of a blinding blizzard, the Cretans of the II Corps' 5th Division managed to secure several heights at the northern end of the Trebeshinë range, but met stubborn resistance at a peak called Punta Nord from the Sforzesca Division and the 53rd Blackshirt Battalion. A fierce Italian counterattack on Hill 1178 was repulsed with considerable loss around the village of Mezgoranit. But Mount Shendeli to the west remained in Italian hands.

This was mountain combat at its most demanding. The designations of the heights that were fought over – Hills 1178 and 1816 (metres) on the first day of the TSH's operations – show the considerable altitudes that the soldiers of both sides had to clamber up, and have enough energy to fight when they got there. The lean and mean Greeks were admittedly better at it than the Italians, who nevertheless showed great determination in attacking what to most of them would have seemed frighteningly unfamiliar and forbidding terrain. Their second attack to re-take Mezgoranit on the night of 15/16 February also ended in failure, with the loss of seven hundred men - two hundred men killed and some five hundred captured. For a week, continuing snowfalls stalled the 5th Division's advance; the division itself in three weeks lost 3,500 men either killed, wounded, captured or debilitated by frostbite, while more than seven hundred and fifty pack mules had perished.

The progress of the I Corps was contested uninterruptedly. In the face of severe Italian artillery fire, the 2nd Division seized a bridge over the Nemerska river and took prisoner some four hundred Italians, including two senior officers. On 19 February, it took the village of Pestan but could not make further headway through the curtain of artillery and tank fire from the 131st (Centauro) Armoured Division that accounted for considerable Greek casualties. Further bad weather halted the 2nd Division's advance along the Tepelenë-Kelçyre line.

February's operations were essentially a contest of who could occupy which strategic height. One of them, running along the west side of the Desnitsa Valley where the main Italian thrust was being planned, was the Mezgoranit peak. The Greek 5th Division's costly seizure of that height showed how hard it was to secure enough flanking positions to be able to fire on the projected Italian route of attack. In response, Geloso beefed up his own front with units of the 59th (Cagliari) Division – which was assigned to the first attack wave – and the 7th, 16th, 29th, 30th and 85th Blackshirt battalions, but all they could accomplish was to confirm what was essentially a stalemate on 8 March, the eve of the offensive.

Cavallero duly drew the conclusions from weeks of inconclusive and bloody fighting. His diary entry for 14 February betrays rueful admiration for the Greeks' skill at bayonet charges but wonders whether it means that they lack proper ammunition! Entries for subsequent days indicate that he felt under intense pressure from constant Greek attacks along his front and worried that the 'inferno of fire' from the efficient Greek mortars and mountain artillery could be shaking his troops' morale.

For weeks, the TSH command in Ioannina had become aware of the concentration of Italian forces on its II Corps front. Aerial observation plus plans found on at least one captured officer had made it quite obvious that the Spring Offensive, or something like it, was imminent. The Italian probes in force were becoming bolder, and apparently better-organized than before. Night assaults were now making use of colour-coded flares that were fired ahead of a probe to illuminate the Greek positions. Engineer teams were observed hacking new trails out of the mountainsides for the infantry to march over. The main blow was expected between Gllavë and Bubesi. Colonel Ketseas was ordered to bring up the 33 Regiment of the 15th Division on the right and the 16 Regiment of the 5th

Division on the left to form a strong buffer under his own separate command seconded to the 1st Division.

But there was some uncertainty on how exactly to meet the expected Italian blow. On 25 February, Papagos conferred with King George II and other senior civil and military officials in Athens on how to keep and hold Tepelenë, a town on a key crossroads. Lieutenant General Markos Drakos, the commander of the TSH, warned that the 1st, 6th and 11th Divisions of the II Corps had been severely mauled and needed at least three weeks' rest to rebuild their strength; moreover, the localized attacks that were made so far turned out to have had little tactical value and resulted only in unnecessary attrition in men and munitions. Drakos recommended suspending even minor offensive operations for some days in order to get the TSH's breath back, as it were, after which both its corps could get on with their original assignments.

Papagos, however, was now faced with a serious dilemma. So far everything had gone swimmingly for the Greeks; the Army's initial objective of ejecting the Italians from Greek territory had succeeded beyond the hopes of even the wildest optimists in Athens. The Army's momentum had carried it over the border and deep into Albania itself in order to form the widest possible buffer zone against a renewal of the Italian offensive. But how wide should that buffer zone be, and where should the Greek advance stop? Technically, Greece in fact had now become an aggressor, entering the territory of neighbouring Albania, an Italian protectorate, by force of arms. Greek government and public opinion, of course, did not read it that way; Greece was winning, and that was all they needed to know. Yet the Army could not go on advancing indefinitely. The war aim of booting the Italians out of Greece had already been achieved four months before. So what was Papagos to do now? The only course of action for him was the potentially unpopular one of changing from an offensive to a purely defensive strategy, placing the I and II Corps along a rough southwest-northeast line in the middle of which Hill 731 stood like a sentinel.

Papagos was also worried about what could happen on the Macedonian and Bulgarian front, where the III Corps was keeping an uneasy watch. He was receiving complaints that the formation of the TSH and the emphasis of maintaining the bulk of the Army in Albania was denuding the north-east sector, and at a time when a German attack there was becoming likelier by the day. In fact, before the war, Metaxas had built a sophisticated one hundred and fifty-five-kilometre line of fortifications, including underground bunkers, modelled on France's fabled Maginot Line, along the top of the Kerkini and Rhodopi mountain ranges on the Greek-Bulgarian border. The proven uselessness of the Maginot Line in 1940 was not lost on the Greek commanders, who realized that the Metaxas Line – designed to keep off a pre-war Bulgarian invader – would similarly be of little use against the superbly-equipped Germans and their Luftwaffe.

The commander-in-chief's decision to maintain the defence line deep inside Albania was to come in for some criticism after the war. Strictly speaking, the criticism went, the Greek Army had already accomplished its prime war aim by repelling the Italian invader. What was to be accomplished by a continued advance, and in foreign territory at that? The losses could not be adequately replenished – the Army was scraping the bottom of the barrel for reserves. Far better, some said, to withdraw to the border and keep a solid defence there to thwart any repeated invasion attempt. It would also free up a considerable body of troops to fight on the north-east border against a German invasion from Bulgaria that was now seen as almost certain. Some senior officers recalled the fiasco of 1922, when a Greek army, after initial heady success in capturing ethnic Greek territory in what is now western Turkey, continued to advance into Anatolia under the whip of a jingoistic media and public, only to meet its Armageddon at the hands of the Nationalist Turks of General Mustafa Kemal. Would the advance in Albania meet the same fate?

Papagos was, of course, perfectly aware of all this. But to him, a withdrawal was out of the question. Much blood had been expended in the fight against Mussolini's legions; at least 12,000 Greek soldiers had been killed since the end of October, and a few hundred more victims of frostbite-induced gangrene or frozen to death. The press and radio in Athens, and the overwhelming bulk of public opinion, wanted the advance to go on; the sight of retreating Italian backs was too good to end. King George II was unwavering in his support for the Army. But the weak government in Athens, bereft of the late Metaxas' strong and inspired guidance, could provide no clear strategic direction. The British military advisers in Athens, moreover, were pressing for a British expeditionary force to move up to the Bulgarian border, where it would need the Greek Army to meet a German attack. Deaf to all alternative suggestions, Papagos counter-argued rather disingenuously that to ask victorious Greek soldiers to pull back after slogging through their winter ordeal was asking too much of them. A soldier's morale, in his view, depended upon his going forward, not back – a reflection of the pre-war French doctrine of *'l'audace – toujours l'audace!'* ('Boldness – always boldness!') in which he had been trained. Any kind of withdrawal would be fatal for morale. And his decision stood.

In a portent of things to come, on 2 March, German forces entered their ally Bulgaria, heading for the Greek border. Soon this disheartening news would reach the troops in Albania, so as a morale-preserving measure Papagos insisted to the men that they would stay put in Albania in order to keep the deep buffer zone they had seized with such hardship. But he also considered an emergency plan for the TSH to link up with the West Macedonia Army Department (TSDM) along the Aliakmon River in northern Greece, in case the Germans managed to get in the rear of the TSH in Albania and cut it off. By now, the overall strategic dilemma – stay in Albania or withdraw in order to confront the Germans – was straining nerves in the Army Staff. A purge of commanders was the result. The TSH commander, Lieutenant General Drakos, known for his cautious approach, was replaced by Lieutenant General Ioannis Pitsikas, ex-commander of the TSDM, the bulk of which was formed by the III Corps under Lieutenant General Georgios Tsolakoglou. The commanders of the I and II Corps of the TSH also were removed, the latter being replaced by Major General Georgios Bakos, who had hitherto led the 3rd Division.

In the final days of February, the 17th Division moved to plug perceived gaps in the planned defensive line in the dip between the Trebeshinë and Shendeli ranges to the west of the Desnitsa river. The move was not easy – in fact, in the intractable Albanian mountains no move was ever easy, hence the Italians' no-choice plan to head in force down the Desnitsa Valley as the simplest way to re-take Kelçyre. Employing commando tactics, one battalion and a company of engineers of the 17th Division hacked out a precarious base of operations on Hill 370, surrounded by a trench that also blocked a road leading west from Kelçyre. They managed to capture an entire Italian company with its anti-aircraft guns and a few light tanks. Meanwhile, it had begun to snow heavily and on 7 March the division, supported by the base on Hill 370, surged through metre-deep snow to secure the Mezgoranit-Shendeli sector, which it accomplished by early afternoon, extending by a dozen kilometres the left flank protection of the main Greek line.

The captured tanks had belonged to the 131st (Centauro) Armoured Division, the only division in Albania to employ tanks. From the outset, the light and fragile Fiats had found it hard going in the mud and snow in the kind of extreme terrain they had not been designed or built for. Early in the war, the Greeks had found a way of immobilizing them by hiding by the roadside and slipping blankets inside the treads to foul the works. Certainly, the squat little Fiats utterly belied the initial high hopes for them, but it was not the fault of the machines per se or of the men who manned them. Almost all the great tank battles of World War Two were fought in great open plains where there was freedom of manoeuvre. The Balkan mountains were about the worst place in the world to use tanks (as the Greeks themselves would shortly find out with their own Vickers light tanks of the 19th Armoured Division in another theatre). But as long as the Twenty-fifth Corps commander, General Carlo Rossi, had the Centauro tanks on his hands, he had to use them any way he could.

Once ensconced at Mezgoranit-Shendeli, the 17th Division began receiving streams of surrendering Italians, most probably from Rossi's corps. According to Greek records at least a thousand Italians with their weapons, including twenty officers, gave themselves up on a single day. Also bagged were four artillery pieces, three anti-armour guns and dozens of automatic weapons and mortars, not to mention food and other supplies. The 17th Division's entrenchment was completed that same night. There still remained the summit of the Shendeli range, but incessant snow and stubborn enemy fire from the north prevented any more advance by the Greeks. Despite the mass surrenders, Rossi's *bersaglieri* were still very much in the fight. They would soon be rushed into an even bigger one.

On the eve of the Italian offensive the Greeks were arranged in a convex umbrella-like line. On the far left was the 2nd Division (facing the Julia) just to the south of the Tepelenë-Kelçyre road and the 17th Division to the north of it, holding on to the southern Trebeshinë range and facing the Legnano and the Wolves of Tuscany. Then came the 5th Division, holding the northern peaks of Trebeshinë and facing off the Sforzesca and Pinerolo. The 1st Division held the tip of the curve and most exposed point at Hills 731 and 717, guarding the entrance to the Desnitsa Valley. Completing the line to the northeast were the 15th and 11th Divisions that faced the Alpine Hunters and Pusteria, ending approximately at Mali Spadarit.

Chapter 4

First and second days

Very early in the first day's attack on 9 March, the Second Battalion's telephone line to the 5 Regiment headquarters was put out of action, as well as the signalling post. The men sent to repair them were almost all killed and wounded. By 7:30 a.m., however, some telephone communication was restored. Kaslas spoke to the sector commander, Colonel Ketseas, who asked him if his battalion was managing to hold its position. 'I told him that all the companies were in place holding on, though I didn't know how many of the men were still alive.'

'Defend your positions to the last,' came the colonel's reply. 'The Country and senior command demand that you keep the honour of arms high.' Kaslas assured Ketseas that he had no intention of abandoning Hill 731, whereupon the line went dead and would remain so for the rest of the day.

In the immediate rear, the Third Battalion of the 19 Regiment of the 6th Division, held in reserve on the right, had been ordered to occupy the height of Spi Kamarate to reinforce the embattled Second Battalion of the 5 Regiment. Its eastern slope abutted the main road between Berat and Kelçyre, which was the only major negotiable route south towards Greece. Its western slope touched the Desnitsa river. Nine Company dug in on the west side of Spi Kamarate out of sight of the Italian artillery, while 10 and 11 Companies plus a machine gun platoon covered the road from the other side. The Third Battalion set up its command post in a cottage on the summit of Spi Kamarate. Theodoros Zikos, the sergeant-major of 9 Company (later to retire as a lieutenant-colonel), oversaw the digging of foxholes that would take two men each. There wasn't much space; moreover, much of it was already taken up by the unburied bloated bodies of Italian soldiers who had fallen there two months before.

When the Italian guns began firing en masse, Major General Vasilios Vrachnos, the commander of the 1st Division, sprinted up to the nearest artillery observation point near his headquarters at Roden to see what was happening. What he saw was an apocalypse of fire and smoke enveloping Hill 731, his division's most advanced position. Momentarily stunned by the sight and sound, he figured that the massive enemy bombardment would be the prelude to the general infantry attack that he and the senior Greek command had been expecting. In fact, since at least mid-February, they were perfectly aware that the massing of Italian troops and artillery around the focal point of the town of Gllavë near the northern tip of the Trebeshinë range had a distinct purpose. Intelligence gleaned from captured Italians was invaluable. Mussolini, too, had been rather too voluble in expressing his aggressive intentions, with the result that the Greeks had plenty of time to prepare for the onslaught. As Vrachnos hurried back to his headquarters to coordinate the 1st Division's defence, Italian shells whistled overhead. 'As long as there are Greeks still alive and can man the machine guns, the position will not fall,' he told Colonel Ketseas, who thereupon issued his order to Major Kaslas on Hill 731 that he must hold on at all costs.

By 8 a.m., the Italian gunners, believing they had totally blasted Hill 731 and its defenders to smithereens, were lengthening their range, probing towards the Greek divisional headquarters in the rear. On the hill itself, Kaslas noticed the change and ordered his battalion to prepare for combat. The uneven lay of the land in front was such that the best tactic in his view was to let the first Italian waves approach as close as two hundred metres, where no natural feature would obstruct the defenders' view, before opening fire. His men crawled out of their holes and shelters, stunned and dazed by the holocaust they had just gone through but with no thought of retreat.

Machine guns were loaded up, bayonets clicked into place. Shortly after 8 a.m., two hours after the start of the Italian cannonade, the first lines of field-grey uniforms could be seen filing forward: the 71 and 72 Regiments of the 38th (Puglie) Division, backed up by the 152nd and 155th Blackshirt Battalions of the 26 Legion, at an estimated distance of about seven hundred metres. The former regiment, advancing in file through narrow defiles, was making for Hill 717, also known as Bregu Rapit, to the east of Hill 731, which was to the left of the latter.

Private Dimitrios Bobos of the 5 Regiment, seconded to Kaslas' battalion, crept cautiously out of his foxhole to view a moonscape of shell craters and uprooted trees. Many soldiers lay dead; all that was left of one man was his stomach and greatcoat. Bobos ran to find Major Kaslas about a kilometre away; outside the major's tent stood a tethered goat trembling all over. Kaslas kept the goat as a valuable source of milk. He pointed to the terrified animal. 'See how the animals sense the horror of war? Who's on Hill 731 now?' Bobos replied that the Greeks were still there, but dangerously few left.

In one of the front trenches was Private Zachariou, the lucky forager, having been transferred to Kaslas' battalion's front-line 5 Company. He remembered the previous night as a mild one, not as cold as usual but almost unbearably humid, with dripping dew soaking the men's uniforms. The trench floors were nearly ankle-deep in wet mud. The initial Italian attack on 9 March struck him as 'a true hell of fire and death'. The entire hill shook in the shell bursts. Zachariou's company lost about half its men in short order; its commander had been wounded but Kaslas had ordered him to stay at his post.

The Italian 72 Regiment, in the lead, came under fire from a Greek platoon in front of the hill that had been cut off from the main battalion position by the artillery barrage. The platoon, under Second Lieutenant Schizas, put up a stiff fight and caused the Italians some losses but, reduced to a mere dozen or so effectives, had to capitulate. While the attackers occupied a northern spur of Hill 717, the forty available guns of the Greek 1st Division artillery opened up, cutting large swaths in the advancing Italian lines. But the men of the Puglie kept on coming, propelled by pressure from behind and their officers' cries of *'Avanti!'* ('Forward!')

When just two hundred metres separated the two sides, the Greek machine guns got in on the act, the heavy Hotchkiss weapons chugging fire and practically stopping the 72 Regiment in its tracks. The Italians hit the dirt, stunned by the unexpected resistance from a place where they had been told there was nothing left alive. More slowly and haltingly now, they continued to move forward, towards 5 Company's exposed right flank and, by 9:30 a.m., had gained some ground, only to encounter a hail of defensive hand grenades. But Kaslas' battalion's supplies of grenades quickly ran out, with the result that, having recovered from its first shock, the 72 Regiment overran the first Greek trenches and launched itself head-on at 5 Company perched on the hill.

Three thousand men of the 63 Regiment of the 59th (Cagliari) Division, minus the division's ailing commander, General Giuseppe Gianni, had also been thrust forward in the first attacking wave but had to halt under a hail of machine gun fire (hence Mussolini's later disparaging remark about Gianni). As Ketseas watched from his vantage point in the rear, Italian columns advancing in irregular formation were scythed down by artillery fire, though several incredibly brave men leaped over the bodies of their comrades and kept on going. These few, however, were halted by a determined counter-charge by the Third Battalion of the 5 Regiment involving the liberal use of bayonets and hand grenades.

Major Kaslas found himself in a quandary. His 6 Company on the left had not yet been engaged, while 7 Company was still in reserve. Taking all the heat were 5 and part of 3 Company. But, with no means of communication, he could neither give orders to his companies nor talk to the sector commander, Colonel Ketseas. Whatever he did would be entirely on his own responsibility. His first decision was to send couriers to order up 7 Company – thus using up the reserve – and request an immediate reinforcement of another company plus a machine gun platoon from the First Battalion of the 51 Regiment at Spi Kamarate, a few kilometres down the valley in the rear. The reinforcement came up quickly. At about the same time, 7 Company formed up alongside 5; within minutes the company bugler sounded the call to advance, accompanied by the Greek battle-dry of *'Aera!'* ('Wind!'). Seven Company's counterattack, in which offensive hand grenades played a large part, caught the front units of the Puglie by surprise and sent them reeling. Already having suffered painful losses, and its morale dented by the unexpected resistance, the entire 72 Regiment broke, pursued by a mere company yelling and howling in triumph and leaping over heaps of bodies.

On the left of the Italian line, the Puglie's 71 Regiment moved on Hill 717 defended by the Greek 51 Regiment's First Battalion under Major Emmanuel Tzanetis, whom Kaslas had replaced on Hill 731 the previous day. Tzanetis, on his own initiative, grabbed a machine gun and called for volunteers to follow him to hit the attackers on the flank; fifteen men did so. Approaching Hill 717, he came across the remains of a Greek unit wiped out by enemy artillery fire, but the unit's machine gun was still serviceable. Tzanetis picked up an ammunition belt he found in a trench and loaded the machine gun. Placing his men in strategic positions on the hill, he began to pour fire into the Italian flank. The action managed to keep the attackers at bay and rescue some of Second Lieutenant Schizas' encircled platoon.

On Hill 731, Grenadier Zachariou heard the order to fix bayonets, but the company commander who gave the order fell gravely wounded immediately afterwards. He was the third company commander Zachariou had lost. In the hellish confusion, it was impossible to tell who, if anyone, succeeded to the command, as the nearest ranking platoon commander had also been seriously wounded and taken to the rear. Major Kaslas walked along the lines, impervious to the crash of enemy shells around him. The ground shook incessantly as if in the throes of a continuous earthquake. 'Well, boys,' he deadpanned, 'as I see, your hill is dancing pretty well. Just imagine that you're taking dancing lessons and it'll be all right.' He walked off, unperturbed, to inspect other parts of the line.

On Hill 717 Major Tzanetis continued to harass the Puglie with cross-fire. At about 10:30 a.m. the Italian wave broke. Ketseas ordered his regimental artillery to shell the retreating enemy resulting in considerable slaughter. Some of Tzanetis' men crawled cautiously around the northeast spur of Hill 717 and discovered a group of about thirty *Arditi* trying to lower themselves from a steep abutment. Tzanetis' detachment slammed into them with bayonets, grenades and the major's machine gun, wiping out about half of them and sending the rest fleeing for their lives.

Meanwhile, General Giuseppe de Stefanis' 24th (Pinerolo) Division had launched an attack on the height of Kiafe Luzit on the Italian right. Kiafe Luzit was one of the high spots at the northern end of the Trebeshinë range, flanking Hill 731 to the west. Joining this attack to the south was the 21st (Sforzesca), which had not got very far when it was stopped by a couple of battalions of the Greek 4 and 16 Regiments which by now, like their compatriots elsewhere on the front, were becoming proficient in the simultaneous use of the bayonet and grenade, a proficiency duly noted by the Italian battalion commanders on the business end. (Pricolo's diary, however, notes that Kiafe Luzit was gained and lost twice, which does not appear in the Greek records.)

The moment arrived when General Alberto D'Aponte, the commander of the Puglie, had to tell Gambara that the initial assault had failed. The furious corps commander proceeded to berate him until – according to Greek radio intercepts – D'Aponte shouted *'Da capo!'* ('From the beginning!') as if ordering a repeat of a symphony. Another battalion of the 71 Regiment was flung against Hill 731;

this time, by sheer bloody persistence, it gained a few footholds on the northern slope and inserted itself into the gap west of Hill 717, rapidly climbing until it seized the smaller height. Hill 731 was now directly threatened from the east. Kaslas and Tzanetis got together a platoon-sized detachment and counter-charged the 71 Regiment with bayonets and grenades and, at close quarters, rifle butts. The melee continued as Italian shells fell like hail. But the Italians held on to Hill 717. So far that day, the Italians had attacked four times, with only the temporary seizure of Hill 717 to show for it.

Around noon, Ketseas ordered up his First Battalion to stiffen Kaslas' Second and be prepared for an attempt to retake Hill 717. That attempt, launched almost immediately, was briefly successful but the Greek command judged that defending two heights at the same time was too costly. The units that had just seized it were withdrawn, and the defence now exclusively concentrated on Hill 731.

Greek casualties that morning had been considerable. Ketseas ordered the hard-hit Third Battalion to the rear, replacing it with the Third Battalion of Colonel Panagiotis Balis' 19 Regiment in reserve that had been placed under 1st Division command. By the afternoon, a carpet of Italian dead and wounded had spread over the slopes to the north of Hill 731. The bodies were densest just in front of the Greek barbed wire. The Italian medics feared to venture out to succour their wounded compatriots, as General Vrachnos had issued orders to fire on all such attempts. Zachariou, for one, was unhappy with the ruthless policy. 'It was just execution,' he wrote many years later. 'We couldn't understand what the sense of those harsh and inhumane orders was. [The Italians] were just trying to save their wounded and bury their dead.' But that was the implacable nature of warfare. Vrachnos' apparent ruthlessness had a concrete tactical aim: the enemy's morale would be seriously dented if successive waves of attackers had to wade through the mangled bodies of their friends. (It is a questionable view, as it could also be argued that a soldier's aggressive fury could be enhanced as he sought to avenge his mates' deaths.) The Greek wounded, on the contrary, could be taken to the rear promptly, while burial details, also in the rear, could work unhindered by enemy shelling.

After a lull of a few hours, the 71 Regiment of the Puglie and 63 Regiment of the Cagliari made another attempt at Hill 731 in the early afternoon. Reinforcing the former were two companies of crack *Arditi*, who advanced with great courage and encircled the defenders at the top. Some Italian detachments got within feet of the outer Greek trenches, to be stopped by Kaslas' men thrusting desperately with bayonets. The churned-up slopes were thick with Italian bodies, but the 71 and 72 Regiments of the Puglie jumped over their fallen comrades to try to seize the height before nightfall; Kaslas' battalion held on, sticking to the rocky terrain like lichen. As the men of the 71 Regiment streamed back downhill in disorder, they found their way blocked by a hail of Greek shells and had to seek safety in the many gullies and ravines branching off the hill. To stem the shelling, Gambara's artillery recommenced its own bombardment all along the Greek 1st Division line as the *Regia Aeronautica* pitched in with bombing and strafing.

Separating Hill 731 from the rest of the Trebeshinë range is the Proi Math ravine. Sergeant Emmanuel Kasimatis of the Second Battalion, 16 Infantry Regiment, was encamped on the south-west side of the ravine. The regiment was in possession of most of the higher peaks to the south. To the north and northeast, Hills 731 and 717 stood out clearly. The Second Battalion's three companies manned the farthest outpost, having spent days and nights hacking foxholes out of the frozen and rocky ground and setting up a barbed wire screen. A company of the 4 Infantry Regiment was held in reserve in the rear. On the eve of the Italian attack, the battalion commander, Major Triantafyllopoulos, walked around the positions offering the men cigarettes and swigs of brandy from a flask he kept with him. He was accompanied by his medical officer who conversed with the soldiers to detect any signs of undue anxiety. 'Bullets seek out those who are afraid,' Kasimatis remembered Triantafyllopoulos saying. 'Isn't that right, doc? And if one grazes you, it will be hot and won't infect. And if you lose a bit of blood, you'll replenish it in a few hours, right?' With words like that, the medical officer need not have worried too much about morale.

The Italian casualty rate on that first bloody day exceeded thirty per cent. But little of the butchery appeared to be perceptible at Gambara's headquarters, where Pricolo was told (and noted in his diary) that the Puglie had seized the summit of Hill 731 and was on its way to encircling the Greek units to the north. Just how this report reached headquarters is no mystery; the mid-level commanders, afraid of the Duce learning of their failure, doctored the despatches from the battle-front – aided of course by the fog of battle in which any advance could be viewed as a 'success'. But it didn't take long for the truth to become known, and when it did, Mussolini balled his fists in anger.

'What the heck is the Cagliari doing?' he stormed. 'Why isn't it advancing? I see nothing of what you're saying!'

Gambara took Pricolo aside and admitted that the day was not going well. The whole success of the initial attack depended on the Cagliari Division's securing of the area to the north of Hill 731, around the village of Bubesi, and drawing Greek forces away from it. General Gianni, the Cagliari commander, from his sickbed (and suspected by Mussolini of malingering) ordered two fresh battalions of the 63 Regiment to storm Bubesi at dusk. As they filed over the dark mountain paths, the men fired into the air, intending to intimidate the enemy, but all they accomplished was to give away their position to three Greek platoons which drove them back with little trouble.

That morning, a diversionary attack had been made against the height of Mali Spadarit, several kilometres north-east of Hill 731, held by the Greek 11th Division. Carrying it out were three battalions of the 12 Alpine Regiment of the Wolves of Tuscany. The seizure of Mali Spadarit was intended to ease the pressure on the Cagliari to the right. It was a domino-like war of heights – there was always another hill next door, and if you didn't seize it, the enemy would. Those heights – and Hill 731 was the textbook example – guarded the valley roads through which men and machines had to move. The Cagliari would be left exposed if Mali Spadarit were not secured.

And the Greek II Corps headquarters knew all about it. Italian security was atrocious: radio messages to and from the Wolves of Tuscany, right down to the timing of the attack and the battalion objectives, were all intercepted by the Greeks. Major General Socrates Dimaratos, the 11th Division commander, ordered an artillery barrage that failed to stop the Wolves who, with great persistence, pushed on towards the front Greek trenches taking horrendous losses. Anticipating success, the Italian artillery lengthened its range, which enabled the defenders to jump out of their trenches and foxholes and fight back.

'Surrender for your own good!' the Alpini shouted.

'No! You'll never take Mali Spadarit!' the Greeks shouted back, backing up their message in fierce hand-to-hand combat. Number 15 Company of the Greek mountain artillery blazed away without mercy and can take credit for the eventual repulse of the Wolves of Tuscany. Dimaratos was shown the text of an agonized message from the Wolves' command:

Mali Spadarit must come into our possession. It cannot be tolerated that the Italian Army is unable to repulse the inferior Greek Army. It is a matter of honour. We owe it to our dead to avenge them and to be worthy of our glorious traditions.

Far from avenging the dead, the abortive assault only added to their number.

As night fell, the air was filled with the sound no soldier who has ever been in combat can ever forget: the groans and screams of the untended wounded and dying. Private Georgios Takos of Kaslas' battalion and the two other survivors of his squad crept over to the mass of Italian bodies on the slope. Trying to ignore the cries around him, Takos found bread and tinned food in the dead Italians' packs. As he and his mates had gone hungry for days, the findings were eagerly consumed. 'God knows how we survived,' he was to write later in life. Part of the explanation was the deadly efficiency of the Greek artillery, which proved superior to that of the Italians through the entire Albanian campaign. On the first day of the battle it fired more than 5,600 shells with a success rate probably proportionally greater than the estimated 100,000 shells fired by the Italians in the opening barrage.

Kaslas was a veteran of the 1920–22 Asia Minor War, when an ill-fated Greek attempt to seize traditional ethnic Greek lands in what is now western Turkey was repulsed by Turkish nationalist forces under General Mustafa Kemal, later revered as Atatürk, the founder of the modern Turkish republic. Kaslas had been taken prisoner and malnourished to the point at which he had temporarily lost his sight. Hence the goat he kept at his headquarters as a source of vitamin-rich milk so that it wouldn't happen again. His previous combat experience no doubt helped him withstand the hellish scenes he was to encounter in Albania. But throughout the Greek Army, the incredibly demanding requirements of fighting over four months in the most arduous conditions, in the worst of weathers, had no doubt toughened up the soldiers to be able to face whatever the Duce could throw at them.

Cavallero, watching the action, was surprised at the tenacity of the Greek defence. 'In the Eighth Corps area the Greek forces were almost equal in number to ours and their artillery was effective and continuous,' he wrote later. As a capable officer, he couldn't help but ruefully admire the way the Greeks had anchored themselves into the rocks, taking advantage of every peak and spur for their defence. On that first morning, on the Fourth Corps front on the left, the 11 Alpine Regiment - against great odds - came within a stone's throw of the height of Mali Spadarit, the 22nd (Cacciatore degli Alpi, or Alpine Hunters) Division made some progress up Hill 931 in the same sector, and the 5th (Pusteria) Division took the village of Selianit after a quick charge. But that was the only good news Cavallero would have that day. 'Despite the advance,' he would write in his memoirs, 'our units found themselves before the well-organized and virtually untouched Greek second-line positions. Moreover, our advance was significantly delayed in comparison with the planned general advance, especially in the central sector.' The sterile staff-speak well conceals the unpleasant surprise that Cavallero and his staff, not to mention Mussolini, experienced. And that was just the first day.

At the same time, the 71 Regiment of the Puglie made another attempt at Hill 731 under cover of darkness. The defenders were alerted, of course, by a brief artillery bombardment that gave the game away. The Italian command, it seems, could not tear itself away from unimaginative adherence to making war by the World War One book; infantry assaults had to be preceded by artillery barrages, and that was that. D'Aponte, the Puglie commander, figured that the fatigued Greeks would be able to put up less of a fight, but he was wrong; this assault, too, collapsed. Informed of the latest debacle, Gianni ordered the Cagliari artillery to cover for his men's retreat. It was a criminally disastrous decision. While the survivors of the 63 Regiment were making their way back, a rain of friendly fire came down, killing and maiming, and making mincemeat out of the newly killed and wounded on the slopes.

The Duce did not hide his disgust at the day's results. At about 8 p.m., he left for the Eleventh Army headquarters at Devol in high dudgeon, taking Pricolo with him. 'I tell you the attack has failed!' he shouted to his air force chief. 'And if an attack does not attain its objectives within the first two or three hours, it's doomed.' Pricolo was surprised at the Duce's sudden intense pessimism. It was the first time he'd seen the Duce so disheartened at a situation which, militarily speaking, had not yet been resolved. Mussolini, as we have seen, also vented his spleen against the ailing Gianni with at least one strong hint that his 'illness' was an act. 'Let's not forget that with just one division and a scouting team, Rommel managed to completely turn around the situation in Libya.'

That evening, Cavallero ordered the shattered Puglie Division withdrawn and replaced it with the 47th (Bari) under General Matteo Negro. De Stefanis' badly-bruised Pinerolo Division was pulled back to the reserves and General Gualtiero Gabutti's 51st (Siena) slotted into its place opposite Trebeshinë. 'The evening found us in full battle,' Cavallero wrote in his diary. 'Our units found themselves up against well-organized and almost intact Greek positions.' That was a considerable exaggeration. The Greek positions, especially after a shattering bombardment, were far from 'well-organized' and at no point were they anything more than flimsy. The Italian commander-in-chief may not have been able to admit even to himself that it is men that win battles, not positions. But most likely he had to justify himself to the Duce who was breathing down his neck. In normal circumstances, an initial upset such as this might have been taken in stride with a change of plan or redeployment of divisions. But Mussolini himself had frowningly witnessed it, and that placed an onerous psychological burden on his commanders all the way down to junior officer level.

After the first repulse of the Italians, the Greek II Corps command, under cover of darkness, sent reserve units to replenish the losses suffered by the 1st Division – fifty-three dead, including two officers, and seventy-seven wounded. Desultory artillery fire from both sides allowed few men to sleep. The division commander, General Vrachnos, asked that restrictions on ammunition consumption be lifted so that he could have more clout. In a single day, the northern sector of the 5 Regiment alone had expended more than 5,500 artillery shells defending Hills 731 and 717, and a lot more were going to be needed. His request was granted.

On the Italian side the problem was how to seize the height of Mali Spadarit, about ten kilometres to the north-east of Hills 731 and 717, in order to outflank the advance positions of Vrachnos' 1st Division. The Italian losses had been considerable. The Julia Division of the Twenty-fifth Corps alone suffered thirty officers killed, eighty-seven others wounded and twenty-four missing, plus sixty-eight enlisted men killed, more than 2,600 wounded and at least six hundred missing – most of them presumably captured.

The following morning, 10 March, was misty and drizzly. The preparatory Italian bombardment, supplemented by air strikes, commenced at 7:45 a.m. With visibility nil, the atmosphere choking and the men cringing in their holes, Major Triantafyllopoulos, the commander of the 16 Regiment's Second Battalion to the west of Hill 731, got on the telephone to his company commanders demanding initial reports. While Sergeant Kasimatis was within earshot, a call came in from the commander of the 16 Regiment, Lieutenant Colonel Christos Ioannou, asking to be briefed. Triantafyllopoulos said he could see Italian infantry (probably the Puglie's 72 Regiment) on their way towards the right of his position, apparently in a flanking manoeuvre. 'I'm preparing to repulse them, I'm in touch with my company commanders, but I've no time now, so you'd better get more observations from your own post.'

'Are they going to get behind you?' Ioannou said with some asperity. 'That's what I want to know.'

'Only over my dead body, sir.'

'Okay, good luck. Whatever you need, I'm here.' The line clicked off.

Triantafyllopoulos turned to one of his company commanders. 'What's the enemy strength?'

'About battalion strength, sir.'

'What formation?'

'Small columns.'

'So much the worse for them.' The major told his companies to remain under cover until the attacking Italian column had crossed the Proi Math ravine and was well up the slope before the Greek position.

'They're getting nearer,' the company commander said nervously.

In reply, the major turned to Captain Kanatouris of the battalion artillery. 'Commence firing.' Within a minute, Kanatouris' shells began to rain down on the Italian column. Kasimatis recalled:

Helmets, weapons and bodies are hurled into the air. The Italians run in a herd to the ridge in their rear. There are shouts, screams and explosions. The machine guns chatter in the direction of the ridge. Soon everything is still except for cries and groans.

A few minutes later, some Italians were seen attempting to regain the position they had been shelled out of. 'Machine gun fire at will on anything that moves,' Triantafyllopoulos ordered. The result was that the few intrepid Italians still going forward quickly withdrew. Kanatouris was ordered to lob a few shells on the retreat. 'Boys, get me some brandy,' the battalion commander said when the action was over.

The shelling lasted just over an hour. East of Hill 731, as the drizzle stopped at about 11 a.m. and the men could raise their heads and breathe again, Sergeant-Major Zikos of the Second Battalion of the 19 Regiment crawled out of his makeshift shelter to see a regiment-strength Italian column on the move. What he saw must have been the First Battalion of the Puglie's 72 Regiment which moved decisively on Hill 731 but after twenty or so minutes had to fall back under Kaslas' battalion's fierce resistance. Then two battalions of the Cagliari's 63 Regiment charged Hill 717 with great determination but in some disorder because of the rough terrain. It was the time when Gambara's guns began to lengthen their range to avoid hitting their own men – which was the moment that the Greeks could effectively counter-attack with a hail of grenades. Though it had the advantage of numbers, the 63 Regiment was eventually thrown back. This was the moment that the Greek 1st Division's 1 Mountain Artillery Regiment, under Lieutenant Colonel Michalis Spyropoulos, let loose with successive salvoes, aiming mercilessly at the Italians trying to find their way back through the wooded gullies, as Kaslas rounded up three Italian privates and a captain.

As the day wore on, the Second Battalion at Kiafe Luzit on the left was reinforced by two more companies of the First Battalion and two machine gun platoons, in case the Italians should try again, which everyone expected them to. 'Let the whole army of *fratelli* [brothers] come on now,' Triantafyllopoulos said. To the south, at Spi Kamarate, Captain Panayotis Koutridis of the Second Battalion, 19 Regiment, was calling his company commanders together to confirm the companies' positions when a shell landed close by, wounding Second Lieutenant Nikolaos Mamalakis, a company commander, in the left leg. Sergeant Major Zikos, a grizzled veteran, somehow personally felt responsible for his young commanding officer and accompanied him as he was taken to the cottage that served as the battalion headquarters. The battalion commander cracked jokes to keep up Mamalakis' morale, but the wounded second lieutenant, ashen-faced and in pain, lifted his service Colt .38 out of its holster and offered it to his immediate subordinate, a reserve second lieutenant, ceding the company command to him. It was not the first time that Sergeant Major Zikos, an experienced serviceman, had seen blood in battle, but the sight of the Second Battalion's first real casualty came as something of a shock. He wrote later:

The loss of our company commander was felt very keenly. For four months we had lived together, he had a gentle manner and the men loved him. He had absolute trust in me. Our company under his leadership was a model of order and discipline, and our morale was of a high order. All the men felt the loss, but the biggest burden of the company fell on my shoulders [as] the two reserve second lieutenants, though fervent patriots and competent officers, were not yet able to command a company.

Mamalakis was transferred to the rear after nightfall, waving to his men from a stretcher.

The second day's morning attack was broken up fairly quickly. By 9:50 a.m., after a fierce fight under pouring rain and hand grenades, the first Italian advance had stalled. The cost to both sides was heavy, especially to the Greek Second Battalion, Zikos' unit, which required replacements from the First Battalion. But the pressure on Mali Spadarit and the Greek 11th Division kept up, with a fresh Italian assault through the mist that managed to seize a spur of the height. The attackers had to advance in thick mud which also hindered the defenders, forcing parts of the 50 Regiment to fall back. At some point, the mist unexpectedly lifted. The 11th Division commander, Colonel Dimaratos, ordered the Third Battalion of the 13 Regiment to counterattack. The spur of Mali Spadarit was clawed back, the first move in a domino effect that, within a few hours, erased any Italian gains on that height.

On the Italian side, for Lieutenant Ajmone Finestra of the 115th Legion of the Puglie Division that had taken the most punishment so far, the dank morning of 10 March was one he would never forget. In the growing light, he watched as the legion's twin unit, the CXV Battalion 'Viterbo', was ordered to push ahead into the Desnitsa Valley in the direction of Kelçyre, probably to try and outflank Hill 731. Finestra's heart sank as he pictured the battalion trying to force its way through the freezing mud with Greek fire pouring down from the heights on either side. A sudden incoming bank of fog hid the Viterbo from view.

Hill 731 was resisting all attacks. Our bombers, flying high, hammered the valley and mountains. Our artillery alternated between supporting fire and barrages; we heard the sound of battle in progress and the mortar shells that tore through the sky with a fearsome shriek.

The CXV Battalion came under immediate attack from the Greeks but appears to have held fast. Finestra heard that it, and other front-line units, had been ordered to hold their gains, whatever they were, 'at all costs'. But the order proved to be of little avail as the Puglie Division by the afternoon had to, once more, admit failure.

The Italian offensive was by no means limited to the Eighth Corps drive against the Trebeshinë sector and its sentinel of Hill 731. Some units of the Ninth Army had been brought into action on the left of the front in support of the main central thrust. One of these was the 2nd (Tridentina) Division whose 5 Alpine Regiment was flung against the formidable heights of Guri i Topit, towering more than 2,000 metres above sea level, where Greek units were dug in. The consensus in the unit was that the Greeks on the summits were not very well armed, or by now they would have been pouring fire down. The Greeks, probably from the easternmost elements of the 11th Division of the II Corps, were taken by surprise, but quickly pulled themselves together to resist. Second Lieutenant Peppino Antolini of the 5 Alpini received a few grenade fragments in the hand; one of his sergeants took a bullet on his helmet, which deflected the projectile and left him with a merely grazed scalp. A Greek soldier with bayonet levelled lunged at Antolini, ripping a sleeve but not his flesh; the lieutenant fired his pistol point-blank at his assailant, to be drenched in his blood. Such was the initial success of the 5 Alpini's uphill charge that the regiment took a dozen or so prisoners. Then, to Antonini's utter chagrin, as he recorded in his diary after the action:

Incredible but true: the command then ordered us to abandon the positions we had seized. So the Greeks reoccupied the twin heights. I'm sure we're going to pay dearly for this mad order.

The comment cleanly encapsulates the tactical chaos that all too often betrayed the raw courage displayed by the Italian rank and file.

Antolini himself, since the first day of the year, had been stationed in the Mount Tomorrit sector in the Ninth Army zone. By March, he and his men had had a bellyful of the merciless ice and snow, haunted day and night by the fear that the Greeks might pounce upon them like ghosts out of the dark. On the night of 27 January, braving temperatures of 20 Celsius below zero, he had led a patrol that failed to detect any of the enemy. Two weeks later his regiment was moved to Guri i Topit, wading through 'mud nearly up to the chest'. They had stopped for the night at Devol, sleeping on the only dry surfaces they could find – gravestones in a local cemetery crawling with giant rats. The upper slopes of Guru i Topit were layered in half a metre of snow. 'The Greeks are above and we below – not a nice situation,' Antolini noted. 'We're living in ever more inhuman conditions, poorly clad… the snow accumulated last night makes supplying impossible, and we're on reduced rations.' In that state, he fended off the bayonet attack and acquitted himself well, only to receive the 'mad' order which made it all futile.

The Greek record of the events of the late morning of 10 March shows that after the failed Italian attempt on Mali Spadarit, a new attack was launched at 11:15 a.m. – again by the much-battered Puglie Division – against Hill 717, only to be driven back with severe losses; minutes later, however, a fresh wave from the Puglie rushed forward over the bodies of their comrades. For at least half an hour the combat was close and bloody, until about 12:30 p.m. when the Italians again broke, the survivors withdrawing to a protective ravine west of Hill 717. Five hours later, an Italian battalion moved to tackle Hill 731 – the seventh such Italian attempt in less than forty-eight hours – but after an hour that, too, had to fall back. The Puglie Division had been severely mauled; one wounded soldier, being taken to the rear, told Lieutenant Finestra that the division was at its last extremity; he saw it in the faces of the men who slouched back.

'That night we couldn't sleep a wink; in front of us men continued to fight, suffer and die.'

It may have been on this day that Giovanni De Pizzol of the 72 Regiment of the Puglie Division looked on with horror as 'our poor brothers' were being slaughtered. 'Our poor friends, sons, fathers, husbands whose families had seen them off hale and hearty, would not return.' Amid the explosions and hail of bullets coming from 'those infernal cowardly Greeks' he prayed to the Virgin Mary until he was wounded. The ambulance on the way to the field hospital resounded with cries such as 'Holy Mother, save me!' and 'Hey, dad and everybody, pray for me.' While recuperating, De Pizzol was delighted to meet a fellow-villager marching towards the murderous front.

> I got up and called out to him with all my strength. He gazed at me a long time, as if to say, 'Who's this?' And I, crying, answered, 'Piero, it's me.' Then he came towards me. We hugged and kissed like brothers, both us of crying. Then he asked me about my wounds and gave me courage.

The Greek 1st Division was not the only one to take it on the chin on 10 March. Geloso had added the 47th (Bari) Division, inserting it between the Puglie and Cagliari to beef up the attack on the sectors of the Greek 11th, 15th and 17th Divisions in the Trebeshinë and Mali Spadarit areas in a multi-pronged probing operation designed to seek out any weakness in the Greek defence line while at the same time hopefully diverting firepower from Hills 731 and 717. At Spi Kamarate, after the wounding of Lieutenant Mamalakis, Sergeant-Major Zikos took over command of a platoon while his own second lieutenant, a reservist, was assigned 9 Company. Seeing and hearing the sounds of battle to the west, he chafed at his inaction. A sergeant came up to him. 'Things are bad on Hill 731,' the sergeant said. 'The

Italians seized the height, but the battalion commander, his staff and some muleteers and his bugler took it back.'

The sergeant was wrong. The height he was referring to was Hill 717, and the Italians in question might well have been the CXV 'Viterbo' Battalion, which according to Lieutenant Finestra did claim some temporary success that morning. It had been thrown back by the 2nd and 3rd Battalions of the Greek 5 Regiment. Such were the losses on both sides, in fact, that henceforth Hill 717 ceased to have any real tactical importance in the battle and remained a devastated stump of rock. But that was far from evident as Zikos fingered his favourite weapon, a Browning pistol that he'd owned since before the war and wondered when he'd ever get to use it. He also had a Bulgarian double-edged combat knife (inherited from his mountain guerrilla grandfather) and a small icon of Saint George that he kept with him all his life.

In the late afternoon, a large bomb fell on one of 5 Company's shelters, killing two senior sergeants. Zachariou still didn't know who was in command of the company, whose members acted and fought pretty much on their own initiative until the 5 Regiment was relieved two days later. Zachariou's four unreal days on Hill 731 marked him for the rest of his life.

> Every minute seemed endless [he wrote in 1989], as if weighed down by the whistle of bullets and roar of bombs and shells passing over our heads. And all the while you expected death any moment. It is difficult to convey it all, even though I lived through it, and even more difficult for any reader who was not there to understand.

After nightfall, as Gambara's artillery fired intermittent tracer shells that lit up the base of the cloud cover with an eerie glow, Mussolini and Cavallero puzzled over the day's lack of results and considerable casualties (not to mention more than five hundred men taken prisoner). The Duce's generals didn't know what to tell him. But he knew what to tell them: it was simply that failure was unacceptable and that the stubborn Greeks would have to be overcome at whatever cost in blood. His ego was dented, and in a man like Mussolini, if he couldn't properly take it out on the enemy, his own soldiers would have to pay.

1. Mussolini viewing the Greek positions from Komarit. (*Marcos Andreou collection*)

2. Major Dimitrios Kaslas.
(*Marcos Andreou collection*)

3. An Italian attack on Hill 731. The second man from the right appears to have just been hit. (*Marcos Andreou collection*)

4. Bersaglieri go into the attack on or near Hill 731. (*Marcos Andreou collection*)

5. Mussolini and General Gambara (right). (*Marcos Andreou collection*)

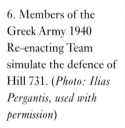

6. Members of the Greek Army 1940 Re-enacting Team simulate the defence of Hill 731. (*Photo: Ilias Pergantis, used with permission*)

7. Framework of an ammunition-carrying mule saddle against a background photo of a Greek Army supply train. (*Hellenic War Museum*)

8. The Greek Army 1940 Re-enacting Team demonstrating a machine gun defence. (*Author's photo*)

GIORGIO DI BORBONE

Capitano del 31° Reggimento fanteria, da Milano, alla memoria.

«Comandante di una compagnia arditi, tre volte volontario di guerra, già ferito in precedenti fatti d'arme in cui si era valorosamente distinto, otteneva, dopo varie insistenze, di rientrare al proprio reparto. In aspro combattimento si lanciava con impareggiabile audacia e sprezzo del pericolo, alla testa dei suoi arditi, contro munita posizione avversaria. Colpito una prima volta, seguitava ad avanzare e giungeva sulla linea nemica conquistandola e disperdendone i difensori con accanito lancio di bombe a mano. Accerchiato da forze soverchianti, persisteva imperterrito nell'impari lotta, finchè, esaurite le bombe ed i colpi della propria pistola contro i più vicini avversari, veniva sopraffatto e cadeva da eroe.»

(Quota 731 di Monastero, fronte greco, 19 marzo 1941-XIX)

9. Unknown artist's impression of the final moments of Captain Giorgio di Borbone, 19 March 1941, on a memorial postcard. (*Constantine Lagos*)

10. Italian–made Gnutti 51cm bayonet (restored). (*Author's photo*)

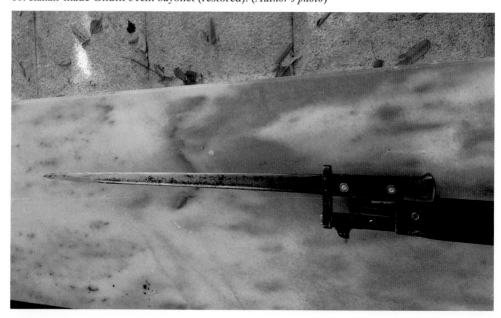

11. The view north from Kelçyre along the Desnitsa Valley, with the Trebeshinë range on the left. (*Author's photo*)

12. The Proi Math ravine, as seen from what remains of the Kelçyre-Berat road. (*Author's photo*)

13. The summit of Hill 731 as it is today. (*Author's photo*)

14. Mortar grenades and helmets recovered recently from Hill 731. (*Hellenic War Museum*)

15. Somewhat neglected memorial to the 38th (Puglie) Division near the summit. (*Author's photo*)

16. Italian shell discovered by the author on the east slope of Hill 731. (*Author's photo*)

17. Hills 731 and 711 (left and right respectively), as seen from the south. (*Author's photo*)

18. Hill 717 and Mali Spadarit beyond, seen from Hill 731. (*Author's photo*)

19. The Greek war cemetery at Kelçyre.
(*Author's photo*)

20. Evangelia Fatsea with a photograph of her grandfather, Sgt Maj Halamabos Kyriakakis of the 14 Regiment, 5th (Crete) Division, still unaccounted for, at the Kelçyre war cemetery, October 2019. (*Author's photo*)

Chapter 5

Third day: Blackshirt blunder

The morning of 11 March dawned foggy and dim, with Italian shells whistling over in the usual nuisance barrage. Some of the shells landed on Spi Kamarate, where Zikos and his platoon huddled in their trenches. At about 9 a.m., the fog began to lift. Zikos noticed a mule, probably belonging to the Second Battalion, standing alone in the desolation about a hundred metres away. As visibility improved, he and his men saw a soldier coming out from behind the animal. The soldier staggered towards the lines, hatless, unarmed, unbuttoned and ashen-faced. 'What happened and why are you in that state?' Zikos asked the soldier when he got to the lines.

After hurling a string of curses at the Italians, the soldier replied: 'They've passed below and are getting near to [our] artillery. I was going along with another fellow with mules loaded with ammunition for Hill 731 and came on the Italians. They almost killed us with their fists. I got away from them by running down a slope.' What he had tangled with were the 26 Blackshirt Legion, plus two battalions of the 72 Regiment, that were pushing down unobserved through the Proi Math ravine behind a reconnaissance squad and approaching a Greek anti-tank battery. The soldier with the mule had been part of a supply team that had got in the Blackshirts' way. So as not to give away their position by the sound of gunfire, the Italians had physically attacked the muleteers and captured them all except the one who had escaped to Spi Kamarate to tell the story.

After two days of futile mass assaults, Cavallero decided he'd have to be a little more inventive. Hill 731 stood in his way, blasted and burned but still there, with the enemy sitting on it. The only way was to outflank it; there had been other such attempts, but only as ancillary moves to the main thrust. The obvious choice was to use the Proi Math (Albanian for 'Big Creek') ravine right under the eastern slope of Hill 731 through which runs the main Berat-Kelçyre road. Cavallero decided to send the 26 Blackshirt Legion down that route – hopefully masked from the Greeks by thick vegetation – to seize points in the Greek rear and pull the defence away from Hill 731.

The only thing wrong with that plan was that it was as obvious as a meat ball on a plate of pasta. Any Greek commander worth his salt would have seen at once that the Proi Math gully offered opportunities for enemy infiltration, and Colonel Ketseas, for one, had already organized a reception for anyone who might try to snake down that path. While tank traps had been dug on the main road, Ketseas stationed battalions of the 19 and 51 Regiments on either side of the gap and called up Captain Koutridis' Third Battalion of the 19 Regiment to replace Kaslas' battered battalion on Hill 731. Artillery batteries were placed on the alert, the gunners' hands on the lanyards awaiting orders to fire. The trap was laid for anyone incautious enough to step into it.

The 155th Battalion of the 26 Blackshirt Legion, under Major Lepri, began making its way into Proi Math before dawn, covered by a curtain of artillery fire. At the same time the First and Third Battalions of the 72 Regiment, plus the 152nd Blackshirt Battalion, made a diversionary move on Hill 731. The Blackshirts hoped to get in the rear of the hill by first eliminating the Greek anti-tank battery at Vinokazit, then veering north to clear the height of Mali Spadarit. But they appear not to have known that shortly beforehand, the tough Macedonians and Peloponnesians of the Third Battalion, 19 Regiment, had entrenched on the height.

The news that the enemy was probing through the Proi Math ravine in an outflanking operation and threatening some of the Second Battalion's artillery was also flashed to the 19 Regiment, whereupon Colonel Ketseas ordered a counterattack at 8:45 a.m. Captain Koutridis moved his companies post-haste to spread out towards the hamlet of Vinokazit, where the Blackshirts were apparently headed. A mad scramble ensued: companies, platoons and squads mixed themselves up in the haste. The battalion medical officer, reserve Second Lieutenant Ioannis Kouvaras, joined them, a Mannlicher rifle in each hand. Zikos' immediate superior, Second Lieutenant Chrysafis Chrysafis, kept repeating as he ran, 'I'm not afraid. I'm not afraid.' Zikos himself felt no fear, only fury and a certain satisfaction. At last he was going into actual battle.

At just the right moment, a ray of sun burst through the overcast sky to light up the 155th Blackshirt Battalion column in tight formation proceeding down the road in the direction of Spi Kamarate. The first to spot them was Second Lieutenant Achilleus Argyropoulos, the commander of a battery of anti-tank guns stationed near where the main road joins the Desnitsa river. He got on the phone to Ketseas, who at once ordered him to open fire. At about the same time Koutridis' battalion on the western spur of Hill 731 poured a rain of machine gun and rifle fire on the rearmost Italian unit, the Second Battalion of the 72 Regiment, as it was passing below. As Colonel Ketseas reported:

> Total panic and confusion prevailed in the Italian ranks when the 75mm guns of the First Platoon of Anti-tank Field Artillery commanded by Second Lieutenant Argyropoulos, blasted them. Cries and groans resounded in the ravine as they were being decimated.

There was carnage at both ends of the Proi Math. The ambush at the north end prevented the Blackshirts in front from retreating. Argyropoulos' guns lengthened their range and hammered the Blackshirts, some of whom fought back as best as they could while others sought safety in the numerous gullies and small ravines on the west side the ravine.

Though the men didn't know it yet, the 26 Blackshirts was essentially leaderless after its commander seems to have disappeared. Major Pellegrini, the commander of the 155th, fell wounded. A young Greek artillery officer, Second Lieutenant Haralambos Mitromaras, in a fit of rage gathered up a handful of volunteers and ran to the fray like an infantry officer, firing wildly into the Italian ranks. It wasn't long before an Italian claimed him. Mitromaras' men rushed the remaining Blackshirts who were firing from behind makeshift barricades of boulders and tree trunks. They stood firm in the face of a storm of Greek bayonets and grenades, until the pile of bodies lying in the Proi Math stream was such as to persuade the survivors to put their hands up, holding handkerchiefs or whatever white material they had on them.

'Major, they're surrendering!' came the shout from Koutridis' battalion on the height overlooking the action. It was about 9:50 a.m., just over an hour after the start of the Proi Math flanking movement. The cries and groans of the wounded resounded off the sides of the ravine. Those who could walk appeared from behind rocks and bushes, bloodied and limping, throwing away their weapons and surrendering to Koutridis' men who tried to treat the wounds as best as they could. One machine gunner of 9 Company had scrambled down the slope to the road and was about to spray the Italian column when a whole squad put up their hands. An Italian officer offered him a wad of Italian lire, apparently in the hope that he might get favourable treatment; the machine gunner refused the money but was gallant enough to offer his captives cigarettes.

Major Pellegrini was found under a bush, being tended by his orderly, who helped him up and walked with him to the Greek lines, his face betraying his contempt: the Blackshirts were made up mostly of the most fanatically ideological fascists. The orderly carried the major's briefcase, which when opened was found to contain the entire detailed battle plan of the Spring Offensive: which divisions were to be aimed at which parts of the Greek line, replete with timings and coloured arrow symbols. It was all there: the assignments of the Puglie, Cagliari, Pinerolo, Pusteria and Cacciatore delgi Alpi Divisions, their objectives and follow-up actions, and tactics to be employed – invariably the mass attack preceded by an artillery bombardment. The plans contained the surprising revelation that after the success of the Spring Offensive Mussolini intended to personally ride into Greece atop a Fiat tank! Naturally the material was sent to Papagos and his corps and division commanders, who now had a much clearer picture of what to expect.

The Blackshirts left at least two hundred and fifty dead at the bottom of the Proi Math ravine; the number of wounded is undetermined, but we can be fairly sure that a good number of grievously wounded subsequently perished, unable to be recovered because of nuisance shelling from their own artillery. About one hundred and fifty Blackshirts were captured, including Pellegrini, two other majors and the unnamed deputy commander of the 72 Regiment, a lieutenant colonel, who took advantage of the confusion to escape. The amount of equipment abandoned in the Proi Math was a windfall to the Greeks: automatic rifles, light and heavy machine guns, mortars, ammunition and food supplies. All went to Ketseas' 51 Regiment, except for eight sacks and four cartons of medical supplies which the 19 Regiment's chief medical officer said would meet the regiment's medical needs for days. He spoke too soon – such was the number of Italian and Greek wounded in urgent need of care that the supplies were only just enough for immediate needs.

The defeat of the Blackshirts in the Proi Math valley had not gone unobserved by the Italian artillery, which intensified its fire in the direction of Kiafe Luzit. For half an hour, the men of the Second Battalion huddled with their terrified Italian captives in their holes as the shells rained down mere feet from the front trenches. When the cannonading stopped Koutridis ordered Zikos to lead a party that would take the prisoners to the 33 Regiment headquarters down the Desnitsa Valley and southwards, away from the immediate danger.

When they were about to cross the river, the Italians began to undress in order to wade or swim across, but Zikos shouted that there was no time for that, so they had to cross fully clothed. He was right to hurry them up, as the group was in full view of several Italian batteries that had begun lobbing shells in their direction. Some of the Italians held what appeared to be sacred books in their hands; Zikos noticed that one had the words 'Santo Antonio' on the cover – probably a life of Saint Anthony. They stopped only when they reached a sheltered ravine to the west of the Desnitsa river and awaited a patrol from the 33 Regiment to pick them up.

While they rested, Zikos had a chance to observe some of the captured men:

> One was an elderly captain who had two rows of decorations. He had fought in Abyssinia. I remarked to him, using sign language, that Mussolini was crazy. He became indignant and replied, 'No.' Then I turned to a soldier and told him the same as I had told the captain, to receive the reply, 'Si.'

Presently an Italian-speaking second lieutenant from the 33 Regiment headquarters showed up to interrogate the prisoners. The Blackshirt captain blamed his soldiers for throwing down their weapons and raising white handkerchiefs when attacked; he said he had no choice but to do the same. It took some time for the prisoners to be rounded up and led to the rear, as many had hidden in defiles to protect themselves from their own artillery fire – and perhaps have a chance to escape. On the way to the rear one of the guards, Sergeant Konstantinos Salvanos of 9 Company, noticed that despite the kind treatment of the prisoners, one Blackshirt major (Pellegrini?) behaved arrogantly to his own junior officers, upbraiding them constantly. 'In general,' Zikos writes, 'we treated the Italian captives in a brotherly fashion.'

The cordiality between captors and captured was remarkable. Sheer relief at being out of the hellhole no doubt prompted most of it. Besides, the defending Second Battalion had sustained no fatalities and had just five men wounded. A bullet pierced both cheeks of one man, who had the pleasure of being treated by a captured medical officer. With certain exceptions, the Greeks showed no overt hostility to their captives and treated them well, fully according to the requirements of the Geneva Convention. This the Italian prisoners appreciated by pretty much behaving themselves on the long journey to internment in Athenian prison camps.

Meanwhile, another portion of the 72 Regiment of the Puglie Division was making its third daily attempt on Hill 731. Lieutenant Finestra was in a special assault group (*Raggruppamento d'Assalto*) tasked with pushing forward to connect with the other units. Packs on backs, weapons in hand, the group got going. Dark thoughts assailed Finestra. His unit was technically in the reserve, yet here it was being ordered into action. That could mean only one thing: the objective of Hill 731 still had not been attained. 'Our last hour has come,' was the only thing that went through his mind. 'I was seized by an odd sensation. I seemed to be on the edge of a cliff, while I marched in silence.' He feared he would never see his home again. As the day progressed, the *Raggruppamento* followed in the footsteps of the CXXI Battalion 'Littoria' and the 121 Machine Gun Company to link up with the 72 Regiment at the foot of the hill.

So far, the Duce had been observing most of the action from his eyrie on Komarit, in the company of Geloso, Gambara and the Fourth Corps commander, General Camillo Mercalli. For the first two days, he had been incessantly bombarding his divisional commanders with orders and advice, but to no avail. He would have been thinking how he could face Hitler once more if his treasured Spring Offensive were to shatter, as it showed signs of doing. On 10 March, the surly weather had grounded his air force, depriving his long-suffering infantrymen, plagued by lice, frostbite and dysentery, of cover. This was a dirty war of the most literal kind. Mario Cervi, the leading Italian historian of the Albanian campaign, described 11 March as 'a sort of stubborn beating at a door that wouldn't open rather than the action of a battering-ram.'

Another piece of information volunteered by the captives of Proi Math was that Mussolini himself was in Albania observing the offensive (though the Greek 1st Division, which issued its report after interrogating the prisoners, must already have known as much). The realization that the Duce's troops were receiving a drubbing under his own eyes was a tonic to the Greeks; taking into account the discovery of Cavallero's plans, this third day of the battle for Hill 731 must be considered a turning point. The Blackshirt defeat in Proi Math was a firm sign that the Duce's offensive was not unstoppable after all and, moreover, the unimaginative Italian tactics were proving quite predictable.

From Zikos' point of view, it was his own Third Battalion that provided the key to success in Proi Math. He relates that it was the nameless mule train private who had escaped the Blackshirts' blows to scramble up to Spi Kamarate who first blew the whistle about what was afoot. He adds that if that had not happened, the Blackshirts could well have slipped undetected to the battalion's own rear, plus that of Hill 731, in which case the outcome of the battle would have been in serious doubt. Ketseas wrote later that 'the Italian incursion had created a dangerous salient for our forces.' That is debatable at best. Almost certainly the Blackshirts' move had been noticed at 19 Regiment headquarters, and opinions differ as to whether Colonel Ketseas or Captain Koutridis gave the initial orders to attack. But the outcome of the encounter is not in dispute, and neither is the fact that the entire Third Battalion, including its cooks and muleteers, joined in the downhill charge with great *élan*.

From his brief exchange with the Blackshirt captain, Sergeant-Major Zikos gained the impression that 'the officers were fascists and the men indifferent.' The dichotomy, of course, was not that clear-cut. They were plenty of men in the lower ranks, such as the late Private Pecoraro, who brimmed with eagerness to fight for country and Duce, while no less a figure than Marshal Pietro Badoglio, who had headed Italy's armed forces at the outbreak of war, and other top-ranking officers such as General Vercellino, took a very dim view of the whole thing. It was true, also, that after the war began a great many soldiers who had started out believing in the Duce's mission lost their faith when they had to go up against the bayonets of an aggrieved nation.

At this point we need to do away once and for all with the pernicious stereotype of the 'unwilling' Italian soldier of World War Two that is a half-truth at best. There is no reason to doubt Zikos' impression of them, though most likely any captured *soldato* might well wish to ingratiate himself with his captors by playing down or hiding his attachment to the Duce's cause. If there was anything, in fact, that kept the Italian soldier facing the muddy death, it was the average man's Catholic upbringing. And as the great majority of them had not known any other leader except Mussolini, they had grown up indoctrinated with the patriotic aspects of fascism and a sense of duty reinforced by the Roman Catholic Church's emphasis on obedience to all levels of authority, from the father of the family, the local priest and the superior officer, all the way up to the Duce and the king. Whether or not they were engaged in an 'unfair' war would not have been an issue to them. Such thoughts are mainly the province of the better-educated urban and middle classes who, in the Duce's army, were a distinct minority.

The diary of farm boy Giovanni De Pizzol is indicative. One entry runs: 'Today there's great joy, yet not without deep sadness for our heroes whose bodies remain on the field of Battle having given all for our Country. Their great heroism and their spirits guide us to our great goal.' There is no trace, either here or in other diary entries, of suspicion that the Italian cause could be anything but right. The capitalization of the words Battle (*Battaglia*) and Country (*Patria*) is a key semantic clue. Silvo Bertoldi, an Italian military historian, considers that the great mass of soldiery in Albania 'never asked themselves who was at fault. They belonged to a country where there was no possibility of disputing things, where everything was accepted as normal and you always obeyed your commander.' The 'great goal' that De Pizzol looked forward to attaining would have been, of course, simply victory in the war, period. According to Bertoldi, the soldiers' 'respect for the sense of duty, the civic virtue that is the highest form of patriotism' kept them risking their lives.

Major Sandro Annoni, a battalion commander in the Eleventh Army's 6th (Cuneo) Division, had taken the trouble to give a sober speech to his men and their families before embarking for Albania. 'I don't promise victory,' he told them, 'but I do promise honour. I'm taking your sons to war and I assure you I will manage their lives like a good family head.' The words, indicating a high level of leadership, were all the more remarkable in that Major Annoni, though he was a veteran of the Abyssinian War and knew Cavallero personally, did not hold a Fascist Party card (when he presumably could have) and was thus kept back on the promotion ladder. He was also single, which in party eyes was suspect, as the ideal man had to be married and have children. But he was a soldier, and it would have been unthinkable for him not to do his duty. It was men like this who redeemed the often-battered reputation of the Italian fighting man.

Then we have the testimony of Lieutenant Vincenzo Ambrosio, a former civil servant, whose dedication to the Duce's cause was total. Though well aware that the majority of the men cursed the war and its hardships, the letters to his father reveal his implacable opposition to that attitude and his view of the Albanian campaign as 'a convergence of the real and constructive efforts of the Italian people'. In contrast to the soldiers' complaints of poor food and clothing and irregular supplies, Ambrosio claimed fervently that in reality the troops had everything they desired, including 'wine and regular cigarettes'. He was one of those undoubtedly sterling characters whose political tastes happened to lean in the direction of fascism and its leader. He exulted in the news that the Duce was there at the front with him. 'This is the great Spring of the Country, papa…' Six days later, on the second day of the Spring Offensive, perhaps below Mali Spadarit, he gave his life for what he venerated. Another initial enthusiast was Corporal Peppino Caramuta of the 139 Regiment of the 47th (Bari) Division. But five months of mud, blood, privation and the obsessive fear of 'the roar of Greek mortars that have killed thousands of our men' changed his mind radically. Though he survived the battle for Hill 731, he was killed the following month. What is beyond dispute, however, is that as the ordeal progressed through to the spring of 1941, what remained of the troops' dedication to regime and country began to suffer serious erosion.

Colonel Ketseas, the sector commander, reported that all three battalions of the 19 Regiment had been severely mauled over three days; the 1st Division command ordered their relief and replacement by other units of the same regiment. Ketseas also had to repulse a fresh attack by the Cagliari's 63 Regiment against Hill 717. Faced with withering defensive fire, the Italians took cover behind the bodies of fallen comrades, some of whom were still alive and weakly begging for water. The 63 was duly driven back with considerable loss, pursued by probing artillery fire. Vrachnos also ordered a replacement for Ketseas himself, but as the Italian threat on the evening of 11 March was still strong, the order was cancelled and he was kept in place. During the night, Koutridis' Third Battalion was moved to the reserves and the much-battered Second Battalion sent back to the east of Vinokazit.

On other fronts, the Greek 15th Division on the right hurled back two companies of Italian infantry that had gone forward after an intense artillery barrage at 8 a.m.; a similar attack at 4 p.m. met with a similar fate. For most of that day, the Italian artillery peppered the whole front of the 15th Division with heavy fire, but without any real result. The Greek 17th Division, holding the left at Mezgoranit at the north end of the Trebeshinë range, repulsed an Italian attack that aimed to seize some high ground there while the *Regia Aeronautica* strafed and bombed the location. In a three-hour after-dark battle, the 17th held firm. The division had not had it easy as, in three days of ceaseless combat, its 29 Regiment in particular had lost a large part of its strength to enemy action and frostbite; moreover, its casualties would likely have been fewer if the men had been able to dig trenches and foxholes in the unyielding rock. The 5th Division, between the 17th and the 1st, was hammered by incessant artillery and mortar fire, suffering nine men killed. The day had similar results for the 11th Division. But none of the defenders retreated an inch. This was partly thanks to the flexibility of tactics ordered by the II Corps command, which at 1 p.m. instructed the 28 and 33 Regiments to send a battalion each to the 1st Division to beef up its defences around Hill 731.

General Vrachnos, the 1st Division commander, issued a congratulatory message to his troops that is worth quoting in full:

My brave officers, non-commissioned officers and soldiers,

Brimming with emotion, admiration and great pride I address myself to you, the Heroes of Trebeshinë, Kiafe Luzit, 731, Spi Kamarate and Bregu Rapit, who for three days in a row held your positions in the face of continuous and bitter attacks by the enemy, the despised invader. Not only did you inflict death from your positions on the thousands of attackers, but with admirable heroism carried out counter-attacks. This attack had been in preparation for months and the enemy had pinned great hopes on it.

My brave comrades, immortal men of our little Greece, that is the enemy that wished to enslave and crush us. He thought that with his thousands of soldiers, his many cannon and aeroplanes, he could break your spirit. To all of You, the heroes of the iron 1st Division, I convey warm greetings, and in the name of our

Country I heartily wish that VICTORY may always adorn your glorious BROW.

Major General Vasilios Vrachnos

Though by our day's standards the rhetoric would seem a bit overblown, it certainly must have been an immense tonic to the troops. In all wars, all too often senior officers are often blamed by the men at the front for being out of touch. By his fulsome praise, Vrachnos showed that he knew how to reward valour. In the Greece (and no doubt the Italy) of the time, such phrasing was not considered in any way artificial or tendentious. It was fully in keeping with Greek national sentiment, which really did demonize the Italians as 'the despised invader'. In such an atmosphere, little distinction would be made between Mussolini and the blameless (for the most part) soldiers who had no choice but to fight under his orders. Vrachnos certainly knew this, yet for his troops' morale's sake he had to pull out all the stops (as indeed, did Winston Churchill during, for example, the Battle of Britain). The commander of the II Corps, Major General Georgios Bakos, messaged the troops that he was 'proud to lead such heroes', adding that his message should be read to all 1st Division personnel, including 'the last private'.

Cavallero was under no illusions. He saw plainly that what he hoped would be the knockout blow against the Greeks had blunted itself but was wary of saying as much to the Duce. He had sent regiments of Bari to help out the badly-pummelled Puglie but had observed their slow and painful progress with consternation. 'The view is disheartening,' he wrote in his diary. 'The soldiers are moving slowly in the mud and in incessant rain.' Through his binoculars, Cavallero could only just discern the grey-green lines struggling forward in the morning mists. 'The Puglie telephones that it cannot go forward as its losses are dreadful. The Greeks continue to stage counter-attacks. In many sectors the battle has become hand-to-hand.' In the third day alone, the 11 Alpini Regiment lost eleven officers and three hundred and twenty enlisted men killed and twenty-five officers wounded. 'The wounded soldiers have not yet been counted,' Cavallero noted.

He added: 'I have ordered [General Alfredo] Guzzoni [the Undersecretary of War and Deputy Chief of the Supreme Staff] to send over all the munitions left in Italy because the Italian Army is here, the war is here, and here is where we have to win.' Hill 731, in short, had become the focal point of the whole Italian war effort. Mussolini telephoned Cavallero from Gambara's headquarters to say that, despite the setbacks, the original plan had to be stuck to at all costs. He relayed an order to General Matteo Negro, the Bari commander, with his opinion that 'the greater the impetus of the men, the fewer will be the losses.' That appeared to be the limit of Mussolini's tactical vision, and none of his commanders, not even Cavallero, dared gainsay him. That vision concentrated almost solely on the prestige of the Italian Army, and by extension his own; winning became its own object. How many of his men's lives would be expended, and what the strategic objective might be that would justify the sacrifice, never, as far as anyone knows, entered his mind.

The Germans, who were closely observing the campaign, were under no illusions. On 11 March, as the Blackshirts were being ripped to pieces in Proi Math, they bluntly told an Italian diplomat in Berlin what they thought of Italian strategy. We can almost see the diplomat's blush as he wrote with dripping sarcasm (presumably in a diary):

As anyone could have foreseen, the Germans are literally furious about our feats of arms on the Albanian front. We walked unprepared right into failure! We really cut a *bella figura* and earned a lot of prestige! We have so much prestige that there's some to spare!

Chapter 6

Fourth and fifth days: 'My boys are gone!'

As a chill northerly wind blew up after dark, the defenders were allowed no rest. Three quarters of an hour after midnight the sky to the north lit up in a Wagnerian backdrop of hundreds of muzzle flashes: Cavallero was hoping to catch the Greeks asleep. If they were, they were certainly jolted awake now, as the shells came howling in. 'Hit the dirt!' echoed in countless trenches and shelters. Tracer shells lit up the objectives that the 139 Regiment of the Bari Division was to attempt.

One battalion of the 139 made for Hill 717, the other for Hill 731. The Greeks were surprised and hard put to keep their lines. These were fresh Italian troops, called up to replace the ravaged Puglie, confident of the surprise value of a night attack; in contrast, Colonel Ketseas' men were tired and badly under strength, decimated by the past three days of combat. But the Bari employed precisely the same unimaginative tactics that had boomeranged on the Puglie and Cagliari: mass assaults on a fanatically-defended height. Cavallero and his generals, it seems, could not bring themselves to believe that the Greeks were capable of resisting so stoutly. To them, it was a mere question of superior force. A night attack may have been an innovation but in essence no different from a daytime operation.

As the Italian artillery flashes illuminated the sky like lightning, the 139 regiment attacked spiritedly but was halted in its tracks by Ketseas' now-familiar combination of Hotchkiss machine guns, avalanches of defensive grenades and mountain artillery. The Bari tried again at 5:30 a.m. – without artillery support this time. The 140 Regiment had replaced the ravaged 139, scrambling over its bodies;

again, two battalions aimed at the respective hills. The 140 made a determined attempt to break the Greek lines but was literally mown down by Ketseas' machine gunners. After an hour's fighting, the Bari battalions pulled back, whipped ragged. In just one night of combat, the division's fighting capacity had been seriously dented.

The impression from the Italian side was later given by squad leader Andreatta of the 115 Legion who remembered 'an eruption of explosions, flashes lighting up almost the whole battlefield, a spectacle that frightened yet inspired'. The legion and the rest of the CXXI Battalion were not exactly in the best condition to fight. During the night, they had leapfrogged the 72 Regiment of the Puglie to the front line, only to spend the hours until morning 'between water and mud, clinging to the terrain, exposed to enemy fire'. That would have been at the northern end of the Trebeshinë range, where a detachment of the Bari attacked at dawn, or on the north-west flank of Hill 731 where the Italians attempted to secure the main road at 9:30 a.m. but were thwarted by shelling.

Though Andreatta was later to claim that Greek resistance was at first feeble, the Greek records show that Ketseas' detachment hit back with more than 2,600 artillery and mortar shells. The bitterest fighting occurred to the east of Hill 731 where, for more than an hour, the grenade, mortar and bayonet wrought great destruction in the Bari's ranks, even though, as the official Greek report said, the Italian artillery action was 'unprecedented'. In this action, the 1st Division lost ninety-nine men killed, including six officers, and three hundred and thirteen wounded. Twenty-eight wounded Italians were captured.

The rest of the day passed relatively quietly, except for sporadic artillery fire from both sides, giving Ketseas the chance to reorganize the defence in his sector. One of the battalions that were moved from the right of the Greek line to beef up Hill 731 was Sergeant-Major Zikos', the Third of the 51 Regiment. As soon as they arrived at the Second Battalion's position on the hill, an executive officer yelled at them to get out of their compact formation, otherwise 'the artillery will kill you'. Zikos relates that, as they couldn't hear any gunfire at that moment, the men blithely ignored the nervous executive officer's frantic shouts. Major Koutridis, Zikos' commanding officer, conferred briefly with Kaslas, his Second Battalion counterpart, in his shelter and arranged temporary positions. Soon afterwards, several shells came howling through the thick morning mist and Zikos and the others hurriedly dug their foxholes.

Zikos, at that point, noticed a solitary soldier leading a pack mule up the slope. Man and beast moved methodically, seemingly oblivious to the shell bursts all around them. When he appeared in a clearing, and thus was particularly vulnerable, the men of the Third Battalion shouted at him to hurry up. The soldier didn't increase his pace, and as he drew near to the battalion lines the men heard him cursing the Italians and Mussolini. Amazingly, neither he nor the mule suffered a scratch. 'He was one of the experienced men,' Zikos noted, 'who had got used to the shelling that was terrifying us.' Thicker fog descended in the afternoon and enabled Koutridis to arrange the exchange of places between his companies and those of the fatigued Second Battalion.

The Third was now ensconced on Hill 731. The battalion's Thermopylaian orders were stark and uncompromising: 'defence to the last man'. The officers grimly told their men that if they retreated even one step, it would be 'the grave of Greece'. Most exposed was 9 Company, holding the summit and extending down the east slope to watch over Hill 717; attached to it was a machine gun platoon and a battery of 51 Regiment artillery. Number 10 Company plus a machine gun platoon was assigned to the west slope overlooking the Proi Math ravine, while 11 Company took position right behind 9 Company on the south slope as a reserve.

Zikos found himself right at the summit, in the most dangerous position of all. The shelters had already been dug by the Second Battalion; a straight line of shallow trenches holding two men each and at most two metres apart. The trenches on the right were somewhat deeper, following the contours of the hill. Only one platoon enjoyed some sort of overhead protection, and a flimsy one at that. There was no communication trench to connect with 11 Company in the rear, no observation post and no barbed wire in front of the line. The 9 Company staff of about a dozen men crowded inside a cabin made of logs and earth, just behind the summit, that had withstood three days of bombardment and was therefore deemed somewhat reliable. The telephone lines had been cut, again, and even visual signalling to the other two companies was difficult.

The apparent disorganization, and the desolation of the place he found himself in, disheartened Zikos. The defence, he figured, surely would have had enough time in the past month or so to build up a functioning position, even if consisting solely of shelters and barbed wire. The two solitary cannon on the hill were placed too close together and hence could be destroyed by a single enemy shell. What shocked him in particular was the sight of a gunner slumped at his post, killed on the first day of the attack. His comrades inexplicably had let him remain there for four days, and only after dark on 13 March was he decently buried. 'How the officers tolerated that was beyond me,' he wrote. This episode could illustrate the callousness generated among some men as a result of months of hardship and the sight of death at close quarters.

Charitably, Zikos put the lack down to the Greek emphasis on counter-attack rather than defence; in February, few had expected the area around Hill 731 to be more than a temporary possession as Papagos' army surged northwards, deeper into Albania. Nonetheless, bitter complaints were heard that the battalion had been put in a hellhole, made worse by the stench from the bodies of Italians scattered around. Koutridis heard the grumbling and strode along the line. 'Don't panic because the enemy has plenty of artillery and mortars,' he exhorted. 'With our digging tools we'll burrow in the earth like ants, and as the ants live, so we'll live.' Zikos didn't feel much better when a grizzled Second Battalion sergeant informed him that the Italians' whole effort from now on would be concentrated on the hill where he stood.

Zikos' task, on 12 March, was to order that the platoon trenches be deepened to 1.3 metres with earthworks in front and behind, and that clear fields of fire be created over the slope that plunged steeply downwards in front of them. Back at the 9 Company command dugout, he primed two cases of Polish-made Wz.24 offensive hand grenades and handed them out to the men of his platoon and the neighbouring one, plus an extra supply of machine gun and Mannlicher rifle bullets. Morale in the front line was not of the highest. One squad sergeant had neglected to set his men to digging, believing that Hill 731 would soon be lost. Zikos bawled out that man and others, but to little avail. He recalled Greek Army Infantry Regulation III, which asserted that 'a well-organized and well-trained army can construct a complete rampart for defence in a single night.' But he was dealing for the most part with conscripts with no previous military experience and suffering various degrees of shell shock.

During an afternoon lull in the shelling, Ketseas sent a team down into the Proi Math ravine to bury the enemy dead and succour any wounded who might be still alive. The team came on a horrifying spectacle: wild beasts were tearing at the bodies, some of them dismembered, scattered along the bottom of the ravine. The officer in charge despaired of burying them all adequately and had to content himself with disposing of only those bodies relatively easy to reach. And even then, the grisly job took up most of the night. As they were labouring, the 1st Division command withdrew Ketseas and his long-suffering 51 Regiment, replacing it with the 19 Regiment of Colonel Panagiotis Balis.

The breathing space was welcomed all along the line. Koutridis' battalion took the place of that of Kaslas, with two companies, 9 and 10, placed on the crown of Hill 731. The First Battalion of the 19

Regiment on the right connected with the 90 Regiment of the 15th Division east of Hill 717. In the rear at Spi Kamarate, the Second Battalion, 19 Regiment, was deployed as a reserve. The Proi Math ravine, and the road running through it, was covered by three anti-tank guns. Colonel Ketseas remained with Colonel Balis for a few days to familiarize him with the situation. Shortly afterwards, the 51 Regiment was formally disbanded and its men allocated to other units, and Ketseas was given command of the 4 Regiment holding Kiafe Luzit, a no less difficult job.

In the morning of 12 March, Mussolini was driven to the Ninth Army headquarters at Elbasan, about ninety kilometres north of the battlefront, to confer with its commander, General Alessandro Pirzio Biroli, who had replaced the reluctant Vercellino in mid-February. On returning to Geloso, he told the Eleventh Army chief in no uncertain terms that the offensive had to continue with no let-up of impetus. He simply could not consider anything other than victory, no matter how many men he lost. That same morning, as the hapless men of the Bari were butting bloodily against the usual stone wall of resistance, Geloso had sent him a pessimistic memorandum to the effect that this particular battle must be considered lost. Three days of fierce combat had torn the Puglie Division to shreds, stunned the Bari and had failed to even dent the Greek positions.

Geloso frankly confessed himself at a loss as to what to do next. At a conclave of generals that afternoon, however, the Eleventh Army commander had recovered his confidence enough to suggest a flanking move against the Greek I Corps positions along the Vijosë river in the west. A breakthrough there would open the way to Tepelenë and threaten the Greek II Corps rear at Kelçyre. He wanted the 7th Tuscan Wolves Division to do it, and the Duce agreed.

Mussolini's habitual frown can be imagined as he pondered the proposal. The Puglie and Bari Divisions were badly pummelled; of the other Eighth Corps divisions slated for the initial attack, he complained, the 24th (Pinerolo) and the 59th (Cagliari), had barely stirred. 'We've got four immobile divisions,' he said, 'and two more available.' One of these was the 51st (Siena) which so far had not been engaged. He went on:

We need to continue this offensive because if we give up the whole cause is lost. The Greeks may create a few more unpleasant situations for us, as has happened in our operations towards Klissura [Kelçyre]. We can't consider any other operations because we haven't got the time.

He was right. Above all, he feared that the Germans would come thundering into Greece from Bulgaria within a few weeks, rendering tragically useless the whole Spring Offensive. Ten days earlier, an Allied expeditionary force consisting of the British 1 Armoured Brigade, the 2nd New Zealand Division and 6th Australian Division had landed in Greece in anticipation of the German threat. To his grim-faced commanders, Mussolini revealed exactly what was bothering him:

Before Germany intervenes we must have a military success, otherwise the Germans will rightly say that the Greeks retreated before them… We have nineteen days ahead of us. It is thus possible to continue the attack. How to continue it? That is a technical problem and I'm in no position to offer an opinion.

If that was an opening for Geloso to contribute a 'technical solution,' he replied lamely that he would consider another attack on the Greek right at Mali Spadarit.

'What about supplies from the air?' the Duce demanded.

'Not very much,' Geloso said.

Mussolini propounded three possible solutions. One was to take Hill 1308 on the Trebeshinë range a few kilometres to the southwest of Hill 731; the second was to push straight down the Desnitsa valley, and the third was to seize Mali Spadarit. He said he favoured the second alternative. Geloso seemed to prefer the Hill 1308 solution as freeing the way to recapturing Tepelenë. 'But that way you'll leave all the rest of Trebeshinë in Greek hands,' the Duce countered, noting that the highest point of the range was 1,900 metres. 'And why are our divisions not advancing?'

Geloso cited the rugged terrain, plus 'the enemy [who] fights well and is well-organized on the ground' and for good measure 'a lack of training on our part, especially of officers'. Cavallero, we are assured, was present at the meeting, but seems to have made no significant comment. He would have been reluctant to stick his neck out in the Duce's presence, and may have been hoping that Geloso, not he, might take the rap for the bloody failures. Mussolini made one other point that unwittingly he shared with General Papagos, the Greek commander-in-chief: the doctrine of continuous motion. 'You must attack tomorrow, otherwise the troops will become rooted to the ground, thinking the action is over.' He well recognized that military morale was always improved by going forward as against staying rooted to a defensive stance; in fact, the principle had been the basis of Papagos' own success. 'The Greeks,' the Duce said, 'must be kept under our fire all day. The antidote to their mortars is speed of movement.' So that was that. Geloso was overruled. That evening the Duce ordered Pricolo, his air force chief, to saturate the whole Greek 1st Division position with aerial bombing, starting the next day.

In the early hours of 13 March, the fifth day of the battle, orders from the Greek II Corps command replaced the worn-out parts of the 51 Infantry Regiment, 1st Division, with the fresher 19 Regiment, 6th Division, plus a battalion from the 67 Regiment, 17th Division. The 1st Division force consisted of three battalions of Colonel Balis' 19 Regiment and one each from the 33 and 65 Regiments covering the right of the front, including the Hill 731 sector, two battalions of the 4 Regiment and two of the 16 Regiment occupying the Trebeshinë sector on the left, plus an artillery battery.

The day broke with a thick layer of fog shrouding the landscape but, around noon, the fog lifted. Gazing north through their binoculars, the Greeks saw columns of lorries and fresh troops coming up to the front over newly-bulldozed dirt roads. The men of the Third Battalion had been hard at work for most of the night strengthening their defences on Hill 731. Sergeant-Major Zikos for the first time could clearly see the enemy positions to the north. About an hour later, the lookouts reported enemy troop movements, plus loaded mule trains, in the general direction of Monastero. The artillery observers relayed the information to the regimental command in the rear. The arrival of the Italian reinforcements was confirmed by aerial reconnaissance by the Royal Hellenic Air Force and Royal Air Force. More cannon fodder.

The atmosphere inside the 9 Company shelter was not cordial. Zikos noted that a Second Battalion second-lieutenant named Psichogios who had stayed to brief the replacements was reading a red-covered book titled *Words of Comfort*. Zikos, an experienced and hardened NCO, makes this curious observation without comment, but the sight of a bookish and sensitive subaltern could not have been encouraging. There was bad blood between the newcomers and the two artillerymen of the Second who had callously left their dead comrade sprawled on his gun for three days and were continually grousing about being kept on the hill. The second lieutenant put down his book after Koutridis, the battalion commander, demanded more information about the enemy troop movements. As Psichogos lacked binoculars, Zikos handed him his own monocular telescope so he could confirm the movements by telephone.

From his eyrie on Komarit, Mussolini watched the action. With him was General Gambara, who remarked that the screen of shellfire seemed quite accurate. Mussolini merely nodded in assent, then placed a call to Cavallero who was at the Bari Division's headquarters with the division's commander, General Negro. 'Tell Negro,' the Duce said over the telephone, 'that I greatly esteem him and am counting on him. Tell him that the more impetus there is, the fewer losses there will be.'

At 2 p.m., with full visibility restored, Gambara's guns went at it again for about an hour. Zikos recalled that bombardment as one of unprecedented intensity. 'We thought we were in the bowels of the earth.' Huddled in the shelter, Second Lieutenant Chrysafis, the 9 Company commander, tried to raise the Third Battalion headquarters by telephone, but the line was cut. From his position at Ballaban, a few kilometres to the northeast, Colonel Balis looked in horror at the inferno, tearing at his hair. 'My boys are gone!' he cried.

As disquieting as the cannonade was, what also worried the men of the Third Battalion was the total absence of answering fire from the Greek lines. Was everyone dead? No-one dared stick his head out of the shelter except Zikos, who was sitting by the exit waiting for a chance to do so. At that moment a shell burst right outside, sending a fragment thudding into the ground to come to rest against his body. 'That almost killed you!' Chrysafis shouted, rather unnecessarily. Zikos, finding he was unhurt, shrugged it off. Two heavy shells hit the roof of the shelter, shaking it and its occupants. For an hour there was no let-up. Lieutenant Chrysafis began to despair. 'We're going to die, Zikos,' he said in a stricken voice.

'God will help,' was the NCO's reply, but he at that moment would have far preferred to die on his feet firing at the enemy than be buried alive under an avalanche of shell-churned earth. There was a Hotchkiss machine gun and a case of ammunition belts in a corner of the crowded shelter; Zikos loaded the gun and handed it to a private in preparation for the inevitable infantry attack. Shortly afterwards the sound of running feet was heard outside the entrance; Zikos for a moment feared it might be the enemy, but it was about twenty terrified battalion members who had fled their trenches in panic and were seeking any kind of shelter, however flimsy. The sight of their faces, contorted with terror, would remain with Zikos for the rest of his life. 'Get out, there's no room,' Chrysafis shouted, drawing his revolver to make his point. The men disappeared. Zikos was convinced that if they had forced their way in, those inside would have risked being crushed to death.

After an hour, the guns fell silent and the Bari's 140 Regiment launched itself against Hill 731 while the Cagliari's 63 Regiment went for Hill 717. Four days of failure seemed to count for nothing as the Italians – mostly fresh troops – threw themselves in thick formations against the Greek 19 Regiment positions with fanatical fury. For the men of the 140, those were truly agonizing moments as they stubbornly ignored their losses and came to within a few metres of the summit. Lieutenant Isaac Lavrentidis, commanding 9 Company in the heat of the fight, figured there was only one way to stem the Italian onrush and save the hill and that was to counterattack desperately. He ordered the company to fix bayonets; the swish of unsheathed steel and muffled clangs as the knives were slotted into place was by now a grimly familiar sound to the attackers. The most vicious hand-to-hand combat now ensued; when a second lieutenant commanding a 9 Company platoon was killed, the rest of the platoon threw itself wildly into the fray with everything they had. At about that time, the 1st Division artillery began lobbing shells into the Italian rear, cutting off avenues of retreat.

Zikos' account of the repulse of the Bari's 140 Regiment is somewhat different. When he judged that the enemy infantry must be close by the Italian shouts he heard from that direction, Zikos hoisted his Hotchkiss. 'I'm going out there,' he said and called for a squad to follow him to the summit of Hill 731, braving the shellfire. He found that his greatcoat hindered his movements, so despite the cold, he threw it off. 'All men at their posts!' he roared. The top was a scene of devastation: the battery guns and the observation post had been destroyed and the bodies of their men lay sprawled around. Zikos, accompanied by a sergeant and three soldiers, ran to the foremost trench on the summit where another sergeant and his men were still alive, as at that point the enemy shells were mostly passing overhead. Fuelled by adrenalin, Zikos jumped into the trench. 'Let's get 'em!' Zikos yelled and the seventeen men in the trench took up firing positions. The Italians were clearly visible now, their grey-green uniforms surging up the slope in a confident stride, in the belief that there could have been no-one left alive on the hill.

Lieutenant Finestra of the 140 Regiment was in the first Italian attack wave of the day. His unit, at first advancing in confidence, was brought up short by furious enemy fire. 'The enemy response was very violent. We were hit by a murderous barrage of fire from artillery, mortars, machine guns and automatic rifles.' (Zikos' few men almost certainly contributed to this.) Stunned momentarily, Finestra's legionaries rallied and stubbornly continued their advance, covered by the 35mm Breda machine guns of Finestra's own 121 Company. According to the lieutenant, they almost made it. 'The peak of Hill 731 was almost within an arm's reach. One more leap and it would have fallen.'

One more leap... Zikos opened up on the 140 Regiment with his Hotchkiss in a long burst that used up a whole ammunition belt. At once, the rest of the men joined in a continuous cascade of fire with machine guns, rifles and grenades. The blast stopped the Italians in their tracks. A cheer went up from the handful of Greeks. 'We're here, you bastards, we're alive and waiting for you!' one man yelled. Nonetheless, they were in a parlous situation. The Italian artillery had got wind of what was going on and was re-directing its fire to the source of resistance. Zikos was thankful that the previous night he had insisted on deepening that particular trench. Meanwhile, 10 Company on the west slope and 11 Company on the east were immobilized by enemy air strikes: twenty-five bombers and thirty strafing fighters. What remained of 10 Company's field guns did what they could, but there was no heavy weapon to oppose the force surging up the hill in the centre.

(Back at his post, Mussolini messaged Negro that he heard the division was doing well; 'I praise you and exhort you to continue thus.' General Guido Lama, the commander of the Eighth Corps artillery, also came in for compliments: 'Keep up until you see the Greeks cave in.' Turning to Cavallero, he said he believed that the Greeks, in effect, already had.)

After stopping the first wave of attackers, Zikos found he had run out of ammunition for his Hotchkiss and sent two soldiers back to company headquarters for more belts. All they could find were cases of Mannlicher rifle bullets; as they were returning with these, both were wounded, one in the leg and the other in the buttocks, but they managed to deliver the ammunition. Zikos took the two soldiers' rifles and began to use them himself, ordering his squad to slacken their fire to economize on bullets. Zikos noticed a group of Italian soldiers dead ahead of him and fired six shots in quick succession. The salvo seemed to scatter the group; he saw stretcher-bearers running up and figured he had neutralized whoever was in charge.

Expecting an enemy charge any minute, Zikos ordered his men to fix their well-worn bayonets. Ammunition was running low, but there were enough hand-grenades to go round. 'We were determined if necessary to die heroically,' he wrote. Instead of charging, the men of the Bari dug in and saturated the Greek position with constant fire from CENSA Model 35 light mortars, a type of weapon developed for infantry use in difficult terrain. Two rounds fell into Zikos' trench. He had just turned to a sergeant with orders to guard against an encirclement from the right when a third mortar round burst between the sergeant and the earthen rampart, sending him flying backwards and killing him instantly. Zikos picked up the body and moved it away, when a fourth round plunged into the trench. After the blast, he looked around to see only a machine gun sergeant still unscathed; the rest of his seventeen-strong squad were dead or wounded, and he himself had been lightly wounded in the right hand.

It was as pure a scene from hell as anything Dante could have imagined. Wounded men pleaded for help. Zikos and the machine gun sergeant dressed as many wounds as they could; one soldier was told to sit on the floor of the trench to stanch the blood from his wounded buttocks. Another soldier gasped: 'Sergeant-Major, write to my mother and tell her I died fighting for my country.' Yet another murmured that he was 'leaving a wife and child'. Zikos tried to keep up the men's spirits as much as he could. The field hospital was far in the rear and the company corpsman couldn't do very much in the cramped space of the company shelter. To make any move at all, transferring the wounded to the rear through the hail of enemy machine gun fire, would have been simply suicide.

Over the roar of battle, Zikos heard the sound of aircraft approaching from the direction of Kelçyre. There were eighteen of them, probably British Bristol Blenheim IVs of the RAF's 84 and 211 Squadrons based at Paramythia in Greek territory. They would also have had Hawker Hurricane escorts of the RAF's 80 Squadron. A wall of Italian flak flew up to meet them. Zikos watched in amazement as the bombers flew through the flak and dived to pummel the front Italian lines, bombing and strafing exposed units, artillery positions and anything else visible. The squadrons also had to tangle with a stream of bombers and escorting fighters sent over by Pricolo; Greek records show that the RAF downed two Italian aircraft and Greek anti-aircraft fire accounted for a third. One British bomber was hit and limped back down the Desnitsa valley. Zikos, watching from his trench, felt nothing but admiration for the allied pilots' skills.

Since about 2 p.m., in fact, the *Regia Aeronautica* had been bombing and strafing the Greek positions with half a dozen bombers and some thirty escorting fighters. Mussolini had kept Pricolo at his side as insurance against any difficulty the infantry might encounter, which was already considerable. Cavallero (so he claimed later) was already having his doubts, but in the interests of keeping his job appears not to have elaborated on them to the Duce. Some two hundred Italian warplanes were sent against the whole Greek II Corps positions to soften them up, especially Hill 1308 on Trebeshinë, but without any real result.

In charge of the defence on that hill was Major Kaslas, who had stayed on to coordinate the action after his Second Battalion of the 5 Regiment had been replaced by the Third of the 19 Regiment. The day's action was, in fact, the 19's real baptism of fire in the battle. During the afternoon Koutridis, the Third Battalion commander, was wounded and was being treated at a field dressing station when a courier from 10 Company ran in with a report that the Italians had overrun part of the company's position and had secured a foothold on Hill 731. The medical officer prepared to evacuate Koutridis to the rear, but instead the major, helped by his orderly, donned his tunic and belt and slung a bag of grenades around his neck. Pistol in hand, he turned to the men around him. 'As many of you as are Greeks and have a Greek heart, follow me.' A good number did indeed follow him with grenade and bayonet, helping him regain 10 Company's position. Zikos noted Koutridis' timely arrival which, he said, sent the Italians reeling, 'adding new bodies to the large number of them already at that place'.

It says much for the Italian infantryman that he was able to demonstrate such valour in the face of fierce odds and under indifferent command. But even Cervi reckons that the courage of the men of the Bari that day was not of the aggressively impulsive kind. It was rather 'a tenacious, stubborn, almost resigned attitude,' a mechanical devotion to duty and adherence to orders whatever the cost, rather than inspired and flashy feats of valour. Moreover, most soldiers knew they had been sent to fight an unpopular war, and thus lacked the spark of enthusiasm so necessary for success in any campaign. As Finestra admitted, 'On that tragic 13 March only heroes could defy death. But we were men with our weaknesses and ideals and, like all men, in the face of death we wanted desperately to live.' There was a lull in the fighting at about 5 p.m., lasting about an hour, after which the Bari Division launched a battalion in what was the thirteenth consecutive Italian attempt on Hill 731. That, too, like the previous twelve, came to grief.

As the sun began to set on that tumultuous day, Zikos gazed out upon the corpses of those *soldati* who had no doubt desperately wanted to live but whom he had helped kill. The drone of the last aircraft had faded into a shell-shocked silence. 'Be patient,' he told his wounded in the trench. 'When it's dark you'll be taken to the battalion dressing station.' Some didn't hear him; they were already dead. Under cover of darkness, the unhurt sergeant carried the wounded men to the rear while Zikos went out to inspect the peripheral positions, ordering the burial of the dead and arranging guard duty. One of the bodies was that of the hapless gunner who had lain over his gun carriage for four days. Zikos found the greatcoat he had thrown off earlier, in the heat of the action, and went to the company shelter where there was general relief. Then the casualty count came in: Zikos' platoon was by far the hardest hit, with sixteen dead and wounded, while the two other platoons of 9 Company suffered one man dead and five wounded. The machine gun squad, however, was completely wiped out except for its commanding sergeant. The company's admin staff had three men wounded. The two companies on the left and right, 10 and 11 respectively, had few casualties.

On 13 March, the Italian Army came the closest it ever would to seizing Hill 731. The morning passed quietly, but in the early afternoon the Italian artillery and aerial bombardment recommenced with renewed fury. Such was the intensity of the Italian bombardment that Lieutenant Finestra's hopes of 'one more leap' were revived. The attack by the Bari had been well-planned. On the hill itself, the Greek communications were in tatters and coordination among the 19 Regiment and its battalions and companies was non-existent. Three mortar rangers were mortally wounded. The shelling and bombing had smashed anything resembling a command structure. It was thanks to the stubborn resistance of hardened NCOs like Zikos that the Greeks only just held on, though the timely appearance of the RAF overhead clearly contributed.

Zikos cites a comment by Second Lieutenant Christos Kintzos of the reserve company crediting him with almost single-handedly turning the tide of the battle for Hill 731. 'It was impossible for us to help,' Kintzos reportedly told Zikos later, 'as we were under such intense artillery fire that any movement on our part would have been disastrous... We were wondering whether the front-line trenches would hold out.' Finestra also wondered, concluding that 'the Italians did not lack courage but luck.' Other factors also played a part. Much credit should go to Colonel Balis, the 19 Regiment commander, who had got over his initial shock and as the fight unfolded quickly, deftly gave orders to individual companies from the reserve Second Battalion to stiffen shaky sectors of the front, including sending a unit of mortars to Hill 717.

Night had fallen, but the bitterest day of the battle was not over. At 9 p.m., yet another Italian attack materialized out of the murk. Greek patrols had detected the movement and had warned the defenders, who got into position in time. A shout of command was heard from the unseen enemy, followed by bursts of machine gun fire. Almost at once, the Greek artillery replied, its shell bursts revealing the silhouettes of the attackers. Within minutes, the shelling combined with a hail of defensive hand grenades had sent this latest attack reeling back with 'blood flowing as if from a spring,' in Zikos' words. A certain amount of confusion clouds this phase of the battle. Zikos himself is unclear about just when this Italian night attack took place, as he seems to be about the night's activity in general. His original account says that the hours of darkness were spent in getting water supplies from the streams beneath the hill, and replenishing food and ammunition supplies.

However, another Italian assault was carried out just after midnight. The unlikely herald of this was Private Panagiotis Mantas of the Third Battalion, who, while on patrol, felt the call of nature and went to answer it in a shell hole. Mantas was the shortest man in the whole battalion, barely 1.5 metres tall. He wore the smallest size of greatcoat, which nevertheless reached down to his ankles. Zikos noted that even his rifle and bayonet were longer than he was tall. However, he was noted for 'discipline and coolness'. The latter quality cemented his reputation that night. As he was squatting, his slight figure covered by his greatcoat, an Italian soldier appeared on the rim above him. In a flash Mantas prodded the man's thigh with the point of his bayonet and ordered him to halt. The Italian dropped his weapon and put up his hands. With his trousers still down, Mantas gathered his greatcoat about him to be technically decent and, at bayonet point, took the Italian to company headquarters. Thenceforth, the diminutive private became famous in the battalion as the man who 'could take prisoners even while taking a shit'.

Zikos observed the prisoner as he was brought in. 'He was wiry and alert, a newcomer to the front.' Under his greatcoat he carried eight offensive grenades, a short-barrelled rifle and a watch. Zikos was at once suspicious that a fresh enemy attack might be in the offing and walked up to the summit to warn the troops there. That's where he learned of Private Mantas' legendary achievement. One can imagine the top of Hill 731 resounding with raucous laughter and perhaps hearty slaps on the back for plucky little Mantas.

As for Cavallero, the sight of Greek shells cutting large swaths in his troop formations did not help his disposition. He also couldn't help seeing RAF Blenheim bombers attacking the Pinerolo Division around Kiafe Luzit. His diary entry of that day contains praise for the Pinerolo for advancing through a 'fiery curtain' of Greek mortar fire from the 4 Regiment. The reports he received told him that the Bari had in fact seized Hill 717 and at least one neighbouring eminence. As we have seen, this was true only momentarily. If Cavallero was aware of the truth he would hardly have communicated it to Mussolini, who was busy heaping praise on Negro for doing 'very well today' and assuring him that the Greek resistance was beginning to crack. 'Our action is starting to have results.'

Chapter 7

'We should call it off'

There was little rest that night for either army. A bitter northerly wind sent the temperature plunging. The soldiers wrapped their greatcoats around them, trying to doze off for a few minutes in their icy holes. Zikos suspected an imminent night attack, and he was right. Under Geloso's personal order that the attacks 'be continued with the greatest possible intensity,' the already exhausted men of the Bari and Cagliari were urged on Hill 731 yet again at 2:30 a.m. in the morning of 14 March. The first to notice them were the outposts of the First Battalion on Hill 717. A detachment of the Cagliari's 63 Regiment had infiltrated a footpath to the west of the hill; a Greek patrol fired on them but, in the darkness, the fire was ineffectual. The Italians continued their progress.

Lieutenant Georgios Ellinas of 3 Company of the First Battalion (19 Regiment) was killed in a futile attempt to halt the infiltration. The Italian advance rolled over the few defenders; the First Battalion called frantically for reinforcements from the 90 Regiment on the right. The reinforcements finally halted the Italian advance, whereupon the recently-ailing General Gianni, the commander of the Cagliari, called for saturation artillery fire. But that couldn't stem the inevitable retreat.

Distracted by the unseen fighting on and around Hill 717, the defenders of Hill 731 found that a new wave of the Bari Division had crept up almost to their front trenches. Two soldiers gave the alarm. Zikos went out to look and saw the Italians had dug in a mere one hundred and fifty metres away. It was a clear, cold night and their helmets glinted in the starlight. He ordered his front line to open fire, to be answered by bursts from three light machine guns. Grabbing a mortar, he fired three rounds back, silencing one machine gun. There were two platoons of the Bari in front, giving covering fire for those behind.

Zikos sent a courier to ask for urgent reinforcements. Half an hour later, six men of the Second Battalion under Sergeant Samaras turned up and began shooting. One soldier, however, merely rested his head against the trench parapet, saying he was ill. The case was similar to one in 5 Company in a nearby sector, where an incoming projectile bounced off a soldier's helmet, denting it, and exploded in a ravine. The soldier had hysterics and was carried, sobbing uncontrollably, to the dressing station in the rear. 'Hey, dude,' the battalion commander said after seeing that the soldier was physically unhurt, 'brave guys don't cry.'

'I can't help it, sir,' the man stammered, alternating between sobs and hysterical laughter. 'Look at my helmet!' The major nodded and addressed a few sober words to the shaken soldier, who was given a couple of days' rest and then sent back to the lines. In the Greek Army, the officers were generally closer to the men than the Italian officers were. It was not so much a matter of class consciousness – there was certainly no lack of haughty martinets in shoulder stars looking down their noses at the 'other ranks' – but of the experience of six months of relentless combat that had quickly weeded out the straw men and phonies and bonded officer and enlisted man together in a common moral purpose.

The men of the Bari stubbornly kept up their fire, forcing the Greeks to expend more ammunition than they expected. The bullets for the Mannlicher rifles were quickly exhausted; Zikos' request for more was answered by a consignment of Hotchkiss machine gun bullets, which would have to do. He wished he had another platoon to back him up, but Koutridis resisted the temptation to send one from the reserve in case a general enemy assault was imminent.

At one point, Zikos noticed that the enemy fire was surprisingly inaccurate, most of the bullets hitting ten or so metres in front of the trenches, just where the hill began to slope downwards. He ordered the right wing of his platoon to fall in behind the central section and kneel behind the men already in the trenches so that they could concentrate their fire.

The twenty-eight men under Zikos were the only ones engaged in active combat that night. Every so often he would order them to yell the 'Aera!' battle-cry to give the impression of greater numbers. As the Italians had come to associate that cry with an imminent furious counter-attack, he hoped it might have an effect. If it did, it was a weak one. Instead of falling back, this time the Bari crept forward relentlessly and, by 5 a.m., had come within eighty metres of the Greek line. The only way to save Hill 731 now was by a firm counter-attack with the most feared of weapons. 'Fix bayonets!' Zikos barked. One nervous soldier spoke up. 'Don't take us down with you, Sergeant-Major.'

Zikos wasn't listening. He intended to employ his Polish-made WZ.24 offensive hand grenades first, before resorting to cold steel. The WZ.24 carried a bigger charge than the defensive fragmentation kind and made a louder noise. 'When I stop throwing my grenades, you start throwing yours,' he told the men. 'Ready to go over the top – go!' Zikos led the way, followed by Sergeant Samaras and the rest, all yelling fearsomely. Twenty metres from the front Italian positions, Zikos hurled two grenades at them, followed by twenty more in short order. The blasts stunned the Italians long enough for Zikos and his men to overrun them in a savage, screaming bayonet charge; where bayonets couldn't be used effectively, rifle butts were swung. An Italian soldier rose and aimed at Zikos, who lunged at him and seized the weapon before it could be fired. As both men struggled for possession of the rifle, Sergeant Theodoros Mylonas rammed his bayonet into the hapless Italian's abdomen.

At this point, a reserve platoon from 10 Company under Lieutenant Isaak Lavrentidis turned up to lend a hand. Lavrentidis threw a couple of Mills defensive grenades at the Italians, who had begun to retreat down the hill, leaving behind their usual quota of bodies. Day was about to break, and as it did so, General Negro's Bari Division artillery began its standard dawn barrage. Lavrentidis, his immediate task over, withdrew his platoon and Sergeant Samaras' squad. 'Stay here,' he ordered Zikos, 'until further orders from the battalion.' Zikos, however, was careful not to reply, 'Yes, sir,' as standard regulations stipulated that after an emergency defensive manoeuvre such as a counter-attack, a unit was required to return to its original position and not stay in place as the lieutenant had ordered. Zikos ordered his platoon to take whatever cover they could from the shelling and when the coast was clear, return to their trenches. When they did, half an hour later, it was with armfuls of captured weaponry, including two light machine guns. Just two men had been wounded, neither of them seriously.

The events of the early morning, when Negro's troops had come perilously close to seizing the hill, had shaken the Third Battalion command. 'Things are very difficult,' Second Lieutenant Chrysafis (the 9 Company commander) muttered in the company shelter, having despaired the previous day. Lavrentidis may have detected a touch of pessimism in the words as, in Zikos' hearing, he rounded on Chrysafis and snapped: 'One step back and it's the grave of Greece.'

Lieutenant Finestra of the 121 Company, CCXXI 'Littoria' Battalion, was very likely in that midnight attack. He reported being encouraged by the Duce's presence at the front. The battalion's progress led him to believe that Hill 731 had actually been taken, if only momentarily. The orders, unchanging, were for the advance to continue 'at all costs'. Squad leader Vittore Andreatta distinguished himself in the action. But such was the 'inferno of dead and wounded' (probably the result of Zikos' counter-attack) that he and the other units were forced back. Yet there were encouraging signs from other sectors. The 24th (Pinerolo) Division on the right of the Bari and the Cagliari on the left reported progress in trying to isolate Hill 731, leading Mussolini to rather hastily conclude that the Greeks were on the ropes.

Around midmorning, Zikos said he was going out to the trenches again, but Chrysafis advised him to stay where he was unless another enemy attack materialized. The sergeant-major insisted on going, on the grounds that the men there needed some encouragement in the face of the constant enemy bombardment. Once at the trenches, he transferred six men to safer positions on the right, leaving just three men at the summit as lookouts and making sure he had a quick path to the top in case of a fresh Italian attack. Shells were raining on the First Battalion position around Hill 717 and the village of Bubesi to the north-east. At 10 a.m., the Bari's 139 Regiment made an apparent feint at the Greek 10 Company position on the west slope of Hill 731, while the 64 Regiment of the Cagliari made for Hill 717. The Greek First Battalion bore the brunt of it. Zikos and the men of 9 Company were able to watch the action unfold.

The feint – if it was that – failed, as 10 Company hit back hard. To the east, the Italians made headway towards the top of Hill 717, but in doing so exposed their right flank to 9 Company. That unit, it will be remembered, was spread out like a diadem on the summit of Hill 731, with fields of fire in three directions. The platoon on its right, led by Second Lieutenant Dimitrios Christodoulou, overlooked the Proi Veles ravine separating Hill 731 from Hill 717. It was thus in an ideal position to pour flanking fire into the Italian columns, followed by a counterattack. As they pulled back, the Italians came within range of the 19 Regiment artillery, which turned the withdrawal into a proper retreat.

Gambara's Eighth Corps artillery observers saw what was wrong and attempted to rectify it by hammering Hill 731 with everything they had. Zikos and his men cowered in their holes against this new inferno of shell and mortar fire. Zikos this time very much feared the end had come for him and his men. He remembered:

Heavy guns, field and mountain, with high explosive and incendiary shells, pounded our positions. Large and medium mortar shells completed the hell of fire. Tree branches collapsed noisily over the trench. Age-old oaks were uprooted and fell on our positions. The smoke from the exploding shells blotted out the daylight. It was impossible for anyone to see who was next to him. The pungent smell of the shells, especially those from the heavy mortars, choked us. We thought they were attacking us with poison gas and looked for our masks… The whole time we knelt in our trench to avoid death from blast compression against the parapet… From moment to moment we expected to be blown to pieces. We hid our hands between our legs so that flesh would not be exposed to the incendiaries… Incessantly we prayed to God, Christ, the Saints and above all the Mother of God.

Zikos' past life flashed before him. Men died all around him. A bullet penetrated one man's cheek and exited through his open mouth. Another man had hysterics, though no-one dared move from his position.

It is a commonplace of warfare that nothing is so destructive of a soldier's morale as the knowledge that he is helpless against forces flying at him out of the air such as artillery shells or aerial bombs. He is pinned down against death that can strike suddenly out of nowhere. He feels like an insect about to be crushed underfoot, whereas his instinct is to be proactive, to do something, to fight a visible foe. One of Zikos' men could stand it no longer. 'What are we sitting here for, Sergeant-Major, being killed by the artillery? Let's attack and get those gunners.' An unrealistic suggestion, yes, but a thoroughly understandable one; if you're going to die, die doing something. The merciless bombardment lasted an hour.

Back at Komarit, Mussolini hoped that this time his mailed fist would break through. Messages from his field commanders suggested that Hill 731 was on the verge of being seized, if it had not been already. Certainly, that was the time that the hill came closest to being taken. Lieutenant Finestra was right when he said that it required only a few more paces. But, as in so many battles, those last few steps are the hardest to take. The closer the Italians got to the Greek positions, the fiercer was the resistance, and when it came to brutal hand-to-hand combat, the hardier Greeks had the advantage. The Bari's 140 Regiment couldn't proceed beyond a murderous curtain of fire.

Captain Koutridis fell wounded, but not seriously enough to be taken to the rear; he stayed on directing his men who, when their ammunition ran out, pulled out their trusty bayonets. By now, any squeamishness over the use of the bayonet would have been burned out of the Greek soldier, who had become a deadly expert in its use. Besides helping conserve ammunition, the bayonet is the ultimate close-order terror weapon; most soldiers, if given the choice, would prefer to stop a bullet than be disembowelled by a bayonet. Its deterrent effect – especially on a force attacking uphill – can hardly be overstated. The Greek Army employed the formidable Italian-made Gnutti, with a 41cm (16.5 inch) needle-like blade of tempered steel and 10cm (4 inch) hilt – roughly twice the length of the standard Italian issue. It can take much of the credit for keeping the Italians off Hill 731.

At 6 p.m., a battalion of the 139 Regiment threw itself against Hill 731 again, this time without the usual artillery warning, only to be driven back by concerted machine gun and artillery fire; Zikos' platoon contributed with another howling bayonet-and-grenade charge. But he dared not advance too far in case he came within range of his own side's guns and, as night fell, the counter-attack was called off. That hectic day cost the 1st Division five officers and one hundred and thirty-five enlisted men killed, and fourteen officers and two hundred and eighty-nine enlisted men wounded. Nineteen men were reported missing. The 19 Regiment, as usual, took the worst of the punishment. Thirty Italians were taken prisoners and a further three were reported to have deserted to the Greek side. The *Regia Aeronautica* carried out at least three hundred sorties that day, in two waves, against points on the Trebeshinë range on the 1st Division's left.

After the usual grim duty of burying the dead, Zikos returned to the 9 Company command shelter to find that his company commander, Second Lieutenant Chrysafis, had been replaced by the steelier Lieutenant Lavrentidis and sent to a safer post with the battalion staff. Also there was Koutridis, the battalion commander, who complained to Zikos that he was using up too much ammunition that was in short supply. The Sergeant-Major replied that he had little choice, as the enemy had been attacking in waves all day and the defensive fire couldn't let up. The platoon was short of defensive grenades. 'If we can get a large number of defensive grenades,' he told Koutridis, 'the hill won't be in any danger.' Koutridis promised him that the ordnance would arrive that night.

There was also a manpower problem of sorts. After every enemy attack, every man who could walk would be detailed to working parties to bury the dead, carry the wounded to the rear, fetch water from the nearest spring or unload food and medical supplies from the mule trains. Precious few were left to guard the trench line. Zikos himself had only fourteen effectives left. Koutridis issued orders that the supplies be carried right up to the front platoons and not offloaded in the rear. He also promised to supply the battalion with sharp axes to shape timber for shelter construction. Captain Konstantinos Rossis, who commanded the 19 Regiment's artillery batteries, was doing a slow burn. In the latest fight, he had lost some of his guns on Hill 731 to the enemy bombardment, and took it as a personal affront from Mussolini, who, he kept muttering, was 'going to pay for this'. By 10 p.m., the entire front was quiet except for the occasional nuisance shelling on both sides.

In the afternoon, during Mussolini's observations of the day's action from his eyrie on Komarit, in the company of Cavallero and Gambara of the Eighth Corps, a pair of RAF fighters had appeared out of the sky strafing the area but failing to hit the observation post. (According to Greek reports, an RAF Hurricane pilot named Brown was hit by fire from an Italian bomber and baled out, landing behind the Greek lines to a hearty welcome.) The watchers scurried for shelter, though Mussolini, to set an example of coolness, made a point of entering last. The Duce was troubled. Six days of pounding at Hill 731 had not yielded even mediocre results; what, he asked Cavallero, was the point of all the sacrifice of lives? The commander-in-chief blamed delays in planning, which had enabled the Greeks 'to take advantage of the time we used to form a front in order to set up a very efficient system of defence'.

> In front of a very well-knit defensive system [Cavallero continued], with centres of fire, the [Greek] troops know how to carry out infiltration tactics and have a strong officer corps. We haven't got such advantages, so instead of infiltration tactics we move in mass and wear down the enemy. If by tomorrow we see them breaking, we can continue the action with maximum intensity. Otherwise, we have to give up.

Cavallero's explanation smacks of disingenuity. Assuming he had such intimate knowledge of the Greek tactics and positional strength, the question arises: why for six days was he doing precisely the wrong thing – staging Somme-style assaults against near-impregnable positions? The presence of the Duce almost certainly had something to do with it; Cavallero of all people knew what his boss wanted to see and hear, and that was attack, attack! Though Cavallero's enemies called him 'the butcher of Italian boys,' he would not have been impervious to the severe losses. On the evening of 14 March, at the Eleventh Army headquarters at Devol, he chaired a meeting of generals to assess the situation.

'If we don't see success, then we shouldn't continue the fight,' Cavallero replied to his fellow generals. 'We should call it off.'

Gambara, the Eighth Corps commander, too many of whose men lay in a carpet of muddy corpses on the north slope of Hill 731, nodded. 'Let's quit right now.' His corps so far had suffered some five thousand casualties; the Twenty-fifth Corps on the right had suffered as badly, and the Fourth Corps on the left had lost one thousand eight hundred dead, wounded and captured – roughly a thousand casualties per division engaged in the whole Eleventh Army. Another factor weighing heavily against the Italians was the brutal fact that, whereas the Greeks could decently bury their dead at night or during lulls in the fighting, the Italians could do nothing for their own fallen; any attempt to gather them up was discouraged by persistent Greek shelling. Therefore, the bloated corpses remained where they fell, a grisly reminder to the fresh waves of attackers coming up. The Greek command, as we have seen, was aware of this and wanted to keep it that way.

But Geloso was all for carrying on, guided by the tragic logic that only ultimate victory could now justify such a bloodletting – to retreat now would be the ultimate ingratitude to the fallen. Hill 731 had taken on an aspect of almost mystical awe – a Golgotha whose mere aspect had become terrifying. And Mussolini couldn't bring himself to abandon the original objective of the Spring Offensive, which was to force a way down the Desnitsa Valley and retake Kelçyre, which would wipe out Greek gains in Albania and clear the way to the Greek border. This was his pet project. Above all, he knew that Hitler was watching, and was loth to have to even slightly alter his grand plan.

Cavallero was given Greek press reports claiming wildly that three Italian divisions had been practically wiped out and some twelve thousand men had been killed in one week alone. Though a gross exaggeration, the figure would certainly boost morale on the Greek home front. Mussolini turned to Gambara. 'How is the troops' morale?' The corps commander replied cautiously that morale was not terribly good after the days of reverses, but its combat quality was deemed to be good enough. It was a classic ambiguous answer, and Geloso leaped on it. The only way to restore morale, he said, was to keep on attacking, otherwise the Greeks would launch a fresh offensive of their own to threaten Vlorë and Tirana.

'If the army needs a spectacular victory, then we have to give it one,' the Duce said after listening to his commanders' comments. 'The best way to accomplish that is to retake Kelçyre... at all costs.' There, again, was that fatal phrase that had cost so much blood to be spilled uselessly, but as far as is known, no general that evening had the nerve to suggest anything else. The Duce concluded:

We have now, thanks to General Cavallero, a front from the Adriatic to Yugoslavia. The initiative belongs to us... For this purpose we selected the appropriate sector. There is nothing to do but to insist.

These words were recorded by Cavallero in his diary. He allowed himself a slight consolation from rumours that King George II of Greece was upset at the extent of the Greek casualties and was toying with the idea of a cease-fire in Albania. This piece of news had arrived via the Hungarian military attaché in Athens, who supposedly was told by the King himself. Though there is little, if any, evidence, to support such a theory, it is true that many in high places, including General Papagos, were seriously troubled about the possible outcome of the clash of titans centring around Hill 731. The Greek Army, though so far resisting successfully and praised to the skies by the national and Allied media, was nonetheless bloodied and battered. If Mussolini's Spring Offensive continued at its current intensity for much longer, the Greeks could well break.

At about that hour the Greek Prime Minister, Alexandros Koryzis, directed his ambassador in London to deliver a long communique to the British Foreign Office:

> In recent days the Greek Army met very violent attacks by the Italian Army which were bravely repulsed. Yet these attacks have become general, and are becoming stronger day by day. Moreover, reports on the presence of Mussolini at the front as well as the chief of the Italian Air Force indicate the Italians' decision to deliver a crushing blow to Greece at all costs.

The prime minister went on to claim that as Italian air power in Albania heavily outgunned that of the Allies, and was wreaking havoc among the Greek ground forces, more RAF help was urgently needed.

> Despite our repeated requests, to both the competent British authorities and to Mr [Anthony] Eden [the British Foreign Secretary] in Egypt, no British air assistance has reached us so far... We appeal seriously to Mr [Winston] Churchill and implore him to consider the extremely critical situation the Greek Army is in and give the required orders so that aerial reinforcements can be sent to the front capable of confronting the powerful Italian forces. It is beyond doubt that the Axis attaches great importance to these attacks, as their outcome would influence the Yugoslav government.

Mussolini's notion that the Greek King was in a defeatist mood was almost certainly wrong. On the contrary, after the death of Metaxas in January, George II had been the very figurehead of the ongoing Greek fight against the Axis. According to the indirect report of the Hungarian diplomat, the King fretted that the 2, 5, 13, 19, 33, 39 and 50 Regiments were 'half destroyed' and that replacement troops sent to the front were ill-trained older reservists. This may well have been an expression of the King's legitimate concerns about manpower as seen through the distorting mirror of Mussolini's wishful thinking. There is not the slightest evidence that George II sought a cease-fire, and he probably would not have lasted long on his throne if he had. If anyone was doubting the Army's ability to hang on, it was some home-front generals and politicians. Encouraged by Eden, George stayed firm.

From the viewpoint of Athens and London there was a bigger picture to look at. The inferno of Hill 731 was a mere detail in a great violent power play with the whole Balkan peninsula at stake. The Wehrmacht and Luftwaffe were poised to surge over the Bulgarian border into Greece as soon as Mussolini stumbled in Albania. The attitude of Yugoslavia was a big question mark: on which side would it throw its weight? If Greece were beaten in Albania, Yugoslavia would probably join the Axis to avoid being encircled by it. Britain was by now committed to helping Greece in the event of a German invasion, but it is to King George's credit that even though he knew that Greece ultimately wouldn't be able to resist, he stuck by the Allies and implicitly encouraged the defenders on Hill 731.

The Greek higher command seems not to have been aware of Mussolini's presence at the front until several days after the start of the Spring Offensive. General Pitsikas, the commander of the TSH who had recently replaced Lieutenant General Drakos and had general supervision of the Albanian operations, in an order-of-the-day on 14 March wrote that he had 'information from various sources' confirming that the Duce was indeed on the scene – nearly two weeks after he had flown in from Italy. It is inconceivable that during that time the Greeks had not cottoned on to Mussolini's presence at close quarters; probably Pitsikas, and his boss Papagos, had deliberately kept the intelligence from the troops for the sake of morale, revealing it only when the brunt of the Italian attacks had passed and there seemed a sporting chance of blunting them altogether. Pitsikas' message was couched in terms that would be considered bombastic and flowery today, but which struck a chord among the rank and file who, almost to a man, fought for purely patriotic motives.

> Greek soldiers [the order-of-the-day ran], by this message I do not intend to remind you of your duty of which you fully realize, as attested by your glowing achievements in recent days, but to express my admiration and the gratitude of the homeland for the ever-greater moral strength you have displayed and for the Wall of China you have raised in protecting the homeland's rights.

Such messages (the rather fatuous 'Wall of China' phrase aside) have their definite usefulness. To have a senior general praising your efforts means infinitely more than having some comfortably-living politician doing it. To men such as Zikos, who at that moment must have been wondering at his own survival so far and still far from confident that he would live through another day, it was a recognition, soldier-to-soldier, that he was doing a commendable job and ought to hang on.

Chapter 8

Exhaustion

The seventh day of the battle, 15 March, opened with an unaccustomed calm. No Italian shelling disturbed the idyllic sunny morning, which the Greeks employed to better dig themselves in. Vrachnos beefed up the flanks and rear of his 1st Division with reserves from the 5th Division on his left and 15th Division on his right. On the previous evening Mussolini, as we have seen, masked any doubts he might have had with a fresh exhortation to keep up the attacks. Papagos, for his part, issued his own order-of-the-day that stressed the men's patriotic and warlike spirit.

This campaign of four months and more which you have carried out victoriously, has covered you with unattainable wreaths of glory. The enemy's efforts are shattered, your will remains unbending and your belief in victory undimmed. The entire army of which You of the central sector so brilliantly represent, and which has written new pages of glory, follows and admires you. I address to you my warmest congratulations. Long Live the Greek Army.

Zikos, like the rest of the 19 Regiment, waited for the morning's expected artillery barrage and infantry assault. But blissful quiet reigned on Hill 731. After a week of hell, it was still in Greek hands – blasted, burned and pounded until all that was left was a lunar landscape with a handful of punch-drunk troops still hanging on to it by the triggers of their Hotchkiss machine guns and blood-stained bayonet blades. If anything, Zikos reflected, the defenders' zeal had become fiercer than ever. The Greek counterattacks that always followed the Italian attacks were attacks of pure blind vengeance rather than anything tactically planned. The men of Zikos' platoon whiled away the time with desultory, sometimes dangerous, activities. One popular hobby throughout the Army was to remove the detonator from an unexploded Italian offensive hand grenade, gently shake out the explosive contents and use the casing as a cigarette case. It was also extremely risky, as one of Zikos' men found out that morning when both his hands were blown off. Naturally, there were strict orders against the practice, but many soldiers persisted, and some inevitably joined the casualty lists as a consequence.

Over at Eighth Corps headquarters, Mussolini awoke in good spirits. His mercurial character was prone to intense mood swings, and he appeared to have put behind him the angst of the previous evening. There was still clout left in the army, Gambara assured him. 'We're involved in an effort including the Fourth, Eighth and Twenty-fifth Corps,' the Duce said, 'in what is a war of attrition against a strong foe.' (This was one of the rare occasions when he had to admit that the Greeks were a tougher adversary that he had imagined.) The objective of the Eleventh Army was not merely to eliminate the eyesore obstacle of Hill 731, he said, but to get through the Desnitsa Valley to Kelçyre. The name of the town was a mantra to him. 'When we have taken Klissura [Kelçyre] the Greek Army will collapse.' He also planned a parallel thrust in the west, on the other side of the Trebeshinë range, directed against Tepelenë, another key crossroads town, from where his forces could swing eastwards for eighteen kilometres to get to Kelçyre and cut off the Greek II Corps. 'We must seize Tepelenë at whatever cost.' Again, that fatal phrase. Cervi cites a dawning realization on the Duce's part that there was no way that the rampart of Hill 731, not to mention Hill 717 and Mali Spadarit, could be overcome by frontal attack. It was a way out for Cavallero, who tried to balance the gung-ho Geloso and the pessimist Gambara without lending undue weight to either.

The men on Hill 731 were too battle-hardened to hope that the lull would last the day, and sure enough, at 1:15 p.m., Italian shells came howling over in intermittent salvoes – essentially nuisance bombardments. But nuisance or no, they were deadly. In the trenches of Zikos' platoon it was a usual form of gallows humour after a round of shell blasts for someone to ask: 'Is anyone dead?' The reply would come: 'No, they're not dead, they're living among us.' Which most often meant that at least one man had been killed, and that the others were poignantly answering on their behalf. The shelling lasted about five hours.

At around noon, lookouts on Hill 731 reported a battalion-strength column moving on the northern tip of the Trebeshinë range on the left. Another column was seen approaching from the north. Colonel Balis ordered up reinforcements to back up the units in that sector. The main Italian attack did not materialize until 8 p.m., when the Bari's 139 Regiment, brought back up to strength by replacements, made an audacious night attack on Hills 731 and 717, hoping to catch the defenders off their guard. The time was well chosen as, towards nightfall, the defenders would relax their vigilance to relieve themselves or look for water in the gullies between the hills. The 139 advanced with great verve, seizing Monastero and most of Hill 717. From there, it poured diversionary fire onto Hill 731 and for some minutes the tactic worked as 9 Company of the Third Battalion, under Lieutenant Lavrentidis in the first line of defence, came under extreme pressure.

Thanks to the morning's observations, the 19 Regiment saw through the Italian scheme; Zikos, for one, was expecting precisely such a night attack and had kept as many men possible alert in the trenches. As the Italians drew closer to the summit, Lavrentidis' men clicked their bayonets into place, took a grenade in each hand and, like ghosts in the darkness, hurled themselves on the attackers. 'Spike 'em!' the Greeks yelled, as steel ripped into flesh. Koutridis, the battalion commander, was wounded but refused to be taken to the rear and stayed where he was, encouraging the men.

The afternoon's cannonade had included Greek positions on Trebeshinë and Spi Kamarate, while units of the Pinerolo Division were poised to bypass Hill 731 from the west – Cavallero's outflanking plan. In response, General Vrachnos sent in the First Battalion of the 67 Regiment from behind the lines to secure Spi Kamarate and be in a position to repulse any enemy infantry. Pitsikas, the TSH commander, meanwhile, worried about the strain on the 1st Division, ordered units of the 8th Division of the I Corps to the west of Kelçyre at the southern end of the Trebeshinë range to secure the lines of supply to Kelçyre from the south, to guard against possible Italian outflanking moves; the 25 Infantry Regiment of the 11th Division was placed at the westernmost point. Pitsikas' tactic was that of an alert boxer in an extraordinarily large ring, keeping his eyes on an adversary who could come at him from at least three directions at once; in a demonstration of tactical flexibility, he would detach units from corps to corps and division to division where he thought they would be most needed so that he wouldn't be blindsided.

Zikos' platoon of 9 Company lost six more men to wounds, reducing his total of effectives to eight. After the last echoes of gunfire died away in the night, Zikos walked over to the battalion headquarters, where Captain Koutridis buttonholed him. The battalion commander fretted that the enemy might use the darkness to infiltrate the ravine to the east of Hill 731 where a single platoon under a rookie sergeant held the path. 'I want you to go and assume command of that platoon,' Koutridis told Zikos. As an NCO, Zikos could not normally command a unit, but Koutridis was willing to overlook protocol as there was no officer available. The sergeant at the path was young and inexperienced. Koutridis added that he would retire Zikos' eight remaining men into a special reserve squad for a well-earned rest and string out the remaining two battalions of 9 Company on the summit of Hill 731 to make up the space. Three more platoons were called up from the 19 Regiment reserves. 'I'll be there before the sun is up, sir,' Zikos said.

Before descending to his new post, Zikos had the satisfaction of receiving a consignment of British-made Mills 36M Mark I fragmentation grenades, which he justly considered far superior to anything he had previously handled, especially the Italian ordnance. The rest of the might was spent hammering and sawing timber – of which the uprooted and shell-torn trees provided plenty – for sturdier shelters and trench linings. About an hour before dawn on 16 March, Zikos hefted a sack of Mills grenades and scrambled down to his new position. Morale in the isolated platoon was bad. The rookie sergeant, Thomas Tamiolakis, was new to the Army and the sector, and was shaken by the wounding of his immediate superior, Second Lieutenant Mamalakis, a week before. He was uncomfortably aware that he was about the youngest man in the unit, which for days had been sitting in position at the mercy of enemy shelling, unable to act. He could not conceal his extreme anxiety. 'One step back and it's the grave of Greece,' Zikos sternly reminded him, in a phrase that by now had become a commonplace. After making sure all was in order, the exhausted Zikos fixed his helmet more securely on his head and draped a tent sheet over himself for his first sleep in three days.

That afternoon, Mussolini had taken a break from his frustrations to travel to the port of Vlorë (Valona) where his daughter Edda had narrowly missed losing her life after the hospital ship on which she had been serving as a Red Cross nurse, the *Po*, was torpedoed and sunk, most likely by a Royal Navy Fairey Swordfish of 815 Naval Air Squadron, Fleet Air Arm, operating out of the Greek base at Paramythia. Edda, who was also the wife of Mussolini's foreign minister, Count Galeazzo Ciano, had spent hours in the water as many wounded men on the ship perished.

While Mussolini was away, Cavallero, Geloso and Gambara, the three commanders most directly involved with the faltering Spring Offensive, took advantage of his absence to discuss the situation freely. Notes of the meeting indicate that it was inconclusive, as all three agreed that the lack of progress and heavy losses of the past week had profoundly affected the troops' morale. Mussolini would return and repeat his Kelçyre-at-all-costs mantra that any officer in his senses now all but ruled out. Diversionary operations were out of the question as they would take time to organize, and time was what they did not have. The perplexity was complete. There seemed to be either an absence of creative tactical thinking or a simple realization that the offensive just wasn't working. They did not give up on the idea itself – the Duce would certainly have had their heads if they had – but decided lamely to 'postpone' further action until a better opportunity to head down that valley to Kelçyre presented itself.

Thus, in the morning of 16 March – apparently without the absent Duce being consulted – orders went out suspending the Spring Offensive. Cavallero explained the decision to his Ninth Army commander, General Pirzio Biroli, trying to put a brave face on it. 'We've saved Italy from collapse, and now we're saving it from disgrace.' Regaining some confidence, he went on: 'The men have fought well. But we're not sunk yet!' He knew the Germans were on the verge of bursting into Greece, and that the Duce yearned for a military victory before that happened. Cavallero's solution this time was to bring up 'a mass of Alpine troops' who knew how to fight in mountainous terrain.

But appearances had to be kept up. While Cavallero planned his next moves, he disguised the lull with intermittent nuisance shelling of the Greek positions while the *Regia Aeronautica* droned overhead looking for targets to bomb and strafe. The pilots were none too successful at this, as by now the Greeks had learned to effectively conceal themselves as soon as they heard the sound of approaching engines. Two shells burst near Sergeant-Major Zikos' trench but he was sleeping so soundly they didn't wake him. The first thing he noticed on waking was 'a heavy burden' on his body which he couldn't shake off, and then realized he was buried alive. Before he could asphyxiate, his men dug him out; Sergeant Tamiolakis, the rookie, was also buried but had his head free so he could call for help. With his trench now destroyed, Zikos and Tamiolakis moved into the neighbouring one. The whole platoon was horribly exposed. Any trees on Hill 717 had long since been smashed and uprooted and there was no vegetative cover at all on the clay soil surface.

Zikos found an able subordinate in Corporal Georgios Dimitriou, 'cool and energetic, the soul of the platoon,' whom he reserved for particularly demanding tasks. During the day, while the Italians lobbed intermittent shells at Hill 731, Zikos forbade any man from exiting his trench. They were told to urinate in empty tin cans and defecate only at night. In the silence, the men could hear the sounds of chopping wood on Hill 731 as the defenders built their shelters. At nightfall, he sent out sentries to watch over the ravine between the hills. Shortly before that, Sergeant Tamiolakis complained loudly of unbearable pains in his feet; he was taken to a field station and diagnosed with frostbite.

Meanwhile, the 1st Division artillery responded to the Italian bombardments. A battery under Lieutenant Kanatouris scored a lucky hit on an Italian ammunition dump, lighting up the dawn sky like a gigantic fireworks display. Colonel Balis monitored whatever enemy troop movements he could detect, concluding that the Italian divisions were in the process of re-forming. The grinding of tank engines and clanking of treads came drifting faintly on the breeze, telling General Vrachnos that the Centauro Division was limbering up for an attempt. Vrachnos had been ready for the tanks for some time, having widened his concealed tank traps across the main road at the entrance to the Proi Math ravine. There were to be no more surprises like the one the 155th Blackshirt Battalion had tried to pull five days before.

When the Duce returned to the front, he tried to keep up the men's morale by visiting various units and field hospitals, keeping up a brave facade that his generals did not share. He did this for four more days which provided a much-needed breathing space for both sides. But the mood in Cavallero's headquarters was gloomy. The Cagliari Division, the hardest hit along with the Bari, had lost some 40 per cent of its effectives. No-one apart from the Duce himself appeared to believe that the ragged Spring Offensive had any chance of success, and even he by now had probably lost faith in his generals' ability to deliver. Yet on the other hand Mussolini, and by extension the Italian military, could not lose face by admitting failure. As a sort of compromise between the two views, the date of 28 March was fixed as the starting point for a fresh attempt at Kelçyre. The intervening fortnight would be used to rebuild strength.

The mood in Athens was upbeat. On 17 March King George issued a fulsome order-of-the-day to the Army in Albania.

> When a week ago the enemy believed he was ready to break you and attempted his powerful offensive effort on which he had pinned so many hopes, you not only held him back but delivered a decisive blow, giving him the reply he deserved as well as a lesson in what Greek spirit and valour can accomplish.

The King's message likened the defenders of Hill 731 to the ancient warriors of Marathon and Thermopylai, and noted, to be fair to the other services, that 'your brothers in the Royal [Hellenic] Navy and Royal [Hellenic] Air Force' were doing their jobs equally well. 'The entire civilized world is dazzled.' Even accounting for the elaborate hyperbole, the King's message greatly heartened the troops in Albania. There could also have been a subtle political purpose: the Army was known to contain left-wing and communist agitators who lost no opportunity to denigrate the monarchy in the hope that a socialist republic could be installed after the war. George II, by portraying himself as supremely appreciative of the sacrifices of the common soldier, was also looking out for himself. Yet these considerations paled before the plain basic fact: the Spring Offensive had been terminally blunted.

Yet, on the Italian side, the offensive seems to have acquired a life of its own. No Italian commander, if he wished to stay in the Duce's good books and keep his job, would dare suggest giving up altogether. Hence Cavallero's plan for 'future action,' which only ensured that Italian boys would go on getting killed for no concrete purpose. It was, however, obvious that the Puglie and Bari Divisions had been whipped to death and were of no further use. They were replaced in the front line by the 51st (Siena) Division of the Eighth Corps and the Centauro of the Twenty-fifth Corps; the fragile Fiat tanks of the Centauro had proven to be an almost uninterrupted embarrassment in the campaign so far but, as long as they were in Albania, Cavallero figured he might make some use of them.

Zikos remembered 17 March as a blissfully quiet, brilliantly sunny day, enlivened only by the occasional nuisance shell. With the pressure momentarily off, the men of the 19 Regiment began wondering about what their own command was up to, especially as Colonel Balis, the regimental commander, had not been heard from. He had been tearing out his hair watching the Second and Third Battalions being plastered on Hill 731, but it didn't escape notice that he hadn't visited the units; military convention demanded that a regimental commander should personally visit his front lines on the third night after their deployment, especially in such hellish circumstances. Understandably, there was a good deal of grumbling about it. To be fair, Balis had more than enough to do at his headquarters at Ballaban but Zikos, for one, thought the colonel ought to have made the effort at least once. Though an NCO, Zikos was far better officer material than many of those in shoulder stars (which he in time would duly acquire).

The men wanted to see all the officers up close. That way they were comforted and encouraged. The one whom they saw almost every night was the battalion commander [Koutridis]. He would visit the company and platoon commanders and the men in the trenches, erect and calm even while mortar and artillery shells burst around him, and not once did he duck for cover. The men admired him.

At about midnight, a staff colonel of the 6th Division appeared on Hill 731 to assess the situation. He was, according to Zikos, the only senior staff officer to take the trouble to talk with the hard-fought men of the Third Battalion of the 19 Regiment. The colonel's report to divisional headquarters described the hill as a desolate mass of earth and rubble sowed with numberless craters. 'It is a miracle how men survived on Hill 731,' he wrote. The Italian bombardment resumed on 18 March, to continue sporadically all day. It was a pure nuisance tactic, designed to fatigue the Greeks and disrupt their supply chains. The task of building shelters, however, continued; the men of the Third Battalion often had to crawl on hands and knees over shell craters and fallen tree trunks to get the necessary timber, losing a few men and mules in the process.

Though the Spring Offensive as it was originally conceived might be formally suspended, a semblance of a fight had to be kept up. Hill 731 still needed to be eliminated for Cavallero's next plan to reach Kelçyre to succeed. There were two reasons for this: first, the Greeks had to be kept busy and fatigued; and second, Cavallero and the other generals fretted that, with the improving weather, Papagos might actually seize the offensive again and drive the Italians back. He had one more ace up his sleeve. Under probable pressure from Mussolini, he appears to have come round from his previous pessimistic stand and concluded that, to salvage whatever credibility his army had left, one more hammer blow at Hill 731, one more attempt to push through to Kelçyre, was required. If the Puglie and Bari Divisions had failed, then someone else would have to try it. Cavallero decided on a special commando-type company formed out of the Siena Division on Gambara's left to operate with support from the tanks of the Centauro to rush the hill in a surprise attack. The operation was predicated on the twin assumptions that the Greek defenders by now would have been on the verge of terminal exhaustion and that a joint armour-infantry strike would do the trick. For this he picked a company of *Arditi* (Daring Ones), Italy's shock troops.

In command of the company was Captain Prince Giorgio Di Borbone, a member of the royal Bourbon family and nephew of King Vittorio Emanuele. Now forty-one years old, he had volunteered for service in World War One as a private, rising to second lieutenant. He had volunteered again when Mussolini's troops invaded Ethiopia in 1935, and a third time when the campaign against Greece was launched. Assigned to the 31 Infantry Regiment of the Siena Division, he was wounded in February but had recovered in time for his new demanding *Arditi* mission. The company had received special training in coordinating with armour at Berat.

The attempt got under way at 6:30 a.m. on 19 March, the eleventh day of the battle, with the usual softening-up barrage by the Italian artillery. The whole 1st Division position from Bubesi to the Trebeshinë range, but concentrating especially on the focal point of Hill 731, was sprayed mercilessly. Again, the defenders huddled in their holes and shelters to protect themselves as best as they could, though some men in outlying trenches were annihilated. A quarter of an hour later, the guns began to lengthen their range – a sure signal that an infantry attack was imminent. Sure enough, three columns of the Siena were soon on their way, the central column consisting of Prince Giorgio's company of *Arditi* consisting of one hundred and fifty-one men, accompanied by four tanks as a screen, firing as they advanced. With astonishing speed, the lead tank surged up the scrubby slopes, followed by Prince Giorgio's assault unit of the 31 Regiment, and scraped and rumbled to the top of the hill, where it stopped to fire in all directions.

The Greeks of the Third Battalion, 9 and 10 Companies, were caught napping. Sheltering from the storm of shells and trying to stay alive (many didn't), they hadn't noticed the enemy advance until it was almost too late. The first they knew of the attack was when one of Zikos' corporals gave a shout: 'Italians at the summit!' Zikos, without hesitation, leaped out of his shelter and organized his platoon in a defensive format. In a nearby shelter, Sergeant Theodoros Mylonas, 'the coolest NCO in the company,' heard Italian shouts outside. 'Don't move,' he cautioned the seven men with him. 'The entrance is low. They won't find us.' But one soldier panicked and, before he could be stopped, ran out with his hands up, calling out, *'Buono Italiano, buono Italiano!'* ('Good Italian, good Italian!'). The particular Italiano he accosted proved to be far from good, as he replied by tossing a grenade at the timid private, seriously wounding him in the back. One yelling *Ardito* emptied his machine gun into the shelter, while another threw a couple of grenades inside. Almost all the occupants were killed, including Sergeant Mylonas, who murmured to the sole surviving soldier just before he died, 'Stanch the blood, stanch the blood.' But his body was too badly riddled for him to be saved.

The whole staff of 9 Company, in fact, had to get out fast to avoid being overrun, retreating to the position of the reserve 11 Company in the rear. The neighbouring 10 Company was also driven back. The unexpected sight of the fire-spitting Fiat tanks was unnerving. Zikos' platoon, meanwhile, had begun to return fire. The 10 Company platoon on his right appeared to have had the fight knocked out of it; the men were on their feet but not doing anything. 'Cease firing and prepare for counter-attack,' Zikos called, hoping to encourage the dithering unit on his right and make a sweep up to recapture the peak. At that moment, Captain Koutridis, the Third Battalion commander, apparently having recovered from his wound, ran up at the head of the reserve 11 Company, its bayonets unsheathed, and charged. The sheer ferocity of the bayonet charge drove the *Arditi* back to the top of the hill; as the Italians retreated, many stumbled into shell craters or tripped over fallen logs, with the result that they were easily slain. Number 11 Company swept past the ruined shelter containing the body of Sergeant Mylonas – and past the body of the Italian who had killed him.

Here the accounts differ. According to some, it was not Koutridis' Third Battalion that counterattacked first, but Lavrentidis' Second Battalion. Zikos, confusingly, is mentioned as sergeant-major in both battalions. Zikos' own account, however, seems more trustworthy. However, all versions agree that whether the leader was Koutridis or Lavrentidis, the bayonet charge against the *Arditi* turned the tide yet again. 'It was a mass butchery', Zikos wrote. 'Scenes of heroism were played out.' He reported seeing one reservist second lieutenant laying out an enemy soldier with a single powerful punch to the head. The wounded who could walk clamoured to be allowed into action; when they were, they despatched wounded Italians wherever they could be found.

In the meantime, the summit of Hill 731 'resembled an erupting volcano' pounded by the artillery of both sides. The armour-piercing machine gun bullets of 9 Company (specifically Second Lieutenant Konstantinos Roundos' machine gun platoon) put the lead Italian tank out of action. Another second lieutenant, Georgios Tzathas, climbed up onto the tank looking for an opening to toss in a hand grenade. He didn't find one, but the growling Fiat tank, its guns now useless, turned on its tracks and headed back down the hill. It hit and uprooted the remains of an oak tree and lurched over it before shuddering to a halt. No-one emerged from the hatch; the crew were probably dead or wounded. (According to one account, some men of 9 Company gathered up beer bottles to use as fuel-filled Molotov cocktails, and it was one of these that Tzathas flung against the tank, followed by others. They had no effect, of course.)

For two hours, the two sides tore at each other with unprecedented ferocity. It was the classic unstoppable-force-against-immovable object situation. The result was that the *Arditi* suffered their worst-ever casualties in the entire Albanian campaign. Their courage was immense. In the valour stakes there was no distinction now between Greek and Italian – the sheer stubborn madness of killing had seized both. 'Go get 'em, boys!' yelled Captain Koutridis over the din of battle. *'Avanti!'* ('Forward!') came the cries from the *Arditi* officers, waving their service pistols as their men collapsed around them. Wounded from both sides were trampled underfoot, their groans and screams adding to the horror.

Yet, as before, it was the deadly accuracy of the Greek artillery that finally broke the Italian impetus. And when the break came, it was sudden. By 8:30 a.m., the north slope of Hill 731 was sown with fresh heaps of mangled Italian bodies and the survivors of the *Arditi* had turned tail. One junior *Ardito* officer had managed to precede the others almost to the summit, only to find himself looking down the barrel of a Greek lieutenant's pistol. Probably glad to be alive, the *Ardito* offered his captor some chocolate from his pack, as well as flasks of coffee and brandy. 'Keep them,' the lieutenant said. 'You'll need them for the long walk to Athens.' (Many prisoners were interned in Athens' Makriyanni barracks beneath the Acropolis, next door to today's Acropolis Museum.) The officer was one of just five prisoners that 9 Company and the Third Battalion took that day; the others were a sergeant, a corporal and two privates. Of the four Centauro tanks involved in the attack, one was put out of action, another was hit by artillery fire and plunged down a cliff overlooking the Proi Math ravine with the loss of its crew, and the other two apparently made it back to the Italian lines.

The Bourbon prince Giorgio was wounded in the initial assault but kept going, blowing a path before him with hand grenades and his pistol. At some point he ran out of ammunition and fell, riddled with machine gun bullets. (He was posthumously awarded the Gold Medal for Military Valour.) The fate of the crew of the lead Centauro tank became known the next day, when Lieutenant Lavrentidis went to inspect it, opened the hatch and found the bodies of the commander, a second lieutenant, and the sergeant gunner, all mortally wounded by armour-piercing bullets. According to the prisoners, as the 31 Regiment of *Arditi* had been moving into position from Gllavë to Monastero the previous evening, Greek shells dropping into the ranks had forced the commanders to change operational plans at the last minute, resulting in some confusion.

The Third Battalion's casualties were three officers and more than thirty enlisted men killed, and forty officers and more than a hundred men wounded – 9 Company again bearing the brunt. Reserves were rushed up from the First Battalion, 33 Regiment, in the rear; in fact, the regiment was poised to replace the 19 Regiment if the latter could no longer hold on. The *Arditi* left at least a hundred dead, many of them victims of shelling during the withdrawal; in fact the entire 31 Regiment was pulled out of the line until it could be rebuilt up to strength. At 10 a.m., a squadron of Italian aircraft appeared overhead, briefly bombing the area behind the hill, but the damage was minimal. Gambara's artillery, as usual, tried to mask the debacle with nuisance fire until about 11 a.m., when the entire battle sector fell silent and the bone-weary troops of both sides were able to rest and regroup.

Zikos and his men gazed down on the fresh bodies covering the ground. Dead Greeks and Italians were found locked together in the paroxysm of fatal combat. But they couldn't stay long in the open as long as the Italian shelling continued. Sometime after 10 a.m., quiet finally descended on the battlefield. As night fell, an eerie sound echoed over the shell craters: the cries of 'four or five' wounded Italians a few metres away. Zikos felt no sympathy for them. The slaughter of the men inside Sergeant Mylonas' shelter had enraged him and his men to the point at which they left the unfortunate Italians crying out piteously all that cold night without lifting a finger to help them. In his account, Zikos claimed that the wounded men could easily have been picked up by their own medics, but were left to suffer because the medics 'were too terrified to approach' Hill 731 again. The explanation sounds simplistic and a trifle callous;

vengeful feelings aside, there was no excuse for the wounded men to be left to die slowly in violation of the most basic rules of warfare. In his memoir, Zikos seems to express some regret, and attempts to provide some vague excuse by asserting that 'war creates hate, and hate removes mankind from its destiny.' It may be accepted as an apology of sorts. Thus ended the eleventh day of the battle.

Most of 20 March, the twelfth day, was taken up with an artillery duel punctuated by sporadic (and ineffectual) Italian air raids. Italian mortar fire aimed at Mount Shendeli in the west killed a major of the 4th Division, some of whose units had been sent to reinforce that sector. A second lieutenant on Shendeli sniped at long range at groups of Italian officers with his machine gun, 'maybe killing some,' in his words. On Hill 731, when night fell and the guns were silent, the desperate cries of the wounded Italians lying in front of the trenches rent the air again; this time, Zikos figured, 'two or three were left alive.' Twenty-four hours later, the cries had been reduced to those of a solitary soldier, who was of course ignored.

At dusk on 21 March, there was an Italian attempt to cut the Tepelenë-Kelçyre road in the south of the sector led by a formation of Centauro tanks, but Greek anti-tank fire quickly broke it up. This, just one of similar isolated operations, appears to have been carried out on the personal orders of Geloso who, as Eleventh Army commander, considered himself the real head of the Italian combat forces in Albania. Cavallero, having officially called off the Spring Offensive and having begun to plan its vague successor, had placed himself under a cloud of sorts. Of all the senior staff in Albania, only Geloso fully backed the aggressive stance of the Duce, while Cavallero's supreme command became nominal only. No official decisions had played a part here; the roles of Cavallero and Geloso gradually inverted themselves by force of circumstance.

The previous evening, Mussolini had called his commanders together to demand an explanation as to why nearly two weeks of fanatical attacks had achieved nothing and why Hill 731, in particular, was still in enemy hands. Time was pressing. Fourteen German divisions were in Bulgaria at the gates of Greece, poised to burst in and bypass his great effort. 'I insist on the need to attack before even one German shell is fired,' he hectored Cavallero. Mussolini praised the commander and his army for having 'erected a wall' against further Greek advances, but cautioned that the 'wall' in the Tepelenë sector was not as stout as it ought to be.

We must give the Italian people the confidence that we have defeated the Greek Army. If this happens, we will be able to carry out the distribution of territory in a way quite different from what would have been possible without our success. The military honour of our nation is at stake. Let us deliver a whipping to the Greeks by 1 April.

Here, plain as day, was the Duce's motivation: he was looking forward to an Axis occupation of Greece – as appeared almost certain – and wanted a share of the booty in the form of territory for an Italian occupation force to administer. If Italy could cut as impressive a military figure as Germany, he figured, it would acquire a powerful bargaining chip towards that end. But pep-talk platitudes aside, the Duce seemed to realize deep down that the game was up. He took aside his air force chief, General Pricolo: 'I've decided to return to Rome tomorrow. I'm sick of this environment. We haven't made a single step of progress. So far they've deceived me. I have utter contempt for those people.'

'Those people' were, of course, his generals. Many, if not most, were relieved to hear that the Duce was leaving; their necks would no longer feel his insistent breath. From Cavallero on down, they knew perfectly well that they had failed against Hill 731. But did it matter so much anymore? They knew as well as anyone that the German Panzers and Stukas were poised to smash into Greece via the Bulgarian border in a matter of days. And that, with near-mathematical certainty, would crush the Greek Army and end the Albanian campaign.

At this point, a brief analysis of Cavallero's tactics is in order. As we have seen, those tactics were based on the principle of an initial overwhelming blow on a narrow front; the resulting breach could then be widened with follow-up attacks supplemented by flanking movements designed to isolate pockets of enemy resistance. Then the whole enemy line could be pushed back. The huge weak spot in that system, however, was that the defence could quickly bring forces to bear on the first thrust and snap the point of it, thus enabling other defending units to be moved back and forth along short lines of communication to neutralize the other ancillary attacks.

The Italians, however hard they tried, could not in the end master the abrupt heights and forbidding crags of the Trebeshinë range to outflank Hill 731. Cavallero's narrow-front battering-ram doctrine assumed that the ram's head would hold; when it was repeatedly blunted or snapped off, there seemed to be no alternative method to fall back on. No fewer than twenty times the Italian commander-in-chief ordered the same futile assault; only once did he achieve a fleeting success which, however, added nothing to the end result. When Geloso varied his tactics, for example on 11 March when he sent the Blackshirt Battalions to infiltrate the Proi Math ravine, they were entrapped by the Greeks who swooped down from the overlooking heights, so that wasn't tried again. The Greeks were too well entrenched in their positions, clinging like lichen, and the Italian command never really found a way of dealing with that.

Twenty years after the war, a report by the Greek Army Historical Department judged that the Italians at Hill 731 were in fact closer to success than they imagined. A major breach in the Greek 1st Division line, said the report, 'would have caused the collapse of the entire Greek formation north of the Aoös (Vijose) river as far as Kelçyre, taking with it the rest of the western front.' That would have meant the abandonment of the Greek positions on Trebeshinë and

Shendeli, leaving the II Corps isolated. The same report judged that the massive Italian artillery barrages did not justify their expenditure of shells as their aim was too often inaccurate. After seeing the costly futility of their daytime attacks on Hill 731, as we have seen, the Italians switched to night attacks, but to no avail.

Chapter 9

Requiem aeternam

As Mussolini took the controls of his aircraft, at 7:45 a.m. on 21 March, to head for Rome with a stop at Bari, he must have wondered what to tell King Vittorio Emanuele, who had been more or less kept in the dark about the Spring Offensive and its negative outcome – in fact, all the King had received were the wildly overoptimistic and inaccurate official bulletins emanating from Cavallero's headquarters. All Italy, in fact, was deliberately and totally misinformed, being told that 'the Greek Army had virtually ceased to exist.' Much of the public, whose menfolk were being massacred, may have taken some comfort from that line. But many in high places knew better, and these people were fobbed off with the 'explanation' that the Duce had never really intended any large-scale assault and that his commander-in-chief had been merely ordered to carry out 'a reconnaissance in force'. Thin at first, the story grew thinner as time went on.

Naturally, Cavallero's reputation took a hit among the desk-bound brass in Rome. His predecessor as Army commander-in-chief, Marshal Pietro Badoglio, sent a message to the King that he was ready to resume command if necessary. In fact, Badoglio even had his own plan to rectify the fiasco in Albania by employing the so-far unused Ninth Army of General Pirzio Biroli to launch another offensive in the east of the country. The Duce was candid enough to give the unvarnished truth to Vittorio Emanuele, though he felt he had to insist that the troops' morale remained 'very high' – the very opposite of the truth. He still harboured a hope that Cavallero's plan to resume hostilities on 28 March might come off.

Mussolini's report to the King, however, couldn't hide the truth that four divisions, the Puglie, Bari, Cagliari and Pinerolo, had been ravaged, with at least one thousand and fifty dead, three thousand two hundred wounded and some five hundred missing in the first three days alone. Nearly half a million men – thirty divisions – had been engaged, as well as about four hundred artillery pieces and four hundred aircraft. And still the Greeks, in the face of this juggernaut, hadn't budged. The Axis had been humiliated, the Allies (essentially meaning Britain) elated. But there was still a war on and, as long as opposing armies faced off in Albania, the mask had to be kept up.

Hardly had the drone of the Duce's aircraft faded over the Strait of Otranto than Cavallero was planning to give the Eleventh Army a week's rest and resume the attacks on 28 March. Mussolini's departure also entailed the departure of certain Fascist Party high officials who had been put in uniform and sent to Albania to show the Italian people that everyone, high or low, had to be involved. Few, if any, were worth the officer's rank they were given. Achille Starace, the ideologue who had cheered on the Duce just before 9 March, was no doubt glad to escape and get back to his easy life in Rome. Of course, neither he nor Mussolini could hear the cries of the dying men sprawled on and around Hill 731.

At dusk on 21 March, Gambara's artillery pounded the Greek rear to interrupt the supply lines. The shells whistled over the Third Battalion's position but caused no damage to it; at precisely midnight the shelling stopped. The main Italian action that day was directed at the 17th Division on Shendeli and the 4th Division in the south around Gjirokaster (Argyrokastro); fatigued units of the former were replaced by fresh troops of the latter. The following day dawned bright and sunny, bringing with it the first welcome warmth of spring. But the stench of the bodies scattered over Hills 731 and 717 didn't encourage any spring-like sentiments. The Italian guns remained silent, which filled Zikos with suspicion: the enemy must be plotting something. Indeed, the enemy was – but it turned out to be something completely unexpected.

For two weeks the Italian bodies had lain uncollected. The acrid odour of decomposition wafted over the Greek lines but the Greek stance, as we have seen, was that if the Italian recovery teams were unwilling or unable to collect their dead in the face of Greek artillery fire, the bodies would have to remain where they were as a deterrent to future attacks. That hoped-for deterrent effect had not, in fact, materialized; the latest fanatically courageous assault by the *Arditi* could attest to that. But it was, by now, obvious to the Italian command that something needed to be done about the abandoned dead and it was General Matteo Negro, commander of the re-formed Bari Division, who decided to do it.

Sometime after 10 a.m. on 22 March, a sudden burst of Greek machine gun fire shattered the silence. The firing was directed at Monastero, where several Italians were seen walking towards the Greek lines holding what looked like white handkerchiefs. The Italians stopped in their tracks when they heard the firing but began walking again when it stopped. When the handkerchiefs were noticed, the firing stopped. At about noon, a platoon look-out reported to Zikos that three Italians, apparently unarmed, were slowly making their way up the slope; one of the men was walking in front, carrying a Red Cross flag held high. Realizing that they were approaching under a truce, Zikos told his men to keep absolutely still and sent a corporal to notify battalion headquarters. Soon, all through the 1st Division, bugle calls were sounded ordering a cessation of fire.

Second Lieutenant Tzathas eyed the Italians suspiciously as they climbed laboriously up the slope from the direction of Hill 717. Lieutenant Lavrentidis ordered the men in his outer trenches to let the Italians through and walked to meet them while they were still about a hundred metres away. There were nine men altogether: Captain Don Luigi Muzzi, chaplain of the 139 Regiment who held aloft the Red Cross flag, two chaplain second lieutenants with white flags, a medical officer and five stretcher-bearers.

Captain Muzzi, through an interpreter, formally requested a brief truce so that the Italian dead could be properly buried. It remains unclear to whom exactly the Italian chaplain made his request. According to Zikos, it was Captain Koutridis whereas other sources cite Lieutenant Lavrentidis. What is clear is that neither officer had the seniority or authority to make such a decision. There were also unexpected security concerns: who could guarantee that the Italian truce team in those few hours of cease-fire wouldn't glean vital information on the Greek positions – especially as the medical officer was carrying a camera? Lavrentidis – or Koutridis – asked Don Luigi to accompany him but had to request that everyone else but one second lieutenant chaplain and the interpreter return to the Italian lines. The medical officer complained – he wanted a complete photographic record of the carnage – but had to comply.

Don Luigi turned to face the vast carpet of bodies stretched before him and murmured a prayer as the Greeks stood respectfully: *'Requiem aeternam, dona eis, Domine... Amen!'* The two chaplains were then blindfolded for security reasons and led by a circuitous route to 9 Company headquarters, stumbling over the bodies of their fallen comrades. Koutridis wanted to know how much time the burial details would need.

'Our commander leaves it to your discretion,' Captain Muzzi replied.

'Do you have written authorization?'

'No. We consider the truce an unofficial one, solely for the purpose of burying our dead. But as we saw on our way here, there are hundreds rather than dozens as we expected.'

'But couldn't you see from your own observation posts the extent of the losses?' Lavrentidis interjected.

Don Luigi was still shaken from the sight of bodies and body parts rotting in the blood-stained mud. He had been able to see

only a small part of the carnage, he replied, on his way up by way
of Monastero and Hill 717. Before being blindfolded, he had been
severely unnerved at the gruesome sights that met his eyes. At this
point in the conversation he buried his face in his hands and sobbed:
'*Dio mio, terribile, terribile!*' ('My God, terrible, terrible!') Captain
Koutridis plied the distraught chaplain with brandy to buck him
up; when Don Luigi was able to, he said: 'Even four days won't be
enough for the task, let alone four hours. Believe me, sir, the Italian
command has no idea of this tragedy.' Koutridis added that his men
would have to keep the burial details under close watch; essentially
they would be hostages while the grim task was being done. But
before anything could be agreed, Army Headquarters in Athens had
to be notified first.

Captain Muzzi and the other chaplain were treated to a frugal
but leisurely lunch. The 9 Company cook prepared some corned
beef meatballs to accompany an otherwise unremarkable meal of
wild greens. Koutridis broke out a bottle of brandy sent to him by
his family back home and poured out generous doses. Don Luigi
displayed his gratitude by handing round tiny icons of the Virgin
Mary as keepsakes. Six hours later, the Headquarters reply arrived:
the truce would apply as of 8 a.m. the following morning (23
March) until 4 p.m., effective along the whole 1st Division sector.
Also, burial of the Italian dead must be undertaken by Greek work
parties in the presence of unarmed Italian chaplains and medics.
Greek Headquarters also demanded that the Italian command
sign a declaration that it was their side that requested a truce. The
beginning and end of the truce would be signalled by the appropriate
bugle calls. Captain Koutridis, as the ranking officer on Hill 731, and
Captain Muzzi signed the initial draft protocol.

The draft, however, required assent from the Italian command so,
at 5:15 p.m., Lieutenant Lavrentidis, on the orders of Colonel Balis
and accompanied only by the interpreter, walked over to the Italian
lines at Monastero, leaving the two Italian chaplains on Hill 731.

Balis had also told him to keep his eyes open and take note of the enemy positions, but the Italians weren't taking any chances either and blindfolded him. The commander of the 139 Regiment greeted Lavrentidis warmly and offered him refreshment but balked at what seemed to him humiliating conditions.

'You may inform General Vrachnos,' the Italian colonel said testily, 'that we merely requested a truce of a few hours in which to bury our dead. Since it has not happened, we don't want it any longer! You may return to your position. So when do you wish the war to resume?'

'I believe, *colonello,* that the initiative is yours,' Lavrentidis replied.

'Would you prefer 11:31 [tonight]?' the colonel snapped.

'Eleven-thirty-one it is,' the Greek replied curtly and began his walk back to the Greek lines, which he reached after 9 p.m. with his discouraging news. Tzathas then accompanied the two Italian chaplains back to their own lines.

What had appeared a promising humanitarian initiative had evaporated thanks to the intransigence of both commands. If there was any real reason why the Italians should not be allowed to bury their own fallen, the Greek Army Headquarters did not give any. Contrariwise, the Italian command had nothing to gain from turning down the Greek conditions, unfair as they might have seemed. According to the official Greek Army Historical Department's account of the Greek-Italian War, the II Corps command initially approved the Italian heralds' request, and implicitly faults the Italian command for turning down the Greek condition that the Greeks do the burying in the presence of unarmed Italian medics. It does not mention the other Greek condition: that the Italians sign a paper saying the truce was their idea. If this last demand seems quite petty and needless, it must be remembered that the unprovoked Italian attack of October 1940 and the subsequent warfare in the snowy mountains of Albania had embittered the average Greek soldier to an extraordinary degree. There would be plenty of men who would fault their senior officers for treating the enemy with kid gloves, even for such a humanitarian purpose. Suspicion also was rife; who could know whether the Italians might use the burial details as a screen for a surprise assault? Sneakier things had happened. And the Greek government naturally would want to rub the Italians' noses in the dirt in this weak moment for them.

Zikos in his memoir avoids explicit blame, but his distress at the outcome is evident. The 22 March, he says 'was a day of peace and a day of mistakes'.

> The men of Hill 731, apart from my platoon, were coming out of their trenches and going up to the Italian dead to grab their weapons, belts, food tins and water bottles, and ammunition....
> There was a lot of unnecessary movement... The Italian observers saw the movements of our men, so the following day was one of losses for us, as their fire was directed precisely at our battle positions.

It was not all callousness, however. Sometime that afternoon, a 9 Company soldier walked over to where the group of wounded Italians had been crying for help for three days. Now just one of them was still alive. The Greek handed him a full flask of water which he gulped down eagerly, and in gratitude embraced the other's knees. As the Greek side was awaiting the reply from Athens, and thus the truce was unofficially in force, Italian stretcher bearers came and took their man away.

Zikos was one of those who feared the Italians might make use of the truce movements of the Italian and Greek personnel to note the Greek positions. His fears were proved right. Right on cue, at precisely 11: 31 p.m., Negro's artillery zeroed in accurately on the very positions they had observed during the day. A 9 Company platoon, under Second Lieutenant Christodoulou, caught the worst of the shelling that wounded him and half his unit (of which a few were killed). But two sides could play that game; when Lieutenant Lavrentidis returned from his futile mission to the Italian lines, he brought details of enemy positions on and around Monastero – where the 139 Regiment was preparing an attack at daybreak and which was promptly shelled by the 1st Division's heavy guns.

Despite the failure of the truce, in the quiet hours before it was broken, some effort, as we have seen, was made to collect the Italian bodies. One of them was that of Prince Giorgio di Borbone of the 31 Regiment of *Arditi,* who was given an elaborate military funeral near Monastero in full view of the Greeks opposite who caught snatches of the hymns borne on the breeze.

Just after midnight, on 24 March, another Italian formation emerged from the darkness to make for Hill 731. The troops appeared to be moving slowly and cautiously behind the screen of an artillery barrage. This attack – the nineteenth since the start of the battle – was halted by 9 Company's grenades and the unmistakable sound of bayonets clicking into place. An hour later, the Italians pulled back, firing to cover their retreat. There appeared to be no rational reason why such futile assaults should continue; most likely Hill 731 had become an obsession – still there like a phantom after the most determined attempts to eliminate it, mocking the Italian command. To strike at it had become a matter of honour. Most likely, this operation was a reconnaissance-in-force, as (to Zikos) it lacked the intensity of the previous eighteen. The left of 10 Company captured six Italians.

At 3:30 a.m., the twentieth attack materialized. As the Greek artillery started up, a white flare lit up the night sky – the gunners' signal to cease fire. In fact, the flare had been sent up by the Italians as a deception. The resulting confusion among the Greek batteries didn't last very long, but long enough to enable the Italian infantry to get closer to the Greek positions than they should have. Nonetheless that attack, too, petered out. But how had the Italians learned the flare signal for the Greek artillery? There was no immediate answer, but the Greek command changed the signals to be on the safe side.

During the rest of that day, an Italian platoon seized a south-facing spur of Hill 717 and began pouring machine gun fire onto Hill 731 until Koutridis' battalion forced it to withdraw. Lavrentidis repulsed a similar enemy advance on the right of the sector, but at the cost of eight men killed and thirty-two wounded. Farther to the right, on the 15th Division front, at least one attempt was made on the Greek lines but, like the others that day, it failed to gain any real result. As no sane Italian commander by now would have believed that Hill 731 would fall with one more big push, these moves were more in the nature of nuisance raids, to keep the Greeks without rest until Cavallero's new offensive, planned for four days later.

The following day, 25 March, was and is a special day for the Greeks. It marks the anniversary of the start of the Greek War of Independence from the Ottoman Empire in 1821, and naturally every soldier at the front would have felt a surge of patriotism and resolve. But just in case, the 1st Division commander, Major General Vrachnos, issued an order of the day likening his men to the original freedom fighters:

> My brave Co-warriors and Immortal heroes, for fifteen whole days, stuck to the ground you earned through your blood through courage and unimaginable heroism, you have received and are receiving the sneaky hammer-blows of the despised enemy... wherever he attempted to approach you, you gave him a hard lesson by means of the bayonet and hand grenade.

Do soldiers bloodied in combat really believe such messages, especially those issued in the rather bombastic terms common at the time? Most probably don't take them quite literally. Yet Vrachnos' words must certainly have been a tonic of sorts; a soldier whose life is daily on the line appreciates some acknowledgement from the brass safe behind the lines, even if it might ring a bit hollow. The Italian attacks were far from 'sneaky' – in fact, they were as obvious as an express train – and Vrachnos would have found little agreement among the troops that the enemy deserved to be 'despised'. There were too many dead comrades for that.

The Italian command, of course, was quite aware of the day's significance to the Greeks. It moved up anti-tank artillery as close to Hill 731 as possible and let loose with a barrage. One shell hit Second Lieutenant Antonios Polychroniades at an observation post, cutting him in two. This was the sign for the men to keep their heads down, as the firing was so close that it was almost impossible to calculate the range; the report of the gun and the explosion of the shell were almost simultaneous. To the left, on the Trebeshinë range, the Greek units were still ankle-deep in snow but on Hills 731 and 717, as well as in the Desnitsa Valley, the sun shone down warmly. Zikos and his platoon spent the morning picking lice off themselves and their grubby uniforms. From his position he looked over at Hill 731:

> I tried hard to see if there was any movement by our men; there was none – the height seemed dead. In the Desnitsa river valley the trees had begun to be in leaf, but Hill 731 presented a strange spectacle. The earth had been churned up and was blackened and burned in various colours by the explosions. Many trees were standing, but without branches, just stumps… Italian bodies and body parts were scattered around our position, numberless bodies around our trenches, a macabre sight that made you think you were in the nether world.

The stench of those bodies was overpowering. The Greek dead had been buried, but far too shallowly, and the odour arose from them, too. The weather was getting warmer, adding to the problem. 'The men moved about like zombies, unshaven and having gone three weeks without a wash, punch-drunk after weeks of battle and looking like ghosts.' Water was running short. The main source, the stream running through the gully between Hills 731 and 717, had been reduced to a trickle which passed over rotting bodies. Recent rains had swelled the Vijosë river, bringing down more human remains. The men of Zikos' platoon filled their water bottles from the muddy pools in shell craters, straining the water through half a dozen layers of bandage before drinking.

That night a new sound emanated from the Italian lines – the raucous tones of loudspeakers blasting propaganda messages in fractured Greek:

> Greek officers and soldiers! Italy loves the Greek people. But it was forced to make war against Greece because your government sold itself to Britain. So, Greeks, you are fighting in vain. Throw away your weapons and surrender!

It is hard to imagine any self-respecting soldier hearing that with anything other than amused contempt. Zikos heard this enlightening message echoing eerily over no–man's–land: 'Boys, come over and surrender to us. Come on, don't get killed needlessly, we'll give you bread.' There would be an interval of classical music and the wheedling would start again. The bit about bread was especially ironic, as throughout the Albanian campaign gaunt Italian prisoners would often hold out their hands pleading for *'pane, pane,'* ('bread, bread'). In fact, that same evening, supply mules finally arrived from the south and delivered satisfactory quantities of food, brandy, cigarettes and dried fruits to the long-suffering men of 19 Regiment.

So far, the Greek 1st Division remained intact with Colonel Balis' 19 Regiment (technically belonging to the 6th Division) covering the immediate front; Koutridis' Third Battalion held Hill 731 and the First Battalion Hill 717, with the Second Battalion strung out in between. One battalion of the 33 Regiment and one of the 67 Regiment held the area of Spi Kamarate in the rear, while the 4, 16 and 31 Regiments were positioned on the left along the Trebeshinë heights, the first two acting as a reserve.

As for Cavallero, his plans for a renewed thrust on 28 March had gone seriously wrong and through no fault of his own. He still had the bulk of Gambara's Eighth Corps facing the Greeks, with the Twenty-fifth on the right and Fourth on the left. Some divisions had hardly been bloodied and remained ready to fight, such as the 5th (Pusteria) and the 29th (Piemonte), and of course there was the virtually unused Ninth Army of General Pirzio Biroli in the northeast. Cavallero had been especially worried about the Greek threat to Tepelenë; the Twenty-fifth Corps, responsible for the Trebeshinë sector, lacked adequate reserves. And that was because those reserves had been abruptly pulled from the corps and sent to plug an emergency in Yugoslavia.

On 25 March, the Yugoslav Regent, Prince Paul, whose government leaned towards cooperation with the Axis, was toppled in a coup led by General Dušan Simović, a former commander of the Yugoslav Army Air Corps. Simović, with the help of the British, replaced Paul with the young legitimate King Peter II. At one stroke, Greece acquired a new ally in the Balkans but the success was short-lived. The coup enraged Hitler who, without thinking out the long-term consequences, on 27 March ordered his troops into Yugoslavia, which he ordered to be 'crushed completely' and its army 'annihilated'. He noted slyly that the Italians, bogged down in Albania, would be grateful for his move; in fact, he decided to wire Mussolini personally with a remarkable demand:

I would cordially request you, Duce, not to undertake any further operations in Albania in the course of the next few days. I consider it necessary that you should cover and screen the most important passes from Yugoslavia into Albania with all available forces.

That, of course, put paid to Cavallero's plan – and just in time, as he would have received his new instructions from the Duce that same day:

> It is clear [Mussolini wrote to Cavallero] that in entering the war against the Axis and joining its forces with those of Greece, Yugoslavia will attempt to attack [us] from the flanks and rear. Thus it is urgently necessary to prepare our defence while Germany attacks from the east to join up with us.

The Duce figured it would take between ten and fifteen days for Cavallero to redeploy his forces in order to squeeze Yugoslavia like a vice. As far as Hill 731 was concerned, the whole strategy had changed. There was no longer any desperate need to punch through the Desnitsa Valley to Kelçyre. The pro-Ally Yugoslavs had to be dealt with first. There was general agreement that the bulk of the Italian forces had to be pulled back from the Desnitsa front to take up positions farther north; Mussolini in particular insisted on keeping the Albanian town of Shkoder (Scutari), that appeared to be threatened by the Yugoslavs. Italian intelligence had broken the Yugoslav codes, and thus the Italian Second Army of General Vincenzo Ambrosio was able to join the *Wehrmacht* in annihilating Yugoslav resistance, as per the Führer's orders. Hitler was on the point of turning the whole Balkan peninsula into an Axis province.

The relief of the Italians being marched away from the hellhole of the past three weeks can be imagined. But Cavallero had no intention of letting off the Greeks lightly. In the days following, he kept his artillery pounding away at Hill 731 and its environs, simply to wear down the defenders. But the Greeks, for their part, were not ready to stop. General Papagos, the commander-in-chief, insisted that the men must be kept engaged to preserve their fighting spirit. In fact, he had the idea of abandoning northern Yugoslavia (today's Slovenia, Croatia and northern Serbia) to the Axis while setting up a line of resistance in the south (today's North Macedonia) in which the combined Greek and Yugoslav armies would take a stand.

Papagos has been severely criticized for this idea. Cervi, for one, considers that he was 'drugged on his Albanian successes' and had little idea of the realities on the ground. For one thing, though the Yugoslav Army was formidable on paper – some 800,000 men under arms – it was in fact riven by political dissention, ethnic rivalries and defeatism and had largely antiquated equipment. In twelve days it was over; Yugoslavia was no more. In Albania, Cavallero could relax while pondering his next moves.

For the men on Hill 731, little had changed. Shells came whistling over daily. On a sunny 26 March, Zikos called over one of his most trusted men, Sergeant Konstantinos Salvanos. Something had been bothering him about Salvanos for some time. The oldest man in the platoon, he had been in jail as a communist agitator; the only way he could secure a pardon was by volunteering for the front, which he did, and he had been sent to 9 Company, Third Battalion, 19 Regiment, 6th Division, in the most dangerous sector. Zikos, knowing his background, had kept a wary eye on him for weeks, but had noticed nothing amiss. On the contrary, Salvanos proved to be the ideal soldier, checking up on guard duty through the night, arranging guard shifts and seeing that all supplies were well under cover. Surprisingly, for a suspected leftist, he made the sign of the cross before every meal and often showed the men photos of his wife and two children. He also never lost his nerve in battle. Zikos was insatiably curious about all this. Was it just an elaborate charade?

'You don't behave like a communist,' Zikos said, confronting him.

'But I'm not a communist,' Sergeant Salvanos replied. 'I'm a tobacco farmer. Just because I protested about low tobacco prices they called me a communist and locked me up.' He turned out to be one of the best soldiers the grizzled Zikos had ever known.

In the evening of 27 March, after the usual irritating day of Italian nuisance bombardments, a mule train turned up with zinc vats full of the first warm food they had in three weeks – beef and pasta. Naturally, it was all wolfed down with more than the usual eagerness, but it must have been a bit tainted, as the following day there was a general run on the latrines, which Sergeant-Major Zikos had to organize in manageable groups to prevent another kind of battle on Hill 731. Apart from that episode, the routine was becoming tedious. At night, the Italian shelling would be replaced by the wheedling tones of the Italian propaganda loudspeakers echoing eerily in the night, and punctuated by the odd mortar round. 'Come on, boys. Don't get killed needlessly...' The boys, of course, ignored it, using the hours of inaction to write letters home.

Cavallero himself considered his mission in Albania over. His troops had fought manfully for Hill 731 – none could have done better – but events elsewhere had eliminated the importance of that objective. As he packed his bags to return to Rome to resume his duties as chief of the general staff, he reflected sadly on the immense cost of the abortive Spring Offensive:

> The losses in men, materiel and transport have been enormous [Cavallero noted in his diary]. The Bari Division has lost almost all its materiel, the 8 Alpine Regiment eighty per cent, the 9 Regiment sixty per cent.

He paid tribute to especially courageous units that had battled heroically, such as the 139 Regiment, but poured scorn on others that he considered had been remiss in their duty, such as the 41 and 42 Infantry Regiments, blaming their lack of morale on their commanders. The commander of the former, Colonel Giovanni Manai, faced a court-martial for withdrawing his regiment in the face of the enemy in December, opening a gap through which the Greeks had poured. He noted also that his troops had to live and fight in sub-zero temperatures and with a lack of air cover in the mist and fog. The losses in officers had been appalling; the 50 Regiment had been without a commander for nearly a week. 'Those Greeks are a weird lot,' he wrote. 'They doze off for an hour and then start fighting again.'

On the Greek side, the inaction caused its own problems. A soldier on Hill 731 was fairly safe if he hunkered down against the enemy shelling, but long periods in a crouching position was likely to seize up the knees; some men could only go to their lookout positions by crawling. And outside was where almost all the shelling casualties occurred. Though the active fighting on Hill 731 was to all intents and purposes over, the Third Battalion suffered a continuing attrition.

About noon on the last day of March, as the spring at last got into its stride and the temperature rose, a courier from 9 Company headquarters arrived at Zikos' platoon with unexpected news: the Third Battalion was at last being relieved. Zikos was asked to send an NCO to headquarters after dark to guide his sector's replacements to the hill. The news triggered an eruption of joy in the platoon, though Zikos was careful to keep everyone on guard against the unexpected. He issued orders to every man in the platoon, wherever he was positioned, to be ready for immediate departure. When it was dark, he sent Corporal Georgios Dimitriou to collect the fresh platoon that would replace his. The shadowy forms of the new arrivals – the First Battalion of 67 Regiment – began to loom out of the murk about an hour later. Koutridis of 9 Company sat down with his replacement to brief him on what he could expect.

That became obvious at almost that instant, when several mortar rounds came thudding in. Zikos' men by now had become experts in judging the time between the firing and the shell bursts and were able to take cover almost instinctively. But no-one had time to inform the new guys massed outside 9 Company headquarters awaiting orders and, sure enough, a few mortar rounds fell squarely into them, killing and wounding three dozen. Their cries and screams could be heard from Zikos' position and he knew what it meant. 'The new company is shattered,' he told his men. 'They're in no position to replace us now.' In fact, he was fuming. He was experienced enough to know that the rules governing unit replacements in a theatre of combat had been shockingly ignored: instead of being immediately assigned to their respective positions, as the regulations stipulated, the new company's platoons had been standing aimlessly around 9 Company headquarters wasting valuable time while the enemy was still active.

The commander of the replacement company rushed out of the shelter and barked at the men to disperse, but of course it was too late. He didn't have enough men left to form a front-line combat unit – that single mortar attack had slashed the company strength by an entire platoon. Yet he had to carry out his task so he sent one platoon up to the summit of Hill 731 to take over there and two more to the eastern slope but, when they reached the position of Zikos' platoon, there were no more men left. The company commander apologetically promised to inform the battalion command but neither Zikos nor any of his men believed him. And when, at midnight on 31 March, they heard the sound of supply mules coming up, their worst suspicions were confirmed – it meant that, alone of the whole Third Battalion, Zikos' platoon would have to stay where it was. It seemed like a bad April Fool's joke.

The month of April opened with intermittent Italian shelling of Hill 731 and its environs. When night fell on 1 April, Zikos and his men hoped they might at last be replaced, but no-one appeared. While the rest of 9 Company rested behind the lines, the men at the front were regaled with the usual nightly cacophony of propaganda broadcasts. The next day, Zikos couldn't help noticing that spring was breaking out in lush vegetation over the landscape except for Hill 731 that stood like a blasted, blackened phantom against the Albanian skyline. He reflected that he had been living in a trench uninterruptedly for more than three weeks, but he preferred it to a shelter. 'The best place is your trench,' he would tell his men, 'and if you get killed it will be in the fresh air. In the shelter you could be buried by earth and tree stumps, as well as not being able to see anything day or night.'

That was the day that the 1st Division was finally relieved from the front to be replaced by the 17th Division, leaving only the 16 Regiment on reserve duty. But the news appeared to be slow to filter down to the 19 Regiment, especially the outlier Third Battalion. By noon on 3 April, Zikos had become thoroughly fed up with waiting to be relieved and sent Corporal Dimitriou to battalion headquarters to find out what was or was not going on. Captain Koutridis, the battalion commander, sent Dimitriou back with the promise: 'As soon as it gets dark wait an hour for the replacements, and if they don't turn up, abandon the position and return to the battalion.' At last they were leaving that corner of hell on earth. Zikos told the men to quietly prepare for the move while making as few movements as possible that might attract enemy attention. Night came with no replacements, so Zikos and his platoon moved out.

'Is Zikos here?' he heard Koutridis call out when he approached the battalion command post.

'He's here,' 9 Company's Lieutenant Lavrentidis replied.

'All right, let's get the battalion out of here.'

Koutridis, obviously relieved not to have to wait any longer, led the Third Battalion south to safety. But even then, they were not out of the woods. Twenty minutes into the march, they entered a zone where Italian heavy shells were coming down; the column wavered a bit, but the officers kept it together. There were no casualties. After an uphill hike lasting three hours, there was a half-hour rest during which Zikos was informed that, of the original one hundred and sixty men of 9 Company's four platoons, fifty-eight were still standing – a casualty rate of over sixty per cent. One-third of the company's mules had been killed along with their drivers. Similar casualties were suffered by 10 Company, with those of 11 Company at about fifty per cent.

Few, if any, had kept their packs and gas masks as the former (French-made) were too much trouble to carry into combat and were thrown away at the first opportunity and the latter (Italian-made Pirelli) were too cumbersome to wear in normal circumstances – besides, it had turned out that no gas was ever employed in the Albanian campaign. Their food tins and water flasks were mostly taken from dead Italians as they were considered superior to Greek Army issue. The night march continued to the Osum river to the east which was reached just before dawn. There, in a wooded area, they stopped to rest, hidden from any Italian aircraft that might appear. They didn't and so, shortly afterwards, the whole 19 Regiment mustered at 6th Division headquarters after their bloody stint as part of the 1st Division at Hill 731. None of them were sorry to leave it.

Chapter 10

Bitter pill

On the last day of March, a German liaison officer, Lieutenant Colonel Speth, turned up at Cavallero's headquarters with a team of German Army 'inspectors' to check out what was happening in the Albanian theatre. The *Wehrmacht* was poised for its big Balkan roll-over, with the Ninth Army of Field Marshal Maximilian von Weichs, put together astonishingly quickly from bases as far away as France, assigned to crush Yugoslavia. Hitler wanted to make sure his Italian allies would do as they were told – that is, stay put. He didn't want any delays or surprises in the Balkans, for he was thinking farther afield.

'How long do you think you can hold your position?' Speth asked.

'At least a month,' Cavallero replied.

The German suggested that it might be wise to pull back from the Tepelenë salient as there was a danger that the Yugoslavs might cross into Albania and hit the Italians from the rear. Cavallero rejected the idea out of hand. He set his face against anything that would even remotely resemble a retreat as an intolerable humiliation in the eyes not only of the Allies but especially of the Germans, to whom the Italian armed forces needed to present a respectable front. He knew perfectly well that Speth was really saying, 'Look, you've failed. Let the real soldiers take over from now on.' He had to content himself with uselessly expending precious shells on Hill 731 to keep up an appearance of bellicosity.

Needless to say, the idea of a Spring Offensive by now had been completely abandoned. Cavallero's strategy, dictated now essentially from Berlin, was to be passive. A week after Mussolini's departure, the Centauro Armoured Division had been withdrawn to protect Shkoder, the shattered Puglie reassigned to the left flank of Pirzio Biroli's Ninth Army near the Yugoslav frontier with the 6th (Cuneo) Alpine Division next to it. Put simply, the Italian Army in Albania would act as an anvil against which the Germans could hammer any Yugoslav resistance as well as prevent the Greeks – and the small British expeditionary force sent to help them – and Yugoslavs from joining forces. Making up this 'anvil' were twenty-one divisions from the Ninth Army (Third and Twenty-sixth Corps) and the Eleventh Army (Fourth, Eighth and Twenty-fifth Corps), with the Bari and 56th (Casale) Divisions in reserve. There were still fourteen Greek divisions plus a brigade in Albania which had to be guarded against.

Beneath the shelter of oak trees and beetling cliffs on the banks of the Osum river, the 19 Regiment was able to have its first real rest. There was plenty of warm food and the hard mental carapace that the men (having faced and seen violent death every day) formed around themselves began to fall away. Memories of fallen comrades were suddenly painful. There was plenty of time to reflect on what they had been through.

> But our consciences were soothed by knowing that we did our duty [Zikos wrote]. Each man of [9] Company called on me and talked about Hill 731. Their morale was high and they considered themselves heroes. I came into contact with the battalion officers and the company sergeant-majors and all the men; they all had the same picture.

Yet the clouds were still there. A bunch of replacements arrived at the battalion, most of them older reservists in their thirties, some of whom had families and, in Zikos' opinion, 'should not have been sent to the front'. Some newly-minted second lieutenants arrived to command the platoons.

The whole game changed completely on 6 April when von Weichs' Second Army barrelled into Yugoslavia and Field Marshal Sigmund List's fifteen-division Twelfth Army smashed its way into Greece simultaneously. Both invasions were preceded by the classic *blitzkrieg* waves of Luftwaffe attack aircraft against which no opponent had yet been able to stand up. The German declaration of war against Greece used the same disingenuous excuse as Mussolini had used the previous October: that Greece, being under the 'control' of Britain, was thus incapable of making its own decisions and needed to be put right. Sections of the Greek Army of Macedonia (the former IV Corps) on the Bulgarian border, especially the 14th Division, stuck to their posts with the utmost heroism; the defenders of Forts Istibey and Rupel, in particular, held their positions in the face of ruthless attacks by air and land, dying with all guns firing and earning the rueful admiration of the Germans whose casualties had been considerable. But such heroism could not change the grim picture: within three days the Germans had occupied Thessaloniki, the main port of northern Greece and chief outlet to the Aegean Sea, and were sending columns into the mountainous territory to the west that soon were threatening the Greek rear in Albania.

On 9 April, Lieutenant General Konstantinos Bakopoulos, the commander of the West Macedonia Army Department (TSDM), capitulated to the invaders. Papagos was enraged. No-one had given Bakopoulos the authority to raise the white flag. Papagos was still firmly convinced that the Greek Army, especially the bulk of it in Albania, could carry on the fight. But as many commentators since have pointed out, he was deluding himself. So far neither the Poles, the Dutch, the Belgians, the Norwegians nor the French, all of whom had reasonably efficient armies, had been able to stand up against Hitler's mailed fist. With his paltry few regiments already overwhelmed, Bakopoulos had no choice. The eastern front was gone.

On the western Albanian front, Papagos was planning an attack on the Italian Ninth Army in conjunction with a Yugoslav advance, set for 8 April. The Yugoslav advance on the Italian positions at Shkoder proved weak and irresolute, no doubt enervated by general pessimism and defeatism in the ranks; Cavallero easily neutralized it and took many prisoners. Shortly beforehand, Mussolini had messaged him that he was about to send over 'three battalions of young Fascists' who, trained in battle techniques, were 'formidable'.

'Send them over,' Cavallero had replied. 'We'll make the best possible use of them.' Such use included moving the army east and south to cooperate with the German advances and outflank the Greeks in Albania. The 53rd (Arezzo) Division of the Twenty-sixth Corps moved to secure the shores of Lake Ohrid at the confluence of the borders of Albania, Greece and Yugoslavia (now North Macedonia) while the Cuneo Division hit at Yugoslav positions. The fight against the Greeks was put on the back burner as the aim now was to join up with the Germans at Struga on the north shore of the lake. This switch of fronts – and strategy – in such a short time was no easy matter. Unlike the swiftly mechanized Germans, most of the Italian troops would have to go on foot, and Geloso, the Eleventh Army commander, suggested a three-day delay to enable his divisions to catch their breath.

But Cavallero was impatient; stymied at Hill 731, he needed to restore his reputation with Mussolini and the haughty Germans who would need little excuse to brand the Italian Army as second-rate. As the Germans rolled unstoppably into Thessaloniki and the adjacent regions of northern Greece, Cavallero telephoned Pirzio Biroli, the Ninth Army commander, to hurry up his own force. 'Get everything together and forge ahead,' he said. 'The Germans are going to be at Struga tonight, certainly by tomorrow. You must be prompt and quick to prevent them from getting there before we do.'

The Cuneo Division had seized the snowy ground overlooking Struga. On 10 April, Major Sandro Annoni, the commander of the Mondovì battalion, whose party non-membership and bachelor status had clouded his promotion prospects, stood scanning the

Yugoslav positions below through his binoculars; he held his head high, as he always did. A bullet smacked into his abdomen, fatally severing the iliac artery. While the rest of the Mondovì moved on, Annoni's body was carried on a stretcher to the rear. (Posthumously awarded the Gold Medal for Valour, Major Annoni was one of the very last Italians to die in the Albanian campaign.) The Cuneo took some 1,500 Yugoslav prisoners, including three generals.

The Yugoslav discomfiture seriously disrupted the plans of Papagos, who seems to have grossly overestimated the Yugoslavs' potential. Wanting more information on the murky situation around Lake Ohrid, he sent a staff major to fly to the scene on a British aircraft and meet General Simović, the ringleader of the pro-Allied coup who was now in desperate straits. Bad weather forced the aircraft to a crash-landing at Bar, which lightly injured the major but seriously shook him. He reached Sarajevo on 11 April but was immobilized by the day-long German bombardment of the city, only reaching Simović's headquarters two days later. Simović was frank: the Yugolav Army had virtually ceased to exist, the Serb and Croat ethnic groups were at each other's throats, and there was nothing left to really fight for. The Italian Second Army, under General Ambrosio, had marched into Ljubljana in the north – indeed, King Vittotio Emanuele had moved to a royal headquarters near Udine in north-east Italy to be closer to the action.

When Papagos' staff major returned to Athens to deliver the grim news, the Greek commander-in-chief realized the game was over. On 12 April, with a heavy heart, he issued an order for all Greek units in all theatres, including Albania, to pull back and join up with the joint Anglo-Greek force attempting to bar the Germans' way into central and southern Greece. The reaction on the Albanian front was one of shock and dismay. Major General George Bakos, the II Corps commander, either refused to believe it or thought that pro-German fifth columnists in Athens had seized control of military policy. On the following day, he issued a curiously-worded four-hundred-word

message to the troops that hit them harder than any Italian artillery
barrage.

> Officers, non-commissioned officers and soldiers:
> In a sad spirit I am informed that some Soldiers and Officers,
> fortunately few, in whose veins no Greek blood flows, have
> deserted to the enemy, the enemy whom you relentlessly pursued
> until yesterday. It is a fact that some soldiers lost their nerve in
> the German invasion of our beloved Macedonia and have run
> to the rear.

This was barb obviously aimed at General Bakopoulos and the
TSDM who had thrown in the towel, to Papagos' fury. Bakos allowed
his bitterness and sorrow to overflow in the rest of the message:

> In the name of God and our sweet Country, I ask that you place
> your fate in the hands of your Officers and myself. Do not be
> misled by clever people who shake your faith in our ideals and
> your courage. Do not be swayed by cowards. We are at a critical
> juncture. The moments are historic ones… I address you at this
> moment as your true Father, because that is what I am. All my
> life, since I was a Second Lieutenant, I have spent in the camps
> among you, and among you my hair has gone grey. Please pay
> careful heed to my Fatherly words: only discipline, cohesion and
> coolness can save us from dishonour… Do not forget my words
> for an instant and that we are Greeks. In God's name do not
> let us be dishonoured after so much glory and such a brilliant
> History.

Bakos' words are surely among the most remarkable ever addressed
by a corps commander to his men in any age. Any sense of class
difference between officers and enlisted men (and there was less of
this in the Greek than in the Italian Army) was now swept away in the

universal grief that months of bitter combat – and winning combat at that – had to come to this. It was as if the ghosts of the warriors of Marathon, Thermopylai and Salamis had risen to shake their fists at the gross unfairness of it all. What had been the use, then, of the desperate defence of Hill 731? (And, for that matter, what had been the use of the twenty bloody Italian assaults on it?)

Did Bakos really believe that 'fifth columnists' had been at work on the home front, influencing even Papagos? Such conspiracy theories are common when affairs turn bad, but there is no real evidence of high-level treachery. Very likely, Bakos wished to preserve his men's morale as much as possible by positing a reason why they were being ordered to retreat – defeatism at home, rather than the more unpalatable truth: that, ever since the start of 1941, the Greek Army in Albania had been in an ultimately untenable military position. In fact, the head of the British expeditionary force, Major General Henry Maitland 'Jumbo' Wilson, had forcefully reminded Papagos of that fact at a tense personal meeting on 11 April. The II Corps in Albania was now desperately needed to protect the western flank of the joint Anglo-Greek force in central Greece. True, in a superb display of military prowess, it had driven back the Italians and had blunted Cavallero's attempt to win back the lost ground. But a withdrawal would have had to come some time. Papagos seems to have believed that, as his army had more or less conquered southern Albania (referred to by many Greeks to this day as Northern Epiros – i.e. the home of an ethnic Greek minority), Greece's frontiers would be extended to the north-west. Wilson's realism and Hitler's panzer divisions well and truly smashed that delusion.

Of course, mutinous rage swept through all ranks at the front. But Zikos, oddly enough, mentions nothing of this, asserting that he and his unit only learned of Papagos' order on 15 April, three days after it was issued. Like a good soldier, he would have automatically obeyed orders, however distasteful, and masked his true feelings. But his silence on the subject, especially in a memoir not sparing criticism and brimming with realism years later, is puzzling.

On 13 April, Cavallero at last was able to move forward. The following day, the 19 Regiment commander, Colonel Balis, visited Zikos' platoon on the march, uttered 'something incomprehensible' and moved on. Almost certainly, the colonel was trying to signal in come cryptic way that a general withdrawal was imminent. On the cloudy and misty morning of 15 April, Zikos was holding a former Italian machine gun post from where he could see the Trebeshinë range and Hill 731 in the distance. The hill, in fact, was already in Italian hands.

Geloso's Eleventh Army, with the 5th (Pusteria) Division in front, and the 2nd (Tridentina) Division of Pirzio Biroli's Ninth Army in the lead, rolled over the shell-blasted landscape abandoned by the Greeks. General Ranza's air force blew up a strategic bridge at Berat. The Greeks occasionally put up token resistance – how could they not? – that slowed up Cavallero's advance. Ranza took a senior Fascist Party figure, Roberto Farinacci, up in an aeroplane to view the advance from on high, but the aircraft caught fire and had to make an emergency landing at Pogradec. Ranza and Farinacci were lucky to escape with their lives. Gambara's much-mauled Eighth Corps was now able to speed down the Desnitsa Valley to Kelçyre and, no doubt to his great satisfaction, grab that elusive prize that had cost so much blood – Hill 731. The slopes were still littered with the bodies of the unfortunates of the Puglie and Bari Divisions, uncollected after the breakdown in truce talks more than three weeks before. Geloso's army moved fast, entering Gjirokaster on 18 April; the Ninth Army's 19th (Venezia) Division covered a hundred and ten kilometres on foot, sniping at the retreating Greeks in front. By now, morale in the Greek Army had all but broken down.

The Third Battalion was assigned to be the rear guard of the 19 Regiment in its march south, with 9 Company the rearmost unit. In the afternoon, an Italian column of the Eighth Corps was spotted snaking down a mule track from Trebeshinë to the Desnitsa river, apparently intending to cut off the Greek retreat to Kelçyre; the 19 Regiment's artillery opened up on the column, decimating it. At dusk, the shadows of Italian troops appeared on the slopes beneath Zikos' platoon which dispersed the attackers in a Hill 731-type grenade and bayonet charge. That same evening, German aircraft appeared over the Desnitsa Valley dropping flares followed by sticks of bombs aimed at the retreating Greek troops. The bombing technique, advanced for its time, awed Zikos, looking down on the scene. At midnight, the Third Battalion was ordered on its feet for a gruelling single-file march through the mountains; the paths were clogged with other units getting away, creating a frustrating traffic jam that slowed all progress to a crawl.

Perhaps it was the lack of rest, perhaps it was the knowledge that they had been beaten without being defeated in the field but, in the early morning of 16 April, what Zikos describes as 'a strange fear' overtook the men.

> They had the impression that an invisible Italian hand would reach out to seize them, and for that reason every man tried to overtake the other and all crowded to the front.

Demoralization was thus quick to set in. The fear of the 'invisible Italian hand' was, in fact, the quite justified fear that they would be captured by the foe they had humbled for five months. No-one wanted to be in that position. A drizzle had been falling since the night. The men's path wound over the top of a cliff slippery with mud; one misstep and a man would tumble hundreds of feet down into a sheer ravine. At the bottom lay the bodies of two mules and their driver who had fallen off during the night. A panic here could result in disaster, and there very nearly was one, had not Captain Koutridis stationed himself at the beginning of the dangerous stretch with his pistol drawn, threatening to shoot any man rushing ahead out of line. But as soon as Koutridis put his weapon back in its holster, all discipline was lost. Zikos had recourse to his cudgel with which he gave a few of the more panicky troops a quick whack so that a decent distance between the men could be kept. There was no loss. To this point had morale in the 19 Regiment, not to mention the whole 6th Division, plunged a mere month after the heroic defence of Hill 731.

The division planned to bypass Kelçyre to the east and negotiate the snow-streaked ridges of Tremisht to reach Leskovik, a mere few miles from the Greek border at Mertzani Bridge. The morning of 17 April found the Third Battalion encamped on Tremisht; craters left by previous bombing raids were full of fresh rainwater with which the men refilled their flasks. It was during this rest that a corporal approached Zikos, claiming that a machine gunner in his platoon had abandoned his weapon. 'How many men are here in your unit?' Zikos asked.

'Ten, sergeant-major.'

'You know the regulations, corporal. The machine gun is abandoned only when the last man has been killed.' To do it in any other circumstance was a capital offence. The corporal indeed knew that. There was then a pause as the hard-bitten sergeant-major eyed the other. 'Did you execute the man who abandoned the machine gun?' The corporal said no. 'Then,' wrote Zikos, 'I beat the corporal with my cudgel until it broke and the corporal ran off in terror.' This was discipline of the strictest type, and quite necessary if the Greeks were to quit Albania in any kind of order.

The going was somewhat easier after that; the paths and roads were not so crowded, and there was no sign of Italian pursuit. Some of the newer unblooded recruits in boredom began firing into the air, annoying the veterans of Hill 731. Koutridis banned the practice on pain of execution but the order continued to be ignored by many, until Lieutenant Lavrentidis, the 9 Company commander, nabbed one offending private and drew his revolver. 'You bastard, I'm taking you out,' he growled.

'Don't kill me, sir,' the private pleaded. 'I've got a family.' Lavrentidis lowered his weapon but warned the private that if he was caught firing into the air again, he was a dead man. That was enough to end the practice. All the men wanted to stay alive to see their homes again. But already events were under way in Greece that would turn their collective home into a prison.

By 16 April, the Germans were barrelling down central Greece towards Athens, driving the outnumbered British and few remaining Greeks before them. Waves of Messerschmitt Bf109 fighters of the Luftwaffe's III/Jagdgeschwader 77 and II/Jagdgeschwader 26 blasted the path through which the panzers would roll, all but eliminating what was left of the British and Greek air components. That week was Greek Orthodox Holy Week, and all the sufferings of Christ's Passion descended on that hapless country. General Wilson was anxious to form a line of resistance below Mount Olympus, and for this he needed the Greeks of the TSH (Epiros Army Department) to hurry over from Albania to beef up his left flank. If that failed, the occupation of Athens was now a mere matter of hours.

For reasons still unclear, the link-up didn't happen. The Greeks later accused Wilson of hiding his true intention to abandon Greece to its fate as hastily as possible without telling them. To be fair to Wilson, he would have been hard put to do otherwise, as he was facing the southern equivalent of the retreat to Dunkirk. There was no way Greece could now be saved and, if he failed to inform the Greeks of this harsh fact, it may be put down to a certain sensitivity to his gallant allies and the hope that they would realize it for themselves. Some did and some didn't, and thus a rift opened in the Greek senior command.

One of those who saw the game was irretrievably up was the TSH commander, Lieutenant General Ioannis Pitsikas, in Ioannina, who messaged Papagos urging an armistice: 'A political intervention is absolutely necessary. The situation is worsening by the hour.' He sent a staff officer to call on the commander-on-chief in Athens.

Pitsikas had probably put his finger on why his force had failed to link up with the British. Yet Papagos could not accept abject surrender, preferring to fight to the last. He knew perfectly well what was in store for the country. 'Greece is going to be occupied by the Axis,' he told Captain Prince Peter, a liaison officer with the British, that day. 'That means we'll all be taken prisoner.' To Papagos, that was the honourable way out. Continued guerrilla resistance in the mountains would be useless and harmful. He actually ordered Prince Peter to be captured when the Germans marched in but the prince said no way, and walked out of the office.

But in this case, Papagos made the more sober calculation. Reports were reaching him of mutinies in the 5th (Cretan) and 6th Divisions where a few summary executions had to be carried out. Major General Katsimitros, the commander of the 8th Division that had smashed the initial Italian offensive in November, added his voice to the call for an armistice, backed up by the commanders of the I and II Corps. The TSH was disintegrating before their eyes. Even worse, the detested Italians were on the march and no Greek soldier in his right mind would ever consider surrendering to them – far nobler, in their view, to give themselves up to the Germans. Papagos himself tended to agree. But his honour demanded that, as long as the British allies were in the country, he had to go on with his duty. Replying to Pitsikas, he asserted that he preferred that 'the Army be dissolved, destroyed or taken prisoner... until such time as Great Britain emerges victorious'.

On 18 April, Greece began to implode at warp speed. King George, Koryzis and Papagos could do little but hold fruitless meetings while the eleven Greek divisions in Albania were left to fend for themselves. On that day, in Athens' ornate Grande Bretagne hotel that served as Greek military headquarters, Wilson – to mollify the Greeks more than anything else – said he might be able to hold at the famous Thermopylai pass in central Greece where Spartan king Leonidas I had defied Xerxes' hordes in 480 BC – *if* Papagos could bring his divisions in from Albania in time. As everyone must have realized at the meeting, those divisions had no hope of covering the distance in any organized form. As the wail of air raid sirens echoed over the city, a telegram from Major General Bakos was read out:

> I have already mentioned, and mention again, that the situation is rapidly worsening. Disorder, disobedience, and the abandonment of positions are on the rise despite rigorous measures adopted, including firing squads.

Amid the deepening despair, Koryzis decided he'd had enough. A mild-mannered former banker, he had never really wanted the prime minister's job, especially at such a critical juncture for a nation. Just after 2 p.m., he told the King he just wanted out. The sheer impossible burden of governing a nation about to collapse was too much for him. George upbraided him severely, demanding that he stay at his post to the end; the advice was hardly wise, as it must only have worsened Koryzis' depression with its imputation of cowardice. The prime minister simply left the hotel – Prince Peter noted that his face was haggard and anguished – went home, locked himself in the bathroom and put a bullet in his head. It was the afternoon of Good Friday.

Panic seized the government. Wilson knew now there was nothing to salvage. On the following day, Lieutenant General Sir Archibald Wavell, the British commander-in-chief in the Middle East, arrived to talk the king and Papagos into approving a British pullout. A telegram from Winston Churchill backed up the demand. King George caved in and the remaining British forces around Athens engaged in a mad rush to the east coast for evacuation by sea, as Luftwaffe Bf109s strafed the packed lorries churning in confusion through the vineyards.

The German Fortieth Corps of General Georg Stumme had, meanwhile, steamrollered across north-central Greece to cut off what was left of the TSH in Albania. On 12 April, the corps' 9th Armoured Division, 73rd Infantry Division and Leibstandarte SS-Adolf Hitler met unexpected resistance from the Greek 13th Division, III Corps, at Lake Kastoria; despite having marched all the way from Pogradec in Albania, the 13th held out for hours but in the end was forced back. Lieutenant General Georgios Tsolakoglou, the III Corps commander, joined the other Greek corps commanders in deciding that it was useless to hold out any longer. On 20 April, Easter Day, he sent three staff officers representing the I, II and III Corps through the lines to the Leibstandarte SS-Adolf Hitler commander, Major General Sepp Dietrich, in Metsovo to negotiate a truce. Dietrich was complaisant, promising Tsolakoglou that the Germans would put themselves between the Greeks and Italians to prevent the supreme shame of the former surrendering to the latter. Papagos protested but to no effect. On 23 April, the King, his family and most of his ministers sailed for Crete, leaving Athens defenceless. For mainland Greece, the war was all but over.

Tsolakoglou's order of the day to the TSH, in the form of a telegram, was curt and to the point:

> Greek Army to retire to Greek–Albanian border [but] Italian Army will not enter Greek territory. STOP Army not considered prisoners of war. STOP Tomorrow mechanized [German] column to move from Metsovo and Ioannina to Gjirokaster, Permet and Leskovik to place [itself] between us and Italians. Road must be free from any vehicle or column.

On receiving the cable, Colonel Ketseas, who had been given command of the 4 Regiment, ordered that the regimental flag be taken down from its staff and hidden in a backpack. (It survived to be delivered to the National Defence Ministry.) Another threat, meanwhile, had raised its head: that of communist defeatism. The outlawed Greek Communist Party had never ceased its agitation in the lower ranks of the Army. As long as Greece was at war with militant fascism, the aims were pretty much the same; but as soon as the surrender was signed, communist cells urged the troops to 'kill your officers before they send you to be killed.' Fortunately, the great majority of troops remained faithful to flag and country even after defeat and, thanks partly to those men, Greece narrowly avoided being dragged into the Soviet bloc after 1945.

But the soldiers still in Albania were in a perilous position. Mussolini, hearing of the Greek surrender to the Germans in northwest Greece, was livid. Here was his chance to be a conqueror worthy of the name and now the Germans were cheating him of his prey. He ordered Cavallero to keep up his aggressive action; on 21 April, a Greek officer under a flag of truce informed the commander of a Milanese cavalry unit that a cease-fire had been declared. He was dismissed with the reply that the Italian Army would recognize no cease-fire until the last Greek soldier had left Albanian territory, and so hostilities continued. The Eleventh Army's Casale Division penetrated the Greek frontier at Kakavia and skirmished briefly with Greek troops before being stopped by a Wehrmacht regiment.

The Germans, ironically, were quite as anxious as the Greeks to keep the Italians away from the front lines. Mussolini demanded to have a say, on the grounds that 'for six months Italian troops have fought the Greeks, with sixty-three thousand casualties'. Though Hitler replied politely to Mussolini's insistence, he had no intention of acquiescing. The Führer was full of admiration for the Greek troops' prowess in Albania and made no secret of it in an address to the Reichstag. He told his generals in Thessaloniki to stall for time while he soothed the Duce with diplomatic platitudes. Only after Tsolakoglou and Dietrich had agreed to surrender terms did the German military attaché in Rome, General Enno von Rintelen, tell the Italians blandly that since there was no more Greek enemy officially, there was really no issue.

The dispirited men of the TSH trudged slowly homewards as Italian aircraft droned over them. Some units crossing into Greece at the Mertzani Bridge were strafed by German aircraft, with some losses. 'In the name of God,' General Pitsikas appealed to Papagos, 'save the Army from the Italians.' But Papagos was now essentially powerless. As for Bakos, so anxious was he to keep his II Corps – the one that had defended Hill 731 and its environs – from Italian captivity that he was relieved when his fellow corps commander Tsolakoglou made his deal with the Germans. There is evidence, in fact, that Bakos aimed to set up an independent state based on Ioannina, with the help of the local bishop, but his division commanders dissuaded him from such a radical step.

The Greeks' sudden departure filled the local ethnic-Greek Albanian villagers with anxiety. One soldier of the 50 Regiment, Private Yannis Beratis, recalled how the women of one village lined the road as the jam-packed lorries left:

All the women, from the youngest girl to the centenarians, watched us in dumb silence, their arms folded over their black aprons, their heads a little to one side, as still as if turned to stone. Then suddenly, as they saw the last of us getting on the lorries, a dirge rose from their lips in unison: 'Why are you leaving? What will become of us alone?' They stretched out their hands to us in supplication, and then raised their aprons to cover their eyes. None of us expected this. The engines roared, the doors shut with a bang. 'We'll be back,' we shouted back.

Of course, no-one went back. The ethnic-Greek women, bereft of their menfolk, had seen the Greeks as liberators. Now they would have to face an Italian occupation and the hostility of the ethnic Albanians in the Italian army. And anyone familiar with Balkan affairs would know how nasty that can be.

Beratis took one last look out of the window next to the driver and saw a twelve-year-old girl kneeling in the mud and crying. She was the daughter of the owner of the home where he had been billeted. That morning, getting rid of some of his gear, he had given her a new green hand-knitted pullover that had been sent to him from Athens, and she was wearing it now, her thin shoulders shaking with grief. 'She, too, raised her apron to hide her bright blue eyes.' Similar scenes were played out along the retreating Greek line.

On 22 April, a day before the Greek King and government fled Athens, the 19 Regiment, with Koutridis' Third Battalion in the lead, formed up in tight echelon at Mertzani to march briskly and in good order to Ioannina. Balis expected to meet Germans on the way and wanted his regiment to make a good impression on them; after all, it had remained unbeaten in battle. At the head of this parade-ground column was Captain Koutridis on horseback. On the way, they met a German mechanized unit heading for Mertzani. Zikos observed the German officers saluting Koutridis, who saluted back and continued the battalion's progress. The 19 Regiment was in a hurry to avoid being captured by the Italians but when, in the late afternoon, it reached Perama on the northern outskirts of Ioannina, a German sergeant stopped the men and ordered them by sign language to surrender their weapons and pile them up in a heap. 'It felt like we were throwing away our bones,' Zikos recalled. They had just made a ten-hour forced march and now the soldier's most valuable possession, his weapon, had been taken away. 'We became an unarmed mob marching with difficulty.' At the village of Mazi, where the regiment was to be formally disbanded, the men fell asleep where they dropped.

All the next day, the men lounged at Mazi, wondering what would become of them. Everyone expected the Germans to come and round them up. As discipline and order had all but evaporated, some men from northern Greece simply deserted and began their long trek home. A group of soldiers were sitting around a campfire that evening when one of them pitched forward, dead. Local young delinquents had got hold of some abandoned rifles and were firing them in the air indiscriminately, and a stray bullet had struck the hapless soldier in the heart. He was the last man of the 19 Regiment to die in the war, in such an obscenely meaningless way. On 24 April, Balis mustered what was left of his regiment and tearfully delivered the disbandment speech. Officers and men said goodbye to one another and set off for their homes, some near and some far.

After getting some rest under a tree, in the evening Sergeant-Major Zikos began his own homeward trek under cover of darkness. It was about fifty kilometres to his home in the village of Lakka Souli and he was careful to avoid the main southbound Arta road for fear of German patrols. He was right to be cautious because a fellow-villager in the regiment, Captain Konstantinos Rossis, had gone on horseback down the main road only to run into a German patrol that relieved him of his horse, papers, binoculars and pistol. The theft of the last item was the most galling as the Führer, in an unusual gesture of respect for the Greek fighting man (and probably to give the Italians one in the eye), had allowed all Greek officers to keep their sidearms. But on a lonely Greek country road, who cared?

Chapter 11

Afterwards

The Italian command officially declared an end to hostilities at 6 p.m. on 23 April. That only meant that the shooting was over, not the aggression. The casualty count from the seventeen days of fighting around Hill 731 remains a matter of dispute. After the Albanian campaign, Mussolini put the number of Italians killed in action in six months at 13,502 dead, though almost certainly that number is far too low, as a staggering 25,067 men were reported missing in action – the majority almost certainly killed, either as a result of being blown to bits, pounded into the mud or dying of wounds in remote locations. Many of the men of the Twenty-fifth Corps were Albanian auxiliaries, and a good number of these would have simply deserted and melted into the mountains.

By Greek calculations, rather more than 18,000 Italians were killed and wounded from the start of the Spring Offensive. The battle for Hill 731 alone cost the *Regio Esercito* some 4,000 casualties against about five hundred for the Greeks (3,000 since the start of the offensive). For the Italians, it was an unsustainable loss rate. Four divisions - the Puglie, Bari, Cagliari and Pinerolo, plus the 26th Blackshirts - lost more than half their strength killed, wounded and captured. Hardest hit was the Puglie, with seventy per cent casualties. And this figure probably does not include the 3,000 or so of all divisions taken prisoner.

Reliable information on Italian casualties in the campaign, in fact, is hard to pin down. A purportedly confidential report drawn up by Cavallero, reported in an Italian magazine in 1957, put the total losses at about 11,800, which includes both dead and wounded.

The Eighth and Twenty-fifth Corps were the hardest hit, with about 5,000 casualties each; the less-affected Fourth Corps suffered about 1,800 casualties. Italian losses also must include the prisoners taken by the Greeks during the battle. The large figure for the missing is also hard to assess. It presumably does not include those known to have been taken prisoner. It would include the many soldiers, like Private Pecoraro until recently, that must still be lying in unknown and unmarked graves in Albania. It also very likely includes some 3,900 deserters, of whom three-quarters were Albanian auxiliaries. (A small number of Slavic-speaking Greeks are known to have deserted in the other direction.) Many of those men would find their way into the various partisan armies that would soon spring up all over the Balkans.

During the entire battle for Hill 731, from the start of the Spring Offensive to the Greek surrender to the Germans, the Greek II Corps (1st, 5th, 11th, 15th and 17th Divisions) suffered about 5,300 casualties. The 1st Division was the hardest hit, with 1,700 casualties, including three hundred and one officers and men killed. The 19 Regiment of the 6th Division, seconded to the 1st Division sector and bearing the brunt of the attacks on Hill 731, had nine hundred and twenty casualties including about two hundred and sixty killed.

If the Greek 1st Division losses seem relatively low in view of the ferocity of the battle, it must be remembered that the division – by far the hardest hit of all the II Corps divisions – was fighting on the defensive from well-entrenched positions. Most of the division's losses, in fact, were the result of Italian artillery fire rather than the fury of close-order combat. Given the colossal disparity in casualty figures, it is reasonable to assume that the Greeks could have held out on Hill 731 indefinitely, as long as Cavallero didn't change his costly and unimaginative tactics. And he would have been highly unlikely to do so, as the idea of mass frontal attacks was ultimately Mussolini's.

On the face of it, and belying his inner feelings, Mussolini was publicly jubilant, sending fulsome congratulations to the men. 'After six months of the bitterest struggle, the enemy has laid down his arms, and victory consecrates our bloody sacrifices.' Hitler must have smiled ruefully at that one; the Italians claiming 'victory' was already too preposterous for the Germans to stomach. The Führer's general staff chief, Field Marshal Wilhelm Keitel, scoffed that the Axis allies 'were like children, wanting to gobble up everything'. Hitler conceded one last sop to Mussolini by allowing Geloso to sign a second surrender document with Tsolakoglou. But the Germans, from then on, remained openly contemptuous of the Italians. And it goes without saying that the Greeks heartily shared the sentiment.

To their credit, and unlike the Germans, the great majority of Italian occupying troops treated the subjugated Greeks in a more or less friendly manner. 'It doesn't take much for the Italian soldier to forget his tribulations,' writes Cervi, and it was a rare Italian who continued to detest the Greeks during the occupation. The two Mediterranean peoples had, and have, much in common. It has been claimed convincingly that the three-year Axis occupation of Greece would have been much harsher had not the Italians mitigated some of the more odious policies of the Germans; for example, thousands of Greek Jews owed their survival to the Italians, who often ignored or blocked German roundup orders.

The machinery of occupation was quick to clamp itself into place. The British and Allied troops were gone, evacuated hastily but losing some 15,000 men in the process. On 23 April King George and the remnants of his government fled to Crete. Four days later, a motorized column of the German 6th Mountain Division entered Athens while the people hid indoors; a captain hoisted the swastika on the Acropolis. General Tsolakoglou agreed to head an occupation government under the German thumb. General Geloso, the commander of the Italian Eleventh Army, was given supreme military authority for the Athens area, apparently as a reward for backing the Duce even when the Spring Offensive was obviously falling apart. The Army, whose divisions had senselessly butted their brains out on Hill 731 and sowed the area with innumerable dead, was now policing the Greek capital.

The Duce and Cavallero ensured that the Italian nation was not allowed to forget the sacrifice of its manhood on Hill 731, now called the *Zona Sacra,* or Sacred Zone. On 10 May, King Vittorio Emanuele visited Albania for a week. The bodies littering the hill and its environs by now had been properly buried. According to the King's aide-de-camp, General Paolo Puntoni, emotion barely registered on Vittorio Emanuele's face when he stopped to see the hill. Cavallero pressed for a memorial to be set up at the summit, though his claim that it would symbolize the 'victorious' battle cannot be taken seriously. The Duce agreed, though he of course failed to mention that the men who were sent to their deaths there were double victims – of both Greek action and his own fallacious ideas of strategy. Yet he was right in supposing that the hill and the blood shed on it constituted a heroic chapter in Italian military history. The Italians had the dubious distinction, writes Cervi, of being 'without doubt the worst-led soldiers in the world, but nonetheless, they proved worthy of their Country'.

On 17 May, Cavallero took off from Tirana to return to Rome. A few minutes into the flight, he asked his pilot to make a detour over Hill 731. He saw that a large white cross had been erected on the summit 'where many heroic sons of Italy now rested'. Rome's official Stefani news agency reported from Tirana on 26 May that the Italian-controlled Albanian government had approved the construction of an ossuary on Hill 731 that would house the bones of those who had fallen in the attempt to seize the hill. The wording of the report gave the strong impression to the Italian public that the battle had been an Italian triumph; in front of Hill 731, it said, the Fourth, Eighth and Twenty-fifth Corps had 'repulsed the enemy'. That phrase stood the whole story on its head, as it gave the completely false impression that the Greeks had been the attackers and the Italians the defenders of Hill 731! It was a classic propaganda technique which in this case, however, fooled few, least of all those who actually were there.

And even the Duce, finally, had to ruefully agree with the Führer that the Greeks had put up more of a fight than he had bargained for. Addressing the Grand Council of Corporations on 10 June 1941, he smoothed over the debacle of Hill 731, claiming that, as a result of the battle, the Greek Army had 'practically ceased to exist as a fighting force'. Yet, probably in order to forestall objections from his listeners, many of whom must have known or suspected the truth, he went on to say: 'One must honestly concede that many Greek units fought courageously.' He attributed it, though, to a fanatical hatred of the enemy inculcated by Greek officers. He ended his rambling speech with a ringing confidence that Fascist Italy on the side of the Axis would help bring into being 'a new Europe'.

As with many of Mussolini's utterances during his long career as Italy's Duce, it is always unclear how much of them he actually himself believed and how much was pure political fluff. He must have been aware that from now on, as never before, he would merely be Hitler's Mediterranean office-boy and a none too reliable one at that. He had put the first spanner in the Axis works when he attacked Greece on 28 October 1940, forcing the Führer to revise his plans for Eastern Europe and the Soviet Union. Now, through the failure of the Spring Offensive, Hitler had been forced to save the Balkan situation with a heavy investment in men and equipment rather earlier than he would have liked. And this, of course, brings up the oft-raised question of whether the Greek achievement in battles such as that of Hill 731 upset the wider German timetable and delayed the onset of Operation Barbarossa, thus altering the whole course of World War Two. The operation's initial starting date had been 15 May, whereas the Germans weren't able to move until 22 June. Ergo, the reasoning goes, Greek military successes at least partly must get the credit.

There are problems with this theory. As early as January 1941, Hitler and his staff had all but written off the Italian prospects in Albania and were already deep into planning Operation Barbarossa. They would already have abandoned what hopes they might have had that an Italian-occupied Greece would secure the Wehrmacht's southern flank for the invasion of the Soviet Union. The occupation of Greece was definitely on their list already. The biggest Balkan prize for Nazi Germany was Romania and its oil, which needed protecting from the south, where Bulgaria and Greece lay. At the close of World War One, the Allies had formed a front in northern Greece above Thessaloniki and Hitler didn't want that to happen again. Greece, with its long and convoluted coastline and myriad islands, would be too useful to the Allies and needed to be occupied anyway.

If there was any single event that delayed Operation Barbarossa, that was the Yugoslav coup of 26 March. It was in direct response to it that a fuming Hitler hastily concluded – as the Oberkommando Wehrmacht minutes show – that he might have to delay Barbarossa for 'up to four weeks'. William Shirer, in his seminal *The Rise and Fall of the Third Reich,* calls the decision 'the single most catastrophic in Hitler's career'. Those few weeks of delay, it is now generally agreed, found the Germans overwhelmed by the fearful Russian winter of 1941–42. Much the same can be said for Mussolini's Spring Offensive. Having placed great Napoleonic hopes on it, he had to watch it smashed against the resistance of a stubborn foe on Hill 731. And just as Stalingrad marked the beginning of Hitler's long fall, so Hill 731 and its heaps of dead sounded the end of Mussolini's years of glory; the casualty lists coming in from the Albanian front had woken the Italians to the folly of the campaign and the incompetence of key commanders, and the Duce's reputation at home never recovered.

But history cannot be written like a series of mathematical functions or algorithms where one factor (even if they are all known) slots automatically into its next phase and a precise result comes out. This is especially true of military history. The fog of war never really goes away. In the heat of battle, human experience and perception are warped and subsequent human memory warps them yet more. It is distressingly common for the researcher to come across two or more completely honest, but completely different, eyewitness accounts of the same event. All too often we are forced to use our own fallible judgement to decide which has more of a 'ring of truth'. This also applies in the wider sphere where we are tempted to assess the significance of a single military event – say the battle for Hill 731 – on the wider conflict in which it was a mere detail.

Though it would be hasty to assume that Mussolini's failure at Hill 731 led directly to the German disaster at Stalingrad, by the same token its existence as a factor cannot be ruled out. While Papagos was languishing in a German *Prominenten* camp, he was told by General Franz Halder, himself an inmate after his ousting as German Staff Chief, that it was Greece's seven-month stalling of the Italian offensive that forced Hitler to delay Barbarossa. Looking at the bigger picture, Mussolini's failure certainly did throw a spanner into the Führer's eastern works, and it remains a moot point whether an earlier invasion of Russia might have succeeded if Hitler had not been forced to divert considerable forces to the Balkans in such a big way.

The battle for Hill 731 – and by extension the entire Greek-Italian war in Albania – was a battle between moral as well as material power. Both sides fought heroically; but the morale on the Greek side was undoubtedly superior. This was a result not so much of ideological differences – few soldiers knew or cared about the pros and cons of fascism as a political creed – as sheer patriotism. It can be fairly said that no Greek soldier, from Papagos on down to the lowliest private, had any real doubt that victory would eventually be theirs. In the words of a Greek Army Historical department report of 1966:

> The commands, the staffs and the commanding officers all were inspired by the unshakeable belief that the much-vaunted Italian Spring Offensive would fail, as all the [enemy] actions since the start of the war had failed.

The Italians laboured under far harder moral conditions. They were away from home in menacingly unfamiliar territory, told to fight an enemy who until recently they never imagined to be such, and stunned by the Greeks' facility with the bayonet and the ubiquitous artillery fire. Yet, if they had been competently led at the divisional and corps level, those disadvantages could have been overcome. Greek writers later claimed that the Italian officers dosed their men with brandy before sending them against the shells and bayonets; the origin of the story is attributed to reports that the breath of Italian prisoners reeked of alcohol. The claim strains credulity. Certainly, men in all combat situations have sometimes had recourse to the bottle to blunt their fear, but to suggest that the Italians' courage was alcohol-fuelled is not only to unacceptably impugn their reputation but to make idiots out of their commanders. A drunk soldier can never be an efficient soldier; in fact, it would make him more likely to do anything but fight.

Mussolini castigated his commanders for alleged incompetence; but what he failed to realize was that he had put those commanders in an impossible position. Cavallero, a very able officer, did his best, but a question must be raised over his use of repeated mass futile attacks against Hill 731. In hindsight, Cavallero appears to have placed too much faith in the preparatory artillery barrages before each assault. These were World War One-era Verdun-type tactics, unsuitable for the craggy terrain of Albania that afforded the defenders plenty of natural cover, not to mention an advantage in height. Instead of charging over open, flat ground – as the British did at the Somme in 1916, even then to their huge cost – the Puglie and Bari Divisions had to go up against steep heights. The thinking here appears to have been that the sight of massed advancing columns would intimidate the defenders as well as knit morale more tightly among the men themselves. That proved to be an illusion. Also, the average Italian soldier was poorly trained, if at all, in mountain warfare, a technique that came more naturally to the Greeks.

It was in their use of artillery and mortars, and the close liaison between them, that the Italians inflicted the most casualties on the

Greeks. From the first day of the battle for Hill 731, Geloso's massed artillery carefully ranged first along the Greek front line and then gradually lengthened the range to six kilometres in the Greek rear down the Desnitsa Valley. These barrages usually lasted about three hours, after which the infantry was sent in. The afternoons usually saw desultory salvoes targeted at the Berat-Kelçyre road as well as preparatory barrages for night attacks. Four days into the battle, these artillery tactics had caused grave damage to the Greek positions.

On the Greek side, a key ingredient in eventual success was the readiness with which the battered front-line units counter-attacked as soon as the Italian infantry had come within range. Whereas the Italians were proficient in screening their attacks with barrages of offensive grenades, the Greek specialty was the bayonet. The bitterest and most brutal fighting occurred during ferocious Greek downhill bayonet charges on an enemy already fatigued from coming up the hill. It was this tactic, more than any other, that assured Cavallero's failure.

Cavallero himself appeared to believe his own delusions to the end. In comments to foreign journalists, he insisted that the whole Italian campaign in Albania had been a 'victory', and that though the Greek soldier was 'a superb fighter,' in the end it was not the Greeks but 'adverse weather and terrain conditions' that were the true enemies.

Have you seen the mountains [he asked the correspondents]? Then you would understand that real significance of the achievements of the Italian soldiers who tamed those unapproachable peaks in the face of heavy fire from a stubborn foe. I fought in the [First] World War at Carso and can assure you that the difficulties that the Italian Army overcame in Albania were incomparably greater than those it faced in the eastern Alps.

He was not wrong there; but what he naturally failed to mention was that the Greeks, too, faced the same incredibly harsh conditions. And in a fight where the problems of weather and terrain were common to both sides, though the courage of the Italians in general was leonine, the Greeks proved to have the superior endurance. Cavallero, though supremely clever, was essentially a managerial-type commander; unlike an inspired leader of men, he thought in purely technical terms: an accurately-calculated x application of men and shells at target y should obtain the desired result z. Beyond that he seemed unable to go, which would explain why he believed that the end result of the Albanian campaign was a 'victory' in that ultimately Greece caved in to the Axis, rather than through any efforts of his own.

Papagos seemed content to quietly accept a quiet life in retirement under the German jackboot; the occupiers had guaranteed his safety as long as he caused them no trouble. But the soldier in him couldn't accept that. Fearing that the communists were taking over the armed resistance movement, he decided to form another. However, in July 1943, before it could take shape, the Gestapo arrested him and four other ex-generals (including Pitsikas of the TSH) and sent them off to prison camps in Germany. At the end of the war, Papagos was again given command of the Greek General Staff, masterminding the civil war against the communist-led forces attempting to install a Soviet style regime and drag Greece behind the Iron Curtain. With that war won and Greece's membership of the free world assured, Papagos was elevated to field marshal, the only non-royal Greek ever to achieve that rank. In 1952, he retired from the Army and entered politics, being elected prime minister on the strength of his military record. He died of cancer in 1955.

Zikos lived quietly in his mountain village for about a year, until a former general named Napoleon Zervas got together a resistance organization to fight the German and Italian occupiers. Though Zervas had been responsible for at least one anti-royalist attempted coup in the past, many patriotic Greeks believed him preferable to the communist groups who were beginning to dominate the resistance movement. Zikos brought his combat experience to Zervas' guerrilla army, the National Democratic Revolutionary League (EDES), and was put in command of the intimidatingly-named Death Company, whose task was to eliminate communists as well as Axis troops, as a captain. The men of the Death Company, armed to the teeth, sported a skull and crossbones on their black berets and Zikos had himself photographed wearing one. (Zervas himself had started out on the centre-left but, faced with the direct communist menace, had veered to the far right.)

In a firefight with German troops in the mountains of Epiros, not far from the Albanian border, on 22 October 1943, Zikos was wounded, but not seriously. He saw the resistance through to its successful conclusion in October 1944, when the last German soldiers left and Greece was free again – to plunge almost at once into a savage civil war between the communist-dominated bulk of the resistance and the British-backed nationalist government of King George II. The communist insurrection took five years to crush, thanks to the energies of Papagos, who was again the Greek Army commander-in-chief, and strong British and American backing. Zikos served through it as commander of the National Army's 581st Infantry Battalion.

In July 1942, General Zervas awarded Zikos the Silver Medal for Valour for his action at Hill 731. That was followed in October 1948 and October 1949 by two Gold Medals, conferred this time by the Army, for fighting the communists. By the time of his retirement as a lieutenant colonel in 1959, he had amassed ten decorations. Twelve years later he wrote his definitive account of the battle for Hill 731, publishing it in 1973. In the book's closing paragraphs he pays a gallant and generous soldierly tribute to his Italian foes, dismissing the popular Greek prejudice of their inferiority in battle.

The reality was completely different. The enemy was tough. His actions were calculated and decisive; the Italians were stubborn fighters. The struggle was waged in front of and over the trenches. The conflict was stupendous, the struggle titanic.

General Bakos, the II Corps commander, accepted the post of defence minister in Tsolakoglou's occupation administration, with his counterpart of the I Corps and three ex-division commanders – all decorated veterans of the Albania campaign – assuming other cabinet posts. The actions of these officers in collaborating with the occupiers naturally came under scathing criticism after the war; Bakos himself was widely accused of harbouring Nazi sentiments. It was the classic case of 'it's a rotten job but someone has to do it.' Tsolakoglou himself believed he was doing his stricken people a service by keeping the civil administration and economy going and acting as a buffer between his masters and a bitterly hostile and starving population. The ex-officers who helped him were no doubt moved by the same considerations. But, unfortunately, it did nothing to help their postwar reputations. In December 1944, two months after the last German left Greek soil, communist insurgents captured Bakos and executed him as a collaborator. Tsolakoglou himself was sentenced to death for high treason but died in jail before the sentence could be carried out.

General Vrachnos, the 1st Division commander, convened his officers on 28 April to inform them that the division was to all intents and purposes imprisoned by the Germans. They agreed to his suggestion that General Bakos, the II Corps commander, should negotiate the fate of the Army. Colonel Ketseas of the 4 Regiment proposed that the Army refuse Axis demands to fight against fellow-Greeks, some of whom had armed resistance as an option, and gained general agreement. That same day, the 1st Division received orders to move to Metsovo in north-west Greece. Vrachnos was arrested by the Italians on 29 September 1942 and transported to Italy as essentially a hostage for the good behaviour of the subjugated Greeks, there to remain until he was freed in May 1945. Three years later, Vrachnos retired from the Army as a lieutenant general and entered politics as a member of the conservative National Rally Party of Field Marshal Papagos and, when the latter won the election of

1952 and became prime minister, served as an undersecretary for the interior. Until his death in 1971, he lobbied the Army Historical Directorate to issue a definitive work on the battle for Hill 731. The lack of response caused him great bitterness that can be felt in a newspaper article he wrote in 1969, lambasting the failure of successive governments to set up a memorial to the men of his division who held on to Hill 717.

> Governments since 1945 until today, as well as the Army leadership, are totally unjustified in this neglect, at a time when memorial services have been held, and monuments and cenotaphs and statues have been put up for battles of less significance than those of the Italian Spring Offensive. They have not said a single word about those who fell and held on to the legendary Hill 731 – out of envy, I imagine – as no member of government since then had been in the government in 1940-1941.

Sadly, this is all too typical of postwar democratic governments. There is understandably a prevailing desire to forget recent horrors and privations, disband the citizen-armies, dispense with militarism and get on with ordinary life. This did not happen in Greece where, until this day the praiseworthy achievements of the Greek Army in 1940-1941 have become knit into the grand national narrative. Yet Hill 731 receives precious little remembrance. In Vrachnos' view, his 1st Division had performed superhumanly against the combined assaults of two Italian army corps, preventing them from barrelling down the Desnitsa Valley towards the Greek frontier. So important was that objective that even Mussolini had gone to the front to lead for himself.

Major Dimitrios Kaslas' post-war life was a curious and rather sad one. In the autumn of 1941 Bakos, now the defence minister in the occupation administration, awarded him the Military Cross Third Class. However, like Zikos, Kaslas fretted at having to live inactive under Axis occupation and joined Zervas' EDES guerrilla resistance group in the mountains. EDES, however, soon found it had to fight two foes at once: the Germans and the communist-led rival resistance army, ELAS. During one skirmish with ELAS, Kaslas was captured but was soon appointed to command the ELAS 52 Regiment. The reasons for his switch of allegiance are far from clear. ELAS, partly thanks to its communist control (and British aid) had become the dominant armed resistance group in Greece and Kaslas might well have thought he could become more useful in its ranks. It is also conceivable that he may been compelled to serve through some threat or blackmail. On the other hand, the available evidence strongly suggests that he could have genuinely converted to far-left views.

With the end of the war and the restoration of a British backed royal government in Greece, Kaslas was classified as a 'dangerous' subversive and packed off to prison camps on the Greek islands. Three years later he was freed and pardoned and retired with the rank of lieutenant colonel. The experience, though, embittered him against the army he had served so well on Hill 731. Plagued by ill-health, Dimitrios Kaslas died in 1966, aged sixty-five. In 1985, a socialist government posthumously promoted him to brigadier in recognition of his services to the wartime resistance. (The Athens Academy placed him on its roster of distinguished officers of the Greek-Italian War.)

After Albania, Cavallero was sent to head the Italian forces in North Africa and promoted to field marshal. But the reverse at El Alamein helped put an end to his career, to the delight of his many enemies at home. When Mussolini was toppled in September 1943 by Field Marshal Badoglio, he attempted to ingratiate himself with the new pro-Allied administration but apparently failed. He remained close to the German commander in Italy, Field Marshal Albert Kesselring with whom he dined in a hotel near Rome on 13 September 1943. The next morning, Cavallero was found dead in the hotel garden with a gunshot wound to the head. The general historical consensus is that he committed suicide, though some sources raise the possibility that the Germans could have murdered him after he refused to collaborate with them.

The course of the whole campaign does not throw a good light on the Italian senior command, in contrast to the brave men at the front. The old phrase 'lions led by donkeys' comes to mind here. After a four-month gradual retreat under Greek pressure, the Duce and Cavallero seemed to have had no original ideas but to fall back on World War One-type mass infantry attacks preceded by an artillery softening-up. There is a strong flavour of the tragedy of the bone-headed 1916 Somme attacks in the relentless hammering at Hill 731 and the heaps of casualties it produced. Cavallero has been severely criticized for insisting on a narrow six-kilometre front for his Spring Offensive, but the sheer intractability of the Albanian landscape probably gave him little choice. To be sure, he did try feints and diversionary flank attacks to ease the pressure on the centre, but they were never pressed forward very resolutely. Too much faith was placed in the big guns and the attack aircraft. When both proved not to be up to the task, it was the infantry that had to pay. The narrow attacking front forced Cavallero to send in his men in dense formations that proved highly vulnerable to artillery shelling and the Greeks' sudden bayonet counter-attacks.

The Greek is a more intractable and complex, as well as hardier character than the Italian, quicker to anger and resentment of wrongs. This, of course, is a sweeping generalization admitting of a great many exceptions. But the whole course of the war in Albania, and especially the bloody climax at Hill 731, appears to have hinged on this difference. The quality of the fighting men on both sides was the same – undeniably high. It was the emotional heat of the Greeks' cause – defence against an unprovoked aggressor – that gave their troops' the will to fight and survive in one of the least hospitable battlefields imaginable. It provided the true bulwark of Hill 731, against which even the most desperate courage of the Italians failed and gave Cavallero (not to mention Mussolini) his keenest frustration.

Another Greek advantage was that the average soldier was fighting on more or less familiar ground. Many hailed from poor mountain villages not unlike those of Albania and had competently handled firearms from boyhood; the transition from hunting to military rifle was easy and, being used to the crude slaughter of animals for food, they were far from squeamish at the sight of blood. They also knew that, when on leave, they wouldn't have far to go home. Most of the Italians, on the other hand, had not grown up anywhere near mountains and a higher proportion were town boys whose baptism of fire was, in consequence, far rougher. Also, they were carried across the sea to an alien and forbidding environment that positively cultivated homesickness and fear of the unknown, as countless soldiers' letters attest. Nevertheless, if the Italian troops had been adequately supplied with apparel and provisions in the terrible Albanian winter, morale could have been kept up. The Greeks, too, suffered badly from hunger and cold and disease, but what kept Hill 731 in their hands was that intangible factor of character – a sheer bloody-minded doggedness and conviction that the enemy had no business taking back even a square foot of what they had been driven from at great cost.

On the other hand, it is an established fact that Italians in tricky situations seemed ready to surrender in large numbers, which surprised even the Greeks. One explanation might be that the privations and sufferings of the troops in Albania had spawned hopes that in Greek hands they might get a bit more to eat and be better sheltered. Officers such as those of the Blackshirts, who were indoctrinated in fascism and contemptuous of the Greeks, remained defiant in captivity. But the great majority of Italian prisoners felt at the very least a sense of relief that their war was over. And, in general, the Greeks treated them well.

Religious faith also loomed large among the soldiers of both sides, buttressing resolve. As we have seen, perhaps the majority of Italian soldiers were country boys brought up under the twin cultural roofs of Roman Catholicism and the Duce's fascist ideology. Though the Vatican essentially opposed fascism and the idea of political dictatorship, on the other hand it saw in the Duce's system of respect for country and family the same values that it had always favoured and deemed essential for society. Pope Pius XII, in office for less than two years in 1940, looked more kindly on this disciplinary aspect of Roman Catholicism than his more liberal predecessor, Pius XI. The view of giving up one's life for one's country was equated to dying for the faith. Some commentators have seen this as a complete surrendering of ecclesiastical to political authority but its effect on the sense of duty of the average Italian soldier is undeniable.

The soldiers' letters home are full of devout prayers for their ultimate deliverance. The chaplain was a key person in the average company and took his boys' spiritual welfare very seriously – they were readier to listen to him than to Fascist Party ideologues in the ranks. 'The chaplain embodied the village priest,' says historian Davide Rodogno. 'The moral aspect was a fundamental component of the health not only of the soldier per se but of the soldiery as a whole.' Faith was the factor that made an otherwise intolerable and ugly conflict bearable for the Italians, many of whom touchingly looked forward, as did Giovanni De Pizzol, to the hour when 'the Holy Virgin helps me return healthy and Victorious.' (He did indeed get home in one piece, never ceasing to thank God for being able once more to see 'my dear parents and brothers, my girl friend and all my friends and fellow-villagers and my great Italy'.) Many Italians made a point of seeking absolution from sins before going into combat. In the evenings, the chaplains would lead prayers 'for us and our loved ones, and then other prayers for our comrades at the front and the poor dead, and thus the day would close.'

On the Greek side, too, Christian faith was very strong, and just as basic an element in patriotism and battlefield valour. In reflecting what helped the Greeks hang on to Hill 731, Zikos credited the versatility and toughness of the average Greek soldier, the excellent camaraderie between officers and men and, to be fair, the sheer strength of the position they were called on to hold. But by far the main factor, he forthrightly asserted, was 'the fighters' faith in God, Christ, the Virgin Mary and all the Saints to whom we prayed constantly'.

> Our faith had reached its apex. We had confidence, and saw clearly, that we lived and breathed under the roof of God. Hundreds of thousands of shells were fired at us but despite that, the number of killed was not large. A single shell from our artillery would kill two or three Italians... One soldier of 9 Company who was blasphemous and for that reason despised by the rest of us, was in an isolated shelter when he received a direct hit from a heavy artillery shell. His body was smashed into so many pieces that it was useless to try and bury him.

It may well be, as is often said, that there are no atheists in a foxhole. But the faith of those Italian and Greek soldiers who were devout was of a different order to a mere taking out of 'spiritual insurance' when death loomed. It was inculcated since childhood and though many, of course, would apparently fall away from the faith growing up (especially those of 'higher' education), faith in a deep sense would never really go away. And at the moment it was needed, it would be there as a prime component of military courage and skill.

A main protagonist of all wars up to about the middle of the twentieth century is the humble yet hardy mule. For centuries this animal, all but unsung, has done all the hard transport work of armies while sharing the dangers with the men. The Albanian campaign was perhaps the last in Europe in which mules played key role in supplying the men at the front. Albania had few roads fit for automobiles and only mule trains could scale its forbidding heights. The affection that supply officers felt for their long-suffering charges can be likened to that which cavalrymen felt for their horses. One such officer, Second Lieutenant Hesiod Tsingos, the 'crazy' company commander of the 14 Regiment who had scaled the snowbound heights of Trebeshinës back in January, described how a mule he was leading slipped while fording an icy torrent:

> The storm was approaching. I tried to help the mule get up, but it couldn't move. It had either broken its leg or got it trapped. I did what I could to raise it up, but in vain. It stayed there motionless and looked at me. I didn't know that animals' eyes could speak... Its look showed it was in despair. I tried to avoid looking at those eyes full of pain. It was just the two of us, alone in a wilderness.

As storm clouds began to gather overhead, Tsingos stroked his mule and spoke to it: 'Hang in there. I'll go and get my platoon and save you. We owe you some of our victory, you know? You've always been faithful and obedient. We'll have you back on your feet.' But Tsingos really had no idea what to do. Night was falling. He had foolishly allowed the three soldiers in his supply train to go on ahead; all he had was an Albanian guide. Seeing the pain in the mule's eyes, he confessed that he cried like a baby. 'I'll stay here with you,' he told the animal between sobs. 'Don't be afraid.'

Then the storm broke and soon Tsingos found himself up to his waist in rushing water. The mule's head began to sink beneath the surface. 'Shoot it! Shoot it!' the Albanian guide shouted. Better the mule should die instantly than be drowned.

> I pulled out my Beretta (captured from the Italians) and pressed the barrel against the mule's head but I had neither the courage

nor the strength to pull the trigger. In that hell I heard the Albanian shouting, 'Shoot it, shoot it!' A salvo of shots was heard.

The shots came from another second lieutenant and three enlisted men who had come to look for Tsingos and rescue him if he was in trouble and had put the mule out of its misery. Tsingos managed to mount another mule. Shivering with shock and fever, he felt nothing but 'a limitless sadness, an unprecedented bitterness permeating my whole being'.

Throughout the ages one of the basic tasks of national leaders has been to mobilize the nation's manpower (and more recently womanpower) when necessary to uphold national interests by force. Today's presidents and prime ministers are no exception; in fact, it would be a pretty poor leader who declined the responsibility. Benito Mussolini in that respect was no different from Winston Churchill, Franklin Roosevelt, or any other 'democratic' politician voted into power. His vision was a clear one – to raise Italy's prestige and power through foreign conquest. It was, of course, a tragically misguided vision, and his own character flaws ensured its failure. But it was nonetheless genuine and had the support of a good many of his compatriots, in and out of uniform.

The Greeks stood in his way and were, of course, quite right to do so. The *Regio Esercito* suffered much the same fate in Greece as the Luftwaffe had in the Battle of Britain a few months before. The Duce's reverses in Albania, however, were overwhelmingly the result of poor intelligence and wrong advice provided by a servile and incompetent cabal, civil and military, rather than anything intrinsically wrong with the fighting qualities of the Italian soldier, who continues to be quite as good as any. That was the great tragedy of Hill 731. Thousands of men were sacrificed for an impossible dream.

The Italians attached far more importance to the memory of the battle. As we have seen, as early as 26 March 1941, before the battle was formally over, Rome's Stefani News Agency had announced the Duce's decision to build a monument on Hill 731 in which the remains of the fallen Italians would be interred. The Fourth, Eighth and Twenty-fifth Corps were held in great esteem. Vrachnos wondered why his 1st Division was not similarly honoured at home. In April 1967, a military junta seized power in Greece; Vrachnos hoped that the martial spirit of its leaders, some of whom were veterans of the Albania campaign, might move them to redress the balance but little, if anything, was done.

Colonel Balis, the 19 Regiment commander, used the tedious months and years of the occupation to set down his experiences in the Italian Spring Offensive and defence of Hill 731 that became an important source for later accounts. Colonel Ketseas, of the 51 Infantry Regiment that first seized Hill 731 and played a key role in the initial stages of its defence, had meanwhile been transferred to command the 4 Regiment. During the occupation, he escaped to the British in the Middle East where, along with many other officers and enlisted men, he joined the Greek Army in exile. Ketseas became second-in-command of the Sacred Band, a crack unit that fought in all the Allied campaigns from El Alamein through to Italy.

General Carlo Geloso, the commander of the Duce's Eleventh Army, was given command of the 93,000 Italian occupation troops in Greece. Hardly had he taken up his new task than he began to chafe under the arrogance of the Germans who looked upon the Italians as second-raters and temperamentally incapable of enforcing ruthless rule. As we have seen, Geloso was able to mitigate the harsher aspects of the Germans' methods, such as saving many Greek Jews from the death camps. But he was a stickler for discipline, often reminding his men to 'always keep in mind that the army is made for war'.

Nonetheless, as the occupation dragged on and the tide of war began to turn, Geloso's occupation troops turned against the whole idea. It became common for inebriated soldiers emerging from taverns to bawl *'Porco Mussolini!'* ('Pig Mussolini!'), no doubt delighting the Greeks and arguably helping lay the foundation for the close postwar friendship between the two nations. But it did not augur well for Geloso who, when Mussolini was toppled in 1943, was arrested and sent to a German prison camp. The following year, the Russians liberated the camp and Geloso briefly became their prisoner before being repatriated. He died in Rome in 1957.

Private Giovanni De Pizzol of the 72 Regiment found himself suppressing revolts against Italian rule in Albania and neighbouring Montenegro, where he recorded his impressions of the local ethnic and religious animosities in detail, before being shipped back to his home near Tezze. Lieutenant Finestra of the 115th Littoria Legion entered politics after the war, becoming a senator with the hard-right *Movimento Sociale Italiano* as well as mayor of the borough of Latina, In 1982 he published his war memoir entitled *Ad Ogni Costo (At All Costs)* ; he died in 2012, aged ninety-one.

The Greek Army has ample reason to be proud of the 1st Division's successful defence of Hill 731. Yet the achievement, as we have seen, has been curiously downplayed at home. One reason perhaps is that it was chronologically too close to the Greek capitulation to the Germans for it to have any real strategic value. To have won a fierce seventeen-day battle only to see Geloso's Italians parading in Athens within weeks disturbs the narrative too much. The sequence is something that just shouldn't have happened. Few books have been written about the battle *per se* – as opposed to copious volumes about the Greek-Italian War in general – but they tell a tremendous story of endurance and valour without, above all, trying to score political or historiographical points.

Something similar has happened on the Italian side, as a lingering sense of shame that Italy fought alongside Hitler's Germany has put the bravery of Italy's soldiers also in the shade. It is hard to find, besides Cavallero's memoirs and Mario Cervi's seminal history, extensive specific narratives about Hill 731. In 1941, a lieutenant named Francesco Gioffreda, who fought at Hill 731 and was wounded, composed a military march to the memory of the battle, called 'Quota Monastero 731' after his return home. Only recently has the piece become available on YouTube; it is subdued and touchingly melodic, evoking reverence while avoiding bombast – the most fitting tribute yet to the brave men of the Italian Eleventh Army who, because they fought like lions for a tragically futile cause, have been in danger of being forgotten by military history.

Chapter 12

For some it isn't over

In the morning of 22 January 2018, teams began digging into a strip of land squeezed between two formidable heights at Dragoti, a village near Kelçyre at the southern end of the Desnitsa Valley. Years of research by Giorgos Sourlas, a Greek former cabinet minister, had indicated that the remains of some seven hundred Greek soldiers were there, buried in a mass grave by the Italians during their move southwards after the battle for Hill 731. It had taken the Greek authorities no fewer than seventy-seven years to talk the Albanians into allowing the humanitarian exhumation to take place. For years, a rusty metal cross had marked the spot. As the diggers unearthed bones and skull fragments, observed by Sourlas, Albanian protesters gathered at a distance shouting anti-Greek slogans.

For the relatives of those soldiers, it has been a long wait. As World War Two gave way to the Cold War, Albania was impressed into the communist bloc. The regime in Tirana became notorious for its Stalinist-type dictatorship, extreme even by Soviet standards, which banned even private cars and mercilessly hounded anyone even mildly suspected of having a religious belief. For forty-five years, this tiny corner of Europe firmly shut itself away from the world as the bones of the fallen Italians and Greeks mouldered under fields and on hillsides, all but forgotten.

To the Italians, however, the memory of the *Zona Sacra* could not be allowed to fade. The thought of their brave men lying untended behind the hardest of iron curtains moved the Italian government in 1962 to open negotiations with the Albanian regime. Two years later, all the identified remains of Cavallero's fallen had been repatriated to Italy for honourable burial; no-one wanted an Italian military cemetery on Albanian soil where no relatives would be allowed to visit and the possibility of politically-motivated vandalism was high. Of course, the remains of many more Italians remained undiscovered, as in the case of Private Matteo Pecoraro of the 8 Infantry Regiment, who was cut down in an assault on Bregu Psarit in January 1941. And of him, that was all that was known.

But his family kept his memory alive. In October 2003 Don Nicola Pecoraro, a priest from Salerno, travelled to Albania to try and find the remains of his uncle Matteo. The death had never been recorded as official. 'You must never forget Matteo,' his mother would say. Matteo's devout sister Giannina was tireless in scouring official records for some indication of his fate. The records indicated the area of Bregu Psarit where the 8 Regiment was in action. As recorded in the Salerno daily newspaper *Il Mattino* on 23 October 2003, on Don Nicola's first visit to Bregu Psarit, his search led him to a local octogenarian woman named Feruze Malko who knew of a spot where an Italian soldier was buried near her home.

Feruze Malko had reason to be grateful to the Italians. During the fight for Bregu Psarit, her house had served as a billet for Italian troops. On 14 January 1941, during a Greek bombardment a shell fragment had wounded her and killed her two-year-old son. She had recovered in a field hospital. She told Don Nicola that tending the grave of the unknown Italian was 'a way of saying thank you' for the care. On Don Nicola's second visit, he was accompanied by the Italian ambassador and military attaché in Tirana and a local team of diggers. Feruze Malko pointed to a small heap of stones and the diggers began shovelling away the mouldy earth beneath.

Twenty-five centimetres down, they came on an intact skeleton in Italian army uniform. Don Nicola's pulse raced. Of course, there was no way of knowing just then whose the remains were; they could have belonged to any one of seven men of the 8 Regiment listed as missing after the battle at Bregu Psarit. Nevertheless, he felt close enough to his goal to reach for his cellphone and call home with the news. The team brought in a metal detector, which located precisely the eight mortar shell fragments that had killed the soldier. But his identity would remain a mystery until the bones were sent for DNA testing at Salerno. There, the following year, the test confirmed that Private Matteo Pecoraro, the well-liked and sensitive young man who had been proud to fight for his country (whatever its leadership), could at last come home. A guard of honour stood to attention over the plain wooden casket in Salerno cathedral as Don Nicola officiated over a memorial Mass for his uncle. He also pledged publicly to search for other unknown Italians who disappeared in what a speaker at the ceremony called 'a useless war,' as well he might.

The scattered bodies of some 8,000 Greeks, however, were done no such favour. With Albania essentially a closed state after the war, no Greek government felt confident of doing any business at all with the hard-line Tirana regime. A half-hearted attempt at talks on establishing a Greek military cemetery in Albania got started in 1973, but with a hard-left communist regime in Tirana and a hard-right military-backed dictatorship in Athens, the attempt fizzled. The Tirana regime's laws were merciless: for example, anyone found guilty of having aided or cared for a Greek soldier during the war faced a long jail term. After Albanian communism collapsed in 1991, new hope surged among the relatives of the missing. Sourlas decided to reopen the campaign for a search for the thousands of bodies known to be under the ground at some one hundred and ninety locations, never properly buried or marked. For years, he had been a fierce critic of what he saw as a lack of official interest in recovering the remains of those men.

Yet post-communist democratic Albanian governments have been hardly more cooperative. For decades, the Tirana authorities have mistrusted the large ethnic Greek minority in the south of the country and to this day continue to fear that setting up Greek military cemeteries, for example, with the Greek flag flying over them could stoke separatist tendencies. Relatives' visits were strongly discouraged, but that didn't faze, for example, Evangelia Fatsea, the granddaughter of (still-undiscovered) Sergeant-Major Haralambos Kyriakakis of the 14 Regiment, 5th (Cretan) Division, II Corps. She wrote in 2005: 'Is there any other case in human history where some people either refuse or cannot be bothered to gather up the bones of their dead heroes?' Every October, Evangelia with her sister and elderly mother make the tiring journey from Crete to the crags of Albania, taking with them a framed photograph of Sergeant-Major Kyriakakis, keeping alive the hope that his remains might one day come to light.

It wasn't until 2005 that Sourlas was able to visit the battlefields of Albania himself. For years ethnic Greeks in the region had been surreptitiously tending the makeshift graves of unknown soldiers in garden plots and fields, and lighting candles over them. Sourlas relates that, during one visit, a local person turned on him and said, 'Where were you all this time?' At Përmet, east of Kelçyre, Sourlas found that a large area previously designated as containing the common grave of 1,400 men had been covered by sports facilities and a newly-laid football pitch. At two churches in Kelçyre, two hundred and eighty-three ossuaries contain the recovered personal items of unknown soldiers, such as watch straps, uniform buttons and shoulder straps. The bones of those men rest in a monastery not far from the town.

That Greece was finally able to have its own men buried in proper military cemeteries in Albania was the result of some Greek diplomatic hardball. In November 2008, the Greek and Albanian governments had finally signed an agreement for two Greek cemeteries to be created on Albanian soil – one at Kelçyre and the other at Bularat, closer to the Greek border. The deal was ratified by the Albanian Parliament in March 2010, yet nothing appeared to have been done to implement this decision. At that time, Albania was signalling its desire to join the European Union. That, of course, required the backing of EU member Greece. Ironically, it took a leftwing Greek government in 2015 to state flatly that Athens would veto Albanian EU membership unless the 2010 agreement were put into effect – a policy, it should be said, that was backed by the entire Greek political establishment. That threat collected minds in Tirana, which gave way in October 2016. Yet such was the Albanian dilatoriness that it took another Greek threat to veto Albania's EU plan to get Edi Rama, the Albanian prime minister, to finally sign the order to set up the cemeteries.

Greek forensic teams continue to DNA test bone fragments recovered at the known burial sites, and at this writing have identified nearly 1,100, leaving some 6,800 samples yet to be analysed. A little over seven hundred and eighty remains are now officially interred in the cemeteries at Kelçyre and Bularat. And yet more remain missing and may never be found.

Hill 731 is still there, but these days it might more accurately be called Hill 725, as the Duce's shells blasted a full six metres off the top. Even today, getting there requires some determination. The most practical way of doing it is to go overland from Greece, crossing the border at Kakavia. One can go by car or by one of the coaches leaving Athens regularly for the seven-hour scenic journey. Alternately, one can fly from Athens to Ioannina, and from there hire a car to Kakavia twenty minutes away. In either car or bus, be prepared for some delay there, as the ever-watchful Albanian police scrutinize your travel documents. Once through, it's twenty more minutes to the first moderate-sized town, Gjirokaster, which boasts a picturesque Old Town and a few excellent modern hotels at rates one-quarter to one-third of what an equivalent hotel would cost in a European city. A list of Gjirokaster hotels can be found on the internet.

An overnight stay at Gjirokaster is advisable, as one needs to be fresh for a further half-hour drive (or bus ride) to Kelçyre. Here, though, a local driver and guide is needed, preferably with a high-clearance jeep or SUV and strong seat belts! The road northwards through the Desnitsa Valley is narrow but good – until just past the small town of Ballaban, where it ends with startling suddenness, giving way to a gravel track. This track – what remains of the wartime Kelçyre-Berat road – gets progressively worse as it winds and bumps around the south western flank of Hill 731, with a sheer drop into the Proi Math ravine on the left. A truly bone-jarring thirty-minute ride brings one to the north end, where the track ends; you complete on foot the hundred or so yards to the top, where a marble monument (sadly vandalized by locals) marks the Greek defence of the hill. Lower down stands an equally battered and insecure memorial to the sacrifices of the Puglie Division.

Caution is required. An unknown number of the many thousands of shells and bombs aimed at Hill 731 lurk unexploded beneath the surface; an especially heavy rain can bring the occasional one up to the top. Shell fragments, cartridges and even helmets continue to litter the slopes around the summit. If the hill were more accessible it would be a souvenir-hunters' paradise. A few deep holes indicate where human remains have recently been unearthed. The guide (such as the one I hired for 50 euros – much preferred over the local currency – for the punishing round trip from Kelçyre) will be willing to join in the search for relics – but stay away from intact-looking rusty shells!

Other than those signs of war, Hill 731 is a most idyllic place. It is as pleasantly green as the surrounding countryside. The only sounds are the hilltop breeze and the distant tinkle of sheep and goat bells. Mussolini's eyrie at Komarit to the north is clearly visible, as are Hill 717 and Mali Spadarit to the north-east. To the west the Trebeshinë range looms as forbiddingly as ever, especially when crowned by a wreath of dark rain clouds and thunder echoes through the Desnitsa Valley. On my own visit in October 2019, as I was strolling back to the jeep a mini-bus full of Italians had just driven up, and I spent a moving few minutes with them at the Puglie Division memorial; after all, to the Italians the hill is still a *Zona Sacra*. One hopes that as more Greeks and Italians with an interest (perhaps a personal one) in Hill 731 make the demanding trip, the Albanian authorities – who desperately want to improve their tourism image – just might fix up the road.

Obtaining a guide can be done through the Greek Army 1940 Re-enacting Team, accessible at www.es1940.gr (e-mails to maran2911@gmail.com). This is a nineteen-member civilian volunteer organization that has painstakingly made its own 1940-era uniforms and insignia, even down to the precise shade of khaki, and obtained genuine Mannlicher rifles and Gnutti bayonets. They are regularly called on to dress up and inject life into pageants and other ceremonies in memory of World War Two.

Of course nothing, not even the most technologically advanced video reconstruction, can recreate the harrowing reality not only of Hill 731 but of countless such bitter battles in history. This book, with its and its author's limited means, is merely a small tribute to the incredibly brave men, Italian and Greek, who did what very few of us, in our day and age, could ever manage.

The fog of war – of any war – never really goes away. And here we might return to George Kitsos, with whose somewhat melancholy reflections this book opens. He went on to write:

> It is possible that in one or two centuries young Greeks will stand in front of pictures hanging on the walls of icy museums and gaze indifferently at the great leaders of 1941 and be unable to imagine how those people did what history says they did.

Such a psychological distance is the root of revisionism, the temptation to rewrite history in light of our own prejudices and the current intellectual fashion and to claim with numbing certainty that we have magically come upon the 'real' story (hoping to earn a handsome profit in the process). A noted British airman, Squadron Leader George 'Johnny' Johnson, an ex-Dam Buster, shortly before his death echoed Kitsos' sentiments a good deal more bluntly in his 2014 book *The Last British Dambuster* (London: Ebury Press, p. 193):

> What do the revisionist historians think they can contribute? These people make me bloody angry. If I were ever to meet one, I would have to hope that someone would hold my hands behind my back. I have only two questions for them. Were you there? Do you have any idea of what it was like?

I will consider this narrative a success of sorts if through the eyes of those who were there I have to some degree tried to recreate, even faintly, the 'idea of what it was like.'

Bibliographical Note

I have chosen not to use footnotes or chapter notes in this book, preferring a general description of my source material at the end. The reason is that the overwhelming bulk of this material is in Greek and Italian, hence not available in English, and it would make little sense to put the customary superscripts in the text, as very few readers would be in a position to refer to the original sources. Therefore I say, in effect, trust me, as I have done everything possible to ensure accuracy in translation.

From the Italian side, the standard text to consult on the Albanian campaign is Mario Cervi's *Storia della Guerra di Grecia* (Milan: BUR 2001), also available in English as *Hollow Legions*. Cervi collates other, earlier material that is now out of print, such as the diary and memoirs of General Ugo Cavallero. An internet search has turned up several intriguing accounts by Italian soldiers at the front, including the moving story of the recovery of the remains of Private Matteo Pecoraro.

Greek sources for the battle of Hill 731 are much more numerous. Field Marshal Papagos' *The War For Greece, 1940-41* (Athens: Bibliophiles 1945) is useful in an academic sense but has been criticized as too dry and technical for a general readership. More specific accounts are to be found in four publications by the Hellenic Army Historical Department: *History of the 1st Division* (Athens 1967), *History of the 6th Division* (Athens 1966), *History of the Greek-Italian and Greek-German War 1940–1941 (Army Operations)* (Athens 1985), and *The Greek Army in the Second World War: Winter Operations – the Italian March Offensive* (Athens 1966).

Of course, the most gripping narratives are told by those who lived through the carnage, and of these by far the best and most detailed is Theodore Zikos' *Clash of Titans: Hill 731* (Athens 1973), on which I have necessarily drawn heavily. A longer and in many ways more detailed account, including background material, is *17 Days in March 1941* by historian Z. Papamichalopoulos (Athens 1967) that pulls together the threads of several versions on the Italian and Greek sides. George Kitsos' *The Italian Spring Offensive* has also proved valuable. The most recent treatment in Greek is *Hill 731* (Athens: Pelasgos 2007) by Georgios Tzouvaras, a retired general, which is useful for such details as maps, battle plans, official communiques and casualty lists. The story of how, after many decades of inaction, the Greek government has begun to exhume thousands of Greek soldiers known to be lying in provisional graves and begun the colossal task of DNA-testing the remains, and of the agreement to set up Greek military cemeteries on Albanian soil, is told by ex-minister Giorgos Sourlas in his *We Did Not Forget the Heroes of 1940-41* (Athens: Livanis) 2019 (in Greek only).

The six-month Greek-Italian conflict has not yet had the coverage it deserves in the English-reading world, as it has been regarded as a sideshow to the more publicized European theatres of the war in 1940 and 1941. Therefore I beg forgiveness of the reader in citing my own *The Defence and Fall of Greece, 1940-1941* (Pen and Sword 2013) that was an attempt to help fill that historiographical gap. The best-selling Greek overview of the campaign, written in a bouncy, patriotic Sunday-supplement journalistic style, is Spyros Melas' *The Glory of 1940* (Athens: Biris [undated]). As a war correspondent, Melas laboured of course under strict military censorship, but allowing for that, most of the time he preserves a certain ring of truth. Denis Mack Smith's *Mussolini: A Biography* (New York: Vintage 1983) remains for me the standard work on the Duce and the political and psychological impulses that moved him to launch a campaign he could not win.

ITALIAN ARMY (*REGIO ESERCITO*)

Commander-in-Chief, Albanian theatre: Gen. Ugo Cavallero

NINTH ARMY: Gen. Mario Vercellino; Gen. Alessandro Pirzio Biroli

Third Corps: (Divs.: 19th Venezia, 29th Piemonte, 36th Forli, 48th Taro, 53rd Arezzo)

Twenty-sixth Corps: (Divs.: 2nd Alpini Tridentina, 4th Alpini Cuneense, 5th Pusteria, 48th Parma, Albanian auxiliaries)

ELEVENTH ARMY: Gen. Carlo Geloso

Fourth Corps (Mercalli): (3rd Julia, 7th Lupi di Toscana) [Julia and Lupi di Toscana later transferred to Twenty-fifth Corps]

Eighth Corps (Bancale, Gambara): (Divs.: 24th Pinerolo, 26 Blackshirt Legion, 38th Puglie, 47th Bari, 51st Siena, 59th Cagliari) [Pinerolo and Bari transferred from Fourth Corps]

Twenty-fifth Corps (Rossi): (Divs.: 11th Brennero, 21st Sforzesca, 23rd Ferrara, 37th Modena, 56th Casale, 58th Legnano, 131st Centauro)

Special Corps (Messe): (Divs.: 1st Alpini Torinesi, 6th Cuneo [units dispersed among other commands], 33rd Acqui)

GREEK ARMY *(ELLINIKOS STRATOS)*

Commander-in-Chief: General Alexandros Papagos

Epiros Army Department (TSH): Lt. Gen. Markos Drakos, Lt. Gen. Ioannis Pitsikas)

I Corps (Demestichas): (Divs.: 2nd, 3rd, 4th, 8th)

II Corps (Bakos): (Divs.: 1st, 5th, 6th, 11th, 15th, 17th)

III Corps (later West Macedonia Army Department) (TSDM) (Tsolakoglou): Not involved in the battle

Index